I0213406

Sitting

At The

Master's Feet

Volume II

A Daily Devotional

Dr. Ronald L. Bernier

Chronological Devotions from 2015

Sitting At The Master's Feet – Volume II

Published by **Vision Publishing**

Ramona, California
ISBN 978-1-61529-197-7

FOR INFORMATION ON ORDERING PLEASE CONTACT:

MASTER BUILDER MINISTRIES, INC
397 Bay Street
Fall River, MA 02724
508-730-1735
or

Vision Publishing
1-800-9VISION
www.visionpublishingservices.com

PRINTED IN THE UNITED STATES OF AMERICA

ENDORSEMENTS

Having stayed in the Bernier house, enjoying meals with his family, suffering through a Red Sox game and participating in the life of the church Dr. Bernier leads, it is without reservation that I endorse his book "Sitting at the Master's Feet." When you stay at someone's home, you see things that even a congregant cannot...and what I have seen with Dr. Ron is a consistent life of devotion to God and family that is remarkable and admirable. When Ron writes these devotions, it is not just something he has researched; it is something he has lived. His writing flows from a Pastor's heart, with integrity and passion. This devotional is filled with wisdom from God, guidance for daily living and will be a blessing to all who read it.

Dr. Stan Dekoven, President, Vision International University
Ramona, California

It is necessary to maintain a healthy and strong faith based on the Word of God. The devotionals written by my friend, Dr. Ronald L. Bernier are so wonderful and great solutions for present day situations. May these devotionals enlighten, teach and encourage as we prepare our hearts for the Lord's coming. I deeply appreciate Dr. Ronald's work, *Sitting at the Master's Feet* and sincerely hope and pray that these devotions will very much be a helpful resource fot the edification of the church.

Dr. Jesroon Levi, Lewis Ministries India, India

One of the highlights of my day, every day, is to enjoy a gem of wisdom from Ron Bernier's daily devotional thoughts; posted on Facebook. Ron is a friend, a co-laborer, a man of God who is deeply committed to the authority of God's Word. He is an intelligent and insightful expositor of the Holy Writ; a precious gift to the Body of Christ in this generation. I am blessed that he has decided to bind his wisdom up and make it available to the wider public. I can't wait for my copy.

Rev. Michael Gantt, General Overseer, Kingdom Covenant Association; Executive Director, Kenya Development Fund,
Brattleboro, Vermont

It's a true gift to be able to share truth in a practical way. You will be encouraged and challenged by these writings of real-life experiences turned into spiritual lessons for everyday life.

Meloni Adams, MTEE Director, Bulgaria

Dr. Ronald L. Bernier's name is held in much esteem among many people across the continents and especially in Eastern Africa; not only for his magnificent ministry and wonderful writing, but also because of his personality, charisma, and gifting of connecting with leaders across the globe. Dr. Ron is a man who walks with God. I am immensely grateful for all he and Vision Publishing have done for the mission. Dr. Ron loves missions and has served so well for so many years. "The Lord recompense thy work, and a full reward be given thee of the Lord God of Israel, under whose wings thou art come to trust" (Ruth 2:12).

Bishop Richard Murungi, MTH, Destiny Community Church
Kenya, East Africa

Since the day of first meeting Dr. Ronald L. Bernier at a BILD Workshop in Ames, IA, I was blessed to have a good friend and a passionate cohort of God's Word.

Whoever has the opportunity to meet Pastor Ron, will be touched by his humility in learning from others, his sincerity in ministry, simplicity in relationships, seriousness in reflective thinking and his mastery in handling the Word.

Pastor Ron and I have followed each other's writings and appreciate and ponder each other's thoughts. On my reading through this manuscript, I intently saw two things that are noteworthy: Pastor Ron handles the devotional material carefully and not leading one toward an individualistic mindset. Rather, his thoughts reflect the issues of individual, family, church, community and global concerns. Secondly, Dr. Bernier handles the verses not as "proof-texts," but he touches the broad picture of the Scriptural and historical contexts in spite of the brevity which is part of the intent of the design of this devotional book.

It is my prayer that the LORD may use Pastor Ron's body of work as a useful tool to educate, encourage, edify and exhort His Church – the Family of Families.

Rev. Dr. R. Dhinakaran Richard, Minister Of The Gospel
Apostolic Leader, EKTA Network
Chennai, India

For a number of years, I had the privilege of sitting under the leadership of Dr. Ronald L. Bernier as part of the teaching staff at East Gate Christian Academy, the academic arm of his Master Builder Ministries. I was blessed to have him take the place of mentor in my son's life, too.

His wisdom and insight have always been hallmarks of his servant leadership, which he has consistently modeled through all the years I've known him. So it was with great joy that I welcomed his daily discipline of Facebook devotionals, seeking them out each morning as he published them anew. They have been a regular part of my reading regimen and I'm thrilled to see his worthy words drawn together into a focused published devotional book for each day of the year. His sound biblical teaching and measured reasoned application of God's Word to life and the world around us is an anchor for those seeking the waters of deeper discipleship and relationship with our Lord. I am happy to recommend this powerful devotional read to all.

Kathyrn Ross, Author And Speaker, Pageant Wagon Publishing
Vineland, New Jersey

We can find many good writings from different people, but if you have had a difficult day or night, and you take a few minutes to read and ponder this daily devotional written by Dr. Ronald L. Bernier, you will be refreshed. As you read the devotion of the day from "Sitting at the Master's Feet", it will give you the hope, strength and the stamina you need to walk with your head up like a mighty warrior. Thank you, Dr. Ronald for your dedication to help many with these inspiring words and for honoring your wonderful grandmother in the first volume with such a great gift and work of art. Congratulations my friend!

Rev. Jose Gabriel Cabral, PHD, Founder And President Of Conquerors For Christ Ministries, Senior Pastor, Conquerors For Christ Church, Founder And President, Care For Children International, Inc., No. Dartmouth, Massachusetts

This daily devotional, *Sitting at the Master's Feet* is simply profound and practical.

Maxim Melousov, D.Min, Lead Pastor, Dnipropetrovsk Christian Church, UKRAINE

I've had the pleasure and honor of knowing Dr. Ron Bernier for nearly a decade. During that time, he's become my pastor, my friend, and my encourager. Until recently, his encouragement came simply through his actions – by his living a life that compels even the most casual observers to ask "how does he do it?" The 'it', by the way, refers to facing the trials of daily life in a ministry of service to a world that sees little need or value in these ideals. It has only been in the past year that I've learned his secret. I know how he does it. And now you are about to find out, too.

In order to live a life that continually points to Christ, Dr. Bernier's actions are firmly rooted in the Word of God. This can only come from knowledge of The Word. Through daily devotionals this knowledge is revealed – bit by bit, day by day, precious verse by precious verse. And each day, Dr. Bernier has drawn closer to God ("But as for me, it is good to be near God. I have made the Sovereign Lord my refuge; I will tell of all your deeds." – Psalm 73:28). There you have it - His secret.

But there's more to it than that. There has to be because in Ecclesiastes 1:4-11, Solomon tells us that there's nothing new under the sun. That includes devotionals. In fact, the concept of devotionals has been around for quite some time with the earliest known Christian example being the Gaelic Felire written in Ireland in the Ninth Century. Jumping ahead twelve hundred years later, a quick search of the internet will yield over 5.7 million sources for devotionals. So why bother with Dr. Bernier's devotionals? What makes his "new" under the sun?

Knowing Ron as I do, I can unequivocally say that what makes his devotionals stand out from all the others is the sincerity of his heart. His heart for "telling of your deeds" is genuine. The stories are real. The relationship is authentic. This is what makes them new in a dark world that prides itself on the latest trend and seeks fleeting popularity and fame above all.

Now you can join him every day as you journey through God's Word with a man dedicated to shining a light in the darkness (2 Corinthians 4:6). Ron sits at the Master's Feet and he'd like you to join him. Bit by bit, day by day, verse by verse.

Dr. Jim Huggins, President/CEO, New Shepherd Films
New Shepherd Entertainment

Time spent in meditation on the Word of God brings forth fruit a hundredfold. I am grateful to Pastor Ronald Bernier for the inspiring devotionals from the Scripture that stir up faith, being both encouraging and applicable to our daily life.

Dr. Peter Kovalenko, Senior Pastor, Kharkov Christian Fellowship
Kharkov, Ukraine

For each person, time is something that one could derive from it – good or evil. We lose a day if we do not receive new knowledge and do not penetrate deeper into the wisdom of God's grace. A reasonable reading of certain books, does not kill time, but makes it even more precious. There are three most difficult things in the world: to keep a secret, to forgive an offense, and to use our free time properly.

The book *Sitting at the Master's Feet* is written with the intention that every day you, dear readers, can extract for yourselves something useful, edifying and instructive. This devotional book contains texts with inspirational commentary for every day of the year. Dr. Ronald L. Bernier devoted a lot of time working on this book to make something special to encourage us and give us advice for every day. Information in this book will be useful for everyone, because it reveals to us the eternal Word of God, bearing a peace and salvation to everyone.

God bless you as you read this book!

Dr. Siarhei Padniuk, Assistant Bishop Of The Belarusian Pentecostal Union, Director Of The Theological Institute, Minsk, Belarus

On behalf of the staff of IDCL, we would like to express our deep gratitude to Pastor Ronald L. Bernier for his participation in the work entrusted to us by God, by strengthening churches and preparing Christians for effective ministry.

Every time Dr. Ron has visited our network of churches and Bible Colleges, his teachings and ministry to churches and pastors were always filled with God-given wisdom and a wealth of practical, pastoral experience. These encounters have left an indelible mark in the hearts and minds of the listeners and have given a dynamic boost to many ministries.

We are sure that the book *Sitting at the Master's Feet* will be a blessing and very useful to every Christian who wants to have a closer walk with God. May God bless this good work.

Valentyna Grenchuk, Operation Manager, Institute For The Development Of Christian Leadership, Kiev, Ukraine

Each day as we come into the Lord's presence, we find comfort, our souls refreshed and we receive the sure mercies of the Lord. David said, 'Both riches and honour [come] of thee, and thou reignest over all; and in thine hand [is] power and might; and in thine hand [it is] to make great, and to give strength unto all.'

Daniel was given supernatural insight, inspiration and vision as he 'kneeled upon his knees three times a day, and prayed, and gave thanks before God, as he did aforetime' (Daniel 6:10).

My prayer is that when you spend time with Dr. Bernier's *Sitting at the Master's Feet* that our Lord and Master will speak to your heart, enriching you so that that you will receive breakthroughs; have knowledge, wisdom and understanding imparted, and that God may reveal the secret things of your life. Let your joy be complete.

Rev. Shadreck Chipunga, National Children's Ministry Superintendent,
Apostolic Faith Mission In Zimbabwe, AFM Berachah Assembly,
Mabvuku, Harrare

God has gifted Pastor Ronald L. Bernier with the means to communicate God's truth with conviction, encouragement, and relevance, yet with simplicity and applicability. During the last couple of years, as I lazily browsed Facebook at the end of the day, my heart always leaped when my eyes encountered a post from Ron Bernier. I knew that in reading what he wrote and taking it to heart, God would use it as a fruitful tool in my goal in becoming Christ-like. I am extremely blessed to know he has compiled these devotions into this book, *Sitting at the Master's Feet*, a book that will certainly be on my nightstand.

Ana Barend, World Surf League (WSL), Women's Chaplain

I deeply believe that a daily devotional time is the secret to expedite victory over every problem in our lives. No one better than Dr. Ronald Bernier, who possesses a tender soul and sensible ears to hear the Holy Spirit, to lead and help us into a deep fellowship with Him every day. Dr. Bernier's devotional is much more than good literature; it is a divine gift to our souls.

Joel Freire Costa, District Superintendent, Brazilian District Council,
President, Assemblies of God Bethlehem Ministries USA

INTRODUCTION & DEDICATION

The year, 2019, will be a year of milestones: My wife and I will each celebrate our 60th birthdays and 40 years of marriage, and our church and school ministry will be embarking on our 25th year of ministry. With the advancing of time also comes a considering of the path that has been walked and the legacy or inheritance that can be left.

My life has been one guided by a love for the Lord, His church, and our family. Doing the simple things in life often has the most lasting influence on others. When God instructed Israel in their new-found freedom as the chosen of God, He gave them a prescription for leaving a mark on succeeding generations:

"You shall love the Lord your God with all of your heart, with all your soul, and with all your strength. And these words which I command you today shall be in your heart. You shall teach them diligently to your children, and shall talk of them when you sit in your house, when you walk by the way, when you lie down, and when you rise up. You shall bind them as a sign on your hand, and they shall be as frontlets between your eyes. You shall write them on the doorposts of your house and on your gates." Deuteronomy 6:5-9

While I hope that the devotions minister to you personally, my greatest motivation has been to preserve a sample of my day-to-day walk with the Lord. I want to leave an inheritance that my family and those who come after me can live their lives accordingly and leave a deposit for succeeding generations.

These devotions have been written in real time. The year is 2015. They are the practical thoughts from everyday life situations, concerns, and testimonies.

I would like to dedicate this year's volume to my wife Bernice, who has made our home one where peace reigns and love is pure. She has always dedicated herself to servanthood, not only in ministry, but to her family as well. Our family greatly appreciates her life giving and nurturing role. These writings are as much her legacy as mine.

PREPARE HIS WAYS

If there is ever a theme that we could embrace for the New Year, it can be seen in Zacharias' prophecy over John. As I read these words this morning, I cannot help but think about our own day and the work to which we have been called. If there is ever a time for a real prophetic voice to rise among the people of God, it is today. I am not talking about the personal make-me-feel-good kind of encouraging words. I am talking about the real prophetic voice of the Lord that prepares us to confess, repent, turn to the Lord and walk in His way.

Zachariah prophesied about John:

"And you child, will be called the prophet of the Highest; For you will go before the face of the Lord to prepare His ways. To give knowledge of salvation to His people by the remission of their sins, through the tender mercy of our God, with which the Dayspring from on high has visited us; to give light to those who sit in darkness and the shadow of death, to guide our feet into the way of peace." Luke 1:76-79

Can you imagine what this meant for the children of Israel in the days preceding the ministry of Jesus? John was to make the way clear. How important is this clear prophetic voice needed as we make way the coming of the Lord in our lives, families, churches and communities?

This is my prayer this morning. I want to be one who will go before the face of the Lord and prepare His ways; proclaiming the knowledge of His salvation, revealing light to those who sit in darkness; guiding feet in the way of peace. May this be a year of proclamation, preparation, planting, plundering and perfecting peace.

Happy New Year to all my family and friends!

JANUARY 2

TODAY...

I have been up since early this morning reading, praying and meditating. I am wondering why we give so much attention and excitement to the first day of the year and then settle like the second day is so much less. I didn't see anyone having parties last night anticipating the second day of the year. There are no posts being written about everyone's joy on the second day. But isn't today a great day also? Life is a gift. If you were able to get up this morning and prepare for work or whatever other endeavor you are planning, isn't that wonderful?

While many tend to live in the past or others long for the future, there is also a great blessing in living in the present. Today is a gift from God. It is a day to listen to His voice. The writer of Hebrews wrote:

"Therefore, as the Holy Spirit says: 'Today, If you will hear His voice, Do not harden your hearts as in the rebellion, in the day of trial in the wilderness, where your fathers tested Me, tried Me.'" Hebrews 3:7-9

As a result of their hardness of heart, the Israelites did not enter the rest of the Lord. But the writer goes on in exhorting us: *"Beware, brethren, lest there be in any of you an evil heart of unbelief in departing from the living God; but exhort one another daily, while it is called 'Today,' lest any of you be hardened through the deceitful ness of sin. For we have become partakers of Christ if we hold the beginning of our confidence steadfast to the end" (Hebrews 3:12-14).*

There is a rest that is promised for the people of God. It is a rest that we can receive by faith and walk in on a daily basis. "Today" is an important day! The Bible says that, "Jesus Christ is the same yesterday, TODAY, and forever" (Hebrews 13:8). TODAY is a great day to celebrate. TODAY is a great day to listen to His voice. TODAY is a great day to rest in Jesus' promises. Let's get excited about TODAY! Give your TODAY over to Him, He will sanctify TODAY so you can glorify Him in it.

JANUARY 3

CHOICES - SHOOT FOR A TARGET OR PAINT A TARGET?

Today is the third day of 2015. For many, even if they have made any resolutions, they are already a distant memory. But if you are hoping for better things in this New Year, you just can't say, "I hope it will be better." You do have a part to play.

Proverbs 17:24 says, *"An intelligent person aims at wise actions, but a fool starts off in many directions."*

There are many things I could say this morning, but let me focus on one in particular. Each one of us must assume responsibility for our lives.

This is not a popular concept because in our culture we have a concept called "political correctness." This basically says, "None of your problems are your fault. Everything bad in your life is somebody else's fault. Blame the environment. Blame the educator. Blame your parents. Blame anybody else, but it's not your fault." But you are never going to be a success in life and you are never going to make your life count if you have this attitude. You must assume responsibility for your own life.

"Each person must be responsible for himself." Galatians 6:5 NCV

The fact is our choices always determine more than our circumstances. You cannot control your circumstances, but you can control your actions and reactions. Charles Swindoll once said, *"Life is 10% of what happens to you and 90% how you respond to what happens to you."*

So in this next year, your actions and reactions will be determined by how you will choose to be different this year. You can shoot for a target, or simply paint the target after you have already shot. The choice is yours.

JANUARY 4

WE HAVE REASON TO REJOICE

For the believer, joy should be part of his or her experience. Joy must also be a decision. The psalmist wrote:

"Let all those rejoice who have put their trust in You; Let them ever shout for joy, because You defend them; Let those also who love Your name be joyful in You. For You, O Lord, will bless the righteous; With favor You will surround him as with as shield." Psalm 5:11-12

Consider these words. Have you put your trust in Jesus? If so, doesn't He defend you? Hasn't He shown you His love? What about His blessing that has surrounded you as His favor has also protected you? This is not only a past or present favor. There is also a future hope that God will continue to provide as He already has done. We need to be reminded of His favor, blessing and protective shield that has been our protection.

In relation to this, how do we respond then to His goodness and promises in our lives? How can we not be joyful? Let's shout for joy! Let's be joyful in the Lord! Let's go in this joy, and exhort our brothers and sisters to be joyful also. When we gather together we can encourage each other in the faithfulness, protection, and blessing of the Lord. We can rehearse God's great faithfulness.

Difficulty, challenges, even hardships may strip us of temporary happiness; however, joy is independent of circumstances. We can be joyful even in difficult circumstances. Joy is something that is settled in our hearts because of who we are and to Whom we belong.

May we gain perspective today and rejoice in the great favor and blessing of the Lord. May our joy be contagious with all the people with whom we have the opportunity to interact. Let the joy of the Lord be your strength.

JANUARY 5

GO ON, MAN, WOMAN, CHURCH, ASK ME!

We are familiar with the reading of Abraham's intercession for Sodom (Genesis 18:16-33), but a key idea is that the earliest manuscripts do not support the reading "*Abraham remained standing before the Lord.*" There is significant textural evidence to indicate that the passage originally read, "*The Lord remained standing before Abraham!*" This begs the question, "Whom was begging whom for the city?" If true, this has tremendous implications for our understanding of the church's responsibility in the city.

Was it God who was advocating Sodom's deliverance before Abraham? Go on Abraham, ask Me - for 50 righteous, 40...10. If Abraham had asked, would God have saved the city for one family? God wanted the city saved. Bargaining stopped - not because God lacked mercy, but because Abraham lacked sufficient nerve. God is saying, "Go on Abraham ask Me, I will forgive, I will starve off judgement."

Consider this thought. Abraham's response to God standing before Him for Sodom was another trial of faith. Could he believe God for the birth of the promised son? Abraham turned to Hagar instead of Sarah and Ishmael was born. Could he believe God for the pregnancy of Sarah? Sarah laughed, and Abraham wavered. Could he sufficiently believe God for the city? He could not; he could not barter with God far enough.

That is God's cry as He stands before us and pleads for the city. One did stand alone for the city. His name is Jesus (see Psalm 2 and Matthew 16:21). We are called by God to be His community, both the foretaste of the kingdom and its present embodiment. All of the city will know of God's kingdom, it will know from our lives together, our witness, and our commitment to the city's broken, hurting and poor.

Are we willing to be the embodiment of the Kingdom of God in our city? Do we have the willingness to reside in the city, to proclaim truth and to work for justice, for what God calls the church to be? This is the cry of God, "Go on, man, ask Me! Go on, woman, ask Me! Go on, church, ask Me!"

JANUARY 6

JESUS BEGAN TO SHOW HIS DISCIPLES...

Jesus did not say it only once, but He stated over and over again to His disciples what would happen to Him. That He must go...that He was destined to go, that it was not optional for Him to go to Jerusalem. It was obligatory for Jesus to do that work which meant the world's salvation. It was part of God's design to go "*to Jerusalem, and suffer many things from the elders and chief priest and scribes, and be killed, and be raised the third day*" (Matt. 16:21).

Why did Jesus have to go to Jerusalem? One primary reason was that Jerusalem was the archetypal battleground between God and Satan for the souls of all humanity. In the Bible, Jerusalem is not simply a city; it is the capital city of the nation of Israel, or the Jewish faith; it was the gathering place of all systems, the religious, political, and economic systems of Israel; it was the spiritual center of the Roman world, and the physical abode of the Law. As the archetypal city, Jerusalem symbolized and stood in the place of all other cities. For Jesus to die in Jerusalem was to die at the spiritual center of the universe.

God's love for the city is exceedingly patient (Luke 13:34-35; 19:41-44). Jesus wept for her. She continually rejected the call of the prophets. Christ longs to see the city become the city of God. Humanity refuses the city of God. Inevitably consequences came upon the city that rejected Christ. The city was destroyed because it refused to recognize the redemptive events occurring in it.

If that was the end of the story, we might just focus on further judgments. And many of God's people seem to be just focusing on that as their message. But the incredible story is that God sent Jesus to the city, not to judge it, but to redeem it. God's heart is that His created order be redeemed (John 3:16-17). We must participate with Christ, take up our cross and follow Him into the city as ministers of His message. There is "Good News" for the city. May we begin to focus on this kingdom message! There has been love demonstrated...and we as His disciples must offer hope as we are committed to speak truth and demonstrate His love. What will this look like for your life? Even today, how might you be an instrument of change?

JANUARY 7

SYSTEMS AND PEOPLE

Over the last couple of days, I have been reflecting and writing about Jesus' focus and saving work for the city. Let me just explain the systems of a city in brief.

The Godly system would include: (1) A religion of relationship (Deut. 6:4-6, 14-16), which is a right relationship with God that develops a right relationship with others; (2) A politics of justice (Deut. 6:6-9, 17-19), where what is right is not just what is convenient; (3) An economics of stewardship (Deut. 6:10-12), where we are called to be responsible with what we have been entrusted.

Opposed to this Godly system is an ungodly system seen demonstrated which includes: (1) A religion of control (religion without relationship); (2) A politics of oppression (weak become slaves of the strong); and (3) An economics of privilege.

Jesus died for the city, its systems, and its people. He also asks us to participate in what He has done; to follow Him, pick up our cross, identify with His suffering, even to lose our lives for His purpose (Matt. 16:22-26). Jesus' death came out of great love and intense commitment to the city, its systems, and its people. He wants us to have this same commitment to minister to the afflicted and comfortable, exploiters and exploited of the systems, and ultimately dealing with principalities and powers, even looking seriously at the corruption in us all.

Our Lord was not crucified in a gothic cathedral on a golden cross placed upon a marble altar between two silver candlesticks. He was crucified on a rugged cross between two thieves, on the city's garbage heap, at the kind of place where cynics talk smut and thieves curse and soldiers gamble. That is where Christ died and that is what Christ died about. There is where Christ calls His church to be. And that is what Christ's call to His church is to be about!

May we consider these thoughts and take proper action!

JANUARY 8

ARE WE MORE LIKE JONAH THAN WE WOULD LIKE TO BELIEVE?

When Jonah realized he was not going to change God's mind, he ran away rather than assume responsibility. After much chastening, Jonah obeyed the word of the Lord and went to Nineveh to proclaim its destruction. The people believed and acted on the message preached, but Jonah could not accept the forgiveness which God exercised toward the people of Nineveh.

The book of Jonah was written in a period of Israel's history when it had become significantly nationalistic and introspective. Israel was withdrawing from all contact with the Gentile world under the reforms of Ezra and Nehemiah. Convinced that God hated the foreign nations even more than they did, the Israelites were eagerly waiting for the Day of Judgment when all the nations would be condemned and only Israel and Judah would be saved.

Jonah's story came as a reminder to Israel that God was as concerned for all the "Ninevehs" of the world as He was for Israel. The Israelites' refusal to share God's "Good News" with the rest of the world was really an attempt to run from the task God had given them, but He would pursue them and work supernaturally in order to have them do His bidding.

We must understand that proclaiming the "Good News" is our mission as well. God has a great concern for all those who have yet to respond to His saving grace.

"For God did not send His Son into the world to condemn the world, but that the world through Him might be saved." John 3:17

The practice and proclamation of His Word is necessary to see the cities of this world turn and respond to God's mercy and grace. We are called to be concerned about this as well. It is time to share the message and believe for change and rejoice in it. Or is there still some of the Jonah spirit in us?

ARE YOU THE COMING ONE? ...

The disciples of John asked this question of Jesus. If not, "*do we look for another*?" (Luke 7:20). Jesus responded to them to report back to John what they have seen and heard. In other words, tell John the words I am speaking and the results that you see happening because of them. We then see in the scripture a summary of some of what Jesus tells them to report:

"The blind see, the lame walk, the lepers are cleansed, the deaf hear, the dead are raised, the poor have the gospel preached to them. And blessed is he who is not offended because of Me" (Luke 7:22-23).

I wonder if someone came to us and asked, "Are you one sent of the Lord?" what would our response be. Would we be able to in some way validate the fact that we are called as His church body? Would there be any signs, results or testimonies that people could confirm that the Lord is present among us; that His anointing is present? Shouldn't there be some visible and tangible change that has resulted in us, and in others, because we are walking with Jesus? Our life should testify and witness this union. And our life work is meant to bring glory to His name.

A few days ago, I saw that a teacher friend have her students study what had been written on the gravestones of others, and then consider what her students might like to see written on theirs. This exercise was to make them think of the importance of their own life. Hopefully, this was a valuable thought-provoking exercise for these students.

What if we were to do this exercise? What would others summarize as they thought of our lives? We do not need to wait till then to find out though. We can begin right now, asking the Lord to manifest His life in and through us, so that when others ask the question, we have something tangible to which to point.

THIS GOSPEL OF THE KINGDOM...

There is much in the news that seems to distract us, as the people of God, from the real mission for which we have been called. Jesus said:

"This gospel of the Kingdom shall be preached in the whole world for a witness to all nations, and then the end shall come." Matthew 24:14

Given the above scripture, there is much we need to ponder about the mission of the church and how much of that focus has been clouded. In this verse is a completed work with a definite goal to accomplish. As a result, consider a few thoughts:

1. God does not reward disobedience, nor will He return until His Church has completed her earthly assignments.

2. "Hard times" or the world-systems' attacks against the Church cannot force God's hand to prematurely remove the Church. God is not moved or manipulated by the enemy.

3. Jesus said the Church would overcome hell's gates (Matthew 16:18); and that the Kingdom of God would leaven the earth (Matthew 13:33) and become a place of refuge for the nations (Matthew 13:31-32).

4. The Church is here as "salt" and "light" and a gift to the unsaved (Matthew 5:13-16).

If the end cannot come until "this gospel of the Kingdom...be preached to the world as a witness" (something seen and heard), the question then becomes what is "this gospel of the Kingdom"? A second question we must ask ourselves is, "How is Christ going to move us from a gospel of you must be born again to the gospel of His kingdom? Anything other than "this gospel" is another gospel. Therefore, we must answer what is "this gospel" of the kingdom?

May we learn to preach “this gospel of the kingdom.”

JANUARY 11

THE PRESENCE OF GOD IN THE CITY

How can the church be the presence of God in the city? Jesus called His disciples "*the salt of the earth,*" "*the light of the world,*" "*a city that is set on a hill.*" But, we who can be what Jesus declared, must be what He declared by having the proper focus. Jesus also said:

"No one can serve two masters; for either he will hate the one and love the other, or else he will be loyal to the one and despise the other. You cannot serve God and mammon." Matthew 6:24

For us to be God's presence in the city, we must have decided not to pursue power (Matthew 7:15-23), possessions (Matthew 6:24-34) or the advocacy of our own little group (Matthew 7:1-6, 13-14). Rather, we must be simply committed to the love of God and the service of the people of our city.

As the church in the city, God has not called us to be above the city, fellowshipping only with God's people while singing, "This world is not my home; I'm just passing through." Nor, are we simply in the city committed to our own welfare without contributing to the city's good.

We are to be the people who live our lives joyfully, hopefully, and profoundly in the city, being the very presence of God to the loneliness, fear and deep hunger of our city's people, systems, and principalities. As we choose and learn to live this way, we can see amazing things happening around us. For God has "thoughts of peace and not evil, to give you a future and a hope" (Jeremiah 29:11). Through our obedience and practice, God's presence will be demonstrated to all who come near.

Lord, help us to be focused on just whom you have called us to be. May our light shine and help others see the correct way to go. May our lives, as salt, flavor and preserve those to whom we have the privilege of relating. May how we relate to others in the proper ordering of our lives and interpersonal relationships demonstrate Your Kingdom government to those we serve. Amen.

JANUARY 12

ALL IN A DAY'S WORK

This morning reading Luke chapter 8, I am thinking about what it is like to walk with the Lord on a given day. We encounter so many various situations where we must exercise faith to be difference makers in our world. We can never fully know the impact we have on the lives of others as we are obedient to God's call on our lives.

On this one day described in Luke 8, Jesus calmed the raging seas; delivered a demon- possessed man; healed a woman who had a long-standing illness simply because she was able to press in and touch Him; and then raise the twelve year old daughter of a man named Jairus. I would say that that was an impactful day! However, Jesus said we would do greater things because He was going to the Father.

The 9th chapter of Luke begins by saying that Jesus "called His twelve disciples together and gave them power and authority over all demons, and to cure diseases. He sent them to preach the kingdom of God and to heal the sick" (Luke 9:1-2).

They, in fact, followed His command and began to see the demonstration of the kingdom as they went. A question we must ask ourselves today is, "Are we preaching this gospel of the kingdom?" If we speak of another gospel, we will never be able to walk in the demonstration and power of Jesus, or see the lives of people adequately changed or radically changed for His purposes. We will instead fill ourselves with excuses as to why we are not experiencing His power and authority.

We serve a great and powerful God. Global climate, demons, sickness and even death are no match for His power. May we grow in our discernment and commitment to the message of this gospel of the kingdom. As the reality of this message saturates our minds and hearts, may we walk in the demonstration of this reality.

Let God arise in our lives! And let His enemies be scattered.

JANUARY 13

LET THESE WORDS SINK DOWN INTO YOUR EARS...

It seems that after every great miracle of Jesus, He tried to orientate His disciples to the mission not the miracle. After the feeding of the five thousand and His asking the disciples who the people say He is, that He said, "*The Son of Man must suffer many things, and be rejected by the elders and chief priests and scribes, and be killed, and be raised the third day*" (Luke 9:22). Associated with that saying was His call for His disciples to deny themselves and take up their own cross and follow Him.

Then we read of Jesus' transfiguration on the mountain where He is seen with Moses and Elijah speaking together about Jesus' mission and what needed to be accomplished at Jerusalem (see Luke 9:28-31), only to come down and face a boy possessed by a demon whom the disciples were not able to deliver. After the boy is healed, everyone is marveling, but Jesus says to His disciples, "*Let these words sink down into your ears, for the Son of Man is about to be betrayed into the hands of men.*"

I have often looked at His previous words, "*O faithless and perverse generation, how long shall I be with you and bear with you? Bring your son here*" (Luke 9:41), as a direct rebuke to the disciples for what they were unable to do. However, as I have pondered this, I am realizing it was a rebuke to the generation of people who continually looked for signs rather than the reality of the Kingdom. The signs made people marvel, but they themselves did not change anyone. It was the consecrated lives, given over to the purpose of God, that could bring about any real change.

What is your focus today? Do you seek Jesus for the signs that you can experience? Or, do you desire to experience Him in the call for which He has called you. For all of us, that will require denial of self and acceptance of the path designated for us to walk. Will we just seek after the miracle, or will we focus on the mission? Only the consecrated Levites were able to carry the Ark of God. Let these words sink down into your ears.

JANUARY 14

GIVE THANKS TO THE LORD

When the ark of God was first placed in the tabernacle of David, he delivered a psalm to be sung before the Lord to Asaph, chief of the Levites, who was appointed along with other Levites to minister to the Lord in that way. The first declaration was to give the Lord thanks. The psalm begins:

"Oh, give thanks to the Lord! Call upon His name; make known His deeds among the peoples! Sing to Him, sing psalms to Him; talk of all His wondrous works! Glory to His holy name; let the hearts of those rejoice who seek the Lord! Seek the Lord and His strength; seek His face [presence] evermore!" (1 Chronicles 16:8-11).

The psalm continues and is a beautiful exhortation of ascribing to the Lord all the thanks and praise of which He is deserving. We, too, have been so blessed by the Lord. It is so easy to forget all that He has done and is doing in our lives. We focus often on the difficulties, or sometimes think erroneously that it is our own abilities that have given us what we have. If we do think this way, then pride rules us, and we have forgotten the grace and mercy of our great God.

This morning, give the Lord thanks for all that He is deserving of. If you compile a list, you will not have enough paper (although it might be a worthwhile exercise). If you cannot think of anything to write down, then perhaps you might need to realize that thankfulness is something that must be more readily cultivated in your life. You might need to train or retrain yourself to understand all that the Lord has done for you.

In practicing thankfulness, in coming into His presence, we begin to find our voice in declaring His goodness to all others we meet. Begin to make this a practice in your life. Start with this prayer and then begin to fill it out.

Thank you, Lord, for more than I can put into words this morning! Help me to express thankfulness in my life and prayer. I do want to thank you for....

JANUARY 15

YES, I HAVE A GOOD INHERITANCE...

This morning as I read Psalm 16, I am thinking of all the joys of being a part of the kingdom of God. The psalmist writes:

"O Lord, You are the portion of my inheritance and my cup; You maintain my lot. The lines have fallen to me in pleasant places; Yes, I have a good inheritance" (Psalm 16:5-6). Again in another verse he writes: *"You will show me the path of life; In Your presence is fullness of joy; At Your right hand are pleasures forevermore." Psalm 16:11*

Yesterday, I had so many greetings and birthday well wishes from so many people; people that I have had the pleasure of meeting, ministering with, or simply being family together. I had greetings from all around this country and others, including India, Kenya, Zimbabwe and Ukraine. Messages were appearing on Facebook, Instant Message, Email, and snail mail. I was trying to acknowledge each one between the different meetings that I also was a part of yesterday and ended up staying up late to get to them all. I so appreciate all the people that have been, and are, such an important part of my life and the life of my family, that I didn't want to miss responding to even one of your greetings.

Coming back to this Psalm, I am reminded of the prayer Paul had for the Ephesians. He prayed for them to receive the spirit of wisdom and revelation in the knowledge of God. That "*the eyes of your understanding being enlightened: that you may know what is the hope of His calling, what are the riches of the inheritance in the Saints, and what is the exceeding greatness of His power toward us who believe*" (Ephesians 1:18-19).

What an inheritance we have in Jesus! What an inheritance we have with the saints! What great hope fills our hearts! What great power is available! Can you see it? Do you believe it? Have you received this wisdom? Yes, I have, and you, too, can have a good inheritance.

Thank you for being a part of this inheritance!

JANUARY 16

HOW MUCH DIFFERENCE DOES PERSPECTIVE MAKE?

I have to get an early start in the morning and thought I would get ahead of my devotional time this evening. With so many situations that I face as an individual and as a pastor, I am pondering one of the readings tonight found in Luke's gospel. Jesus was comparing the eye as being the lamp of the body. Obviously, a lamp's effectiveness in how well it emits light. Jesus said:

"When your eye is good, your whole body is full of light. But when your eye is bad ("unhealthy" in the ESV*), your whole body is full of darkness. Therefore take heed that the light which is in you is not darkness. If then your whole body is full of light, having no part dark, the whole body will be full of light, as when the bright shining of a lamp gives you light" (Luke 11:34-36).*

I remember when my children were growing up, and we had conversations at the supper table about the day's events, how often I would try to help them to see another side to the situation they had been evaluating and judging. Why was this so important? If they could not see another side to the issue, they might take offense instead of responsibility. They might also be judgmental instead of allowing grace, mercy and forgiveness to flow. Giving someone the benefit of the doubt first, or perhaps going to someone and clarifying just what the intent or motive, was if any at all, they could reconcile with others more readily.

We live in a day where offense is so easily accepted and differences bring many to a boiling point way too soon, often without justification. So what causes all of this? Isn't it how you and I see something? How we perceive things affects our countenance, our witness, even our attractiveness and usefulness to others. Be careful how you see. Take heed that what you let in is light and not darkness.

Is there something that you may need to look at differently than you have been? Ask the Lord to give you His eyes. Then you will no longer grope in the dark but be enlightened that others may come to the light also.

JANUARY 17

WHAT ARE THE RIGHTEOUS TO DO?

I have been thinking through how God evaluates the city. In the book of Jonah, God calls the city a great city, even though its wickedness is crying out to Him. He calls a reluctant prophet to cry out to it, so that the city might repent and avert judgment. In Genesis, He also comes down to evaluate another city, Sodom, as to what has been cried out against it because of its great wickedness. As a judge, the Lord evaluates for Himself and brings proper judgment.

In Sodom's case Abraham intercedes with the Lord but does not intervene. He prayed a far off but did not bid the Lord that he could go and warn the inhabitants of the city of the impending judgment. Also, Lot, whose presence was in the city, did not proclaim the word of the Lord, nor was there any substantial practice or influence that seemed to come from his family, but all they could do was run from the city in self-preservation. So we have intercession without intervention; and presence without practice and proclamation. Somehow, we need to have these various components to really make a difference: prayer, presence, practice, and proclamation.

One thing that is clear is that God loves the people of this world. He bids us to give our lives in such a way that they may know this love also. Which one of these areas is most challenging to you? Think of how Jesus modeled all of these areas: prayer (He was always in communication with the Father), presence (He came into this world to identify with us in every way and yet without sin), practice (Jesus practiced what He preached. His life was a testimony to the Word of God) and proclamation (Jesus proclaimed the "Good News" of the Kingdom in truth and power).

Until we, as the people of God, get this together, we will struggle with the victory in which are meant to walk. As people and churches, we must give serious thought to incorporate prayer, presence, practice and proclamation! This is what the righteous must do! Only in this way will we have the integrity to be able to help others in a meaningful way. Through Christ we can do it!

JANUARY 18

DRESSED AND LIGHTS ON!

I am reminded of some of the times when I have traveled a long distance and have arrived to certain destinations late at night, worn from the traveling and yet, someone was there to receive me and make sure that I had some food and refreshments. They could have long ago been dismissed for the day, but instead they waited for my arrival and went out of their way to be present, ready, willing to serve. There are other instances when someone was not at their post, and you can imagine what difficulties that might present.

When Jesus spoke of our need to be ready to await Him, He said:

"Stay dressed for action and keep your lamps burning, and be like men who are awaiting for their master to come home from the wedding feast, so that they may open the door to him at once when he comes and knocks. Blessed are those servants whom the master finds awake when he comes." Luke 12:35-37 ESV

Just for added information, a wedding feast could last for multiple days. So, those who awaited their master had to keep alert with the lamps lit, ready at any moment for his coming.

I wonder if we understand what this means. What does it mean to be ready; to have our lamps lit; to be fully dressed? Can we be called on in a moment's notice? If we slack off, abandon our post, we will not be where we are supposed to be and will miss the visitation and the assignment given to us.

You and I can only be blessed if we are ready, dressed for action, and with our lamps burning. This is the substance of which faithfulness is made. There is an action to what we believe. Being ready requires action, thoughtfulness and preparation. There is an endurance and perseverance required. Waiting is not inaction, but all action necessary to be a dutiful servant. Let us be prepared and ready for every good work.

JANUARY 19

GOD IS OUR VINDICATOR

There is a law of sowing and reaping in the kingdom of God. In our family, we sometimes refer to it as a revolving account. What you do to others will often be done onto you in some capacity or another. However, this is not the motivation for what we do, but simply the results of what we do.

In reading Psalm 41 this morning, I am reminded of this same idea. The psalmist writes:

"Blessed is he who considers the poor [helpless or powerless]; The Lord will deliver him in time of trouble. The Lord will preserve him and keep him alive, and he will be blessed on the earth; You will not deliver him to his enemies. The Lord will strengthen him on his bed of illness; You will sustain [restore] him on his sickbed" (Psalm 41:1-3).

What a powerful psalm; how we care for the powerless of this world will be noticed by God! And when we find ourselves powerless, He will be our power. He delivers us from trouble; preserves us; blesses us on the earth; protects us from our enemies so that they do not overcome us; even strengthens us and sustains us when sick to restore us once again. What great and wonderful promises!

If you find yourself strong today, use that strength to lift others up. If you find yourself weak, be encouraged that the Lord is able to strengthen you and lift you up.

May all of us continually sow to the capacity we have opportunity, considering others who are in a disadvantaged state or in a particular need. And when we are in need, may we have faith in an all-powerful God who does not slumber or sleep to cause us to arise!

May the Lord be your strength and encouragement today. May all you sow be done with love and in faith in an all-powerful God.

JANUARY 20

THE NARROW WAY

As Jesus was traveling someone asked Him:
"Lord are there few who are saved?" Luke 13:23

In thinking about that question, I wonder how many really pondered the question or even the answer that Jesus gave to the question. For in our day, there is either a too casual thinking about entrance to the Kingdom of God, or no thought at all. Jesus responded:

"Strive to enter through the narrow gate, for many will seek to enter and will not be able." Luke 13:24

The interesting thing is that those standing outside the closed door may even say, "*we ate and drank in Your presence, and You taught in our streets*" (Luke 13:26). As if their proximity to Jesus' presence or their geographical location in relation to His work made enough of an association that He must receive them. Maybe they were thinking, "You know, I know some people who know You. I lived near to where You were doing Your work. I saw some of what You were doing in my time." The answer Jesus gives is:

"I tell you I do not know you." Luke 13:27

Here He reveals the way through the narrow gate. It is through Himself. He is the way, the truth, and the life. No one comes to the Father except through Jesus (see John 14:6). Any other way will not work. Any other door will not give entrance. Any other philosophy, religious expression, or human works cannot open the door. Wide is the way to destruction, but narrow is the way to life.

Here is the important question that each of us must answer: "Do we know Jesus?", and just as important, "Does Jesus know us?" The real answer to that question has eternal ramifications for all of us. Let us enter the narrow gate, through Jesus our Lord.

JANUARY 21

LIVING BY GOD'S GRACE

Well I am setting off on a typical day. Hospital visits, pastor's meeting, preparation for a memorial service, leadership training, building logistics, preparation for hosting the overflow shelter (dates might change to sooner), Bible study and whatever will come as a surprise or need. Your list might be different, but still very important. What I am thankful for is God's grace which is always sufficient, not only to us as individuals, but to us as the church. Paul writes:

"God has dealt to each one a measure of faith. For as we have many members in one body, but all the members do not have the same function, so we, being many are one body in Christ, and individual members of one another. Having then gifts differing according to the grace that is given to us, let us use them." Romans 12:3-6

What a pleasure it is to be part of the body of Christ. Every one of us who has presented ourselves as a living sacrifice to the Lord can prove what His will for our lives is. We do so by allowing the Lord to direct our thoughts and ways according to His magnificent grace and wisdom.

You and I have been given grace gifts. These gifts are not the same. The measure of faith differs. But that does not mean that one gift or function is more important than the other. We are members of each other and therefore what we contribute has significant impact on the whole.

Each one has a unique purpose. Yet, that purpose cannot be realized in isolation and apart from the functioning body. While our gifts may differ, they differ according to the wisdom of God. What is important is that each of us is called to use the gifts we have. If we do, it will be a blessing to all we are associated with and we will be builders in the Kingdom of God. If we do not, something is missing for all of us.

May we deploy what we have been given for the building up of others and therefore display the wisdom of God.

JANUARY 22

I SHALL NOT WANT...

Psalm 23 was among my morning readings today; what a beautiful psalm. I encourage you to read it in its entirety. It is all about the Lord and what He does for those who are hid in Him. The shepherd imagery is used. How a shepherd cares for and directs his sheep is raised to another level for how the Lord our Shepherd cares for us.

The Lord our Shepherd feeds, nourishes, protects, restores and leads. He removes fear because of His presence. He guides with able strength that no matter how difficult the path, we are assured He will bring us through, even if correction is needed, or we must be defended. He causes us to be strengthened and gives us a platform even as our enemies watch, knowing they will not have the advantage. We are anointed from on high, even more than we can contain.

As a result of all of this, and even more so, David declares:

"Surely goodness and mercy shall follow me all the days of my life; and I will dwell in the house of the Lord forever." Psalm 23:6

Can you even take in all that the Lord has done, is doing, and will do for you and I? Being our Shepherd, He satisfies our very being. We are not in want. We do not need to strive. We do not need to fear. We have assurance, above all else, that He will be with us, no matter what we face. And ultimately, our dwelling place is with Him forever.

You and I get to experience all of this here on the earth in some wonderful measure. But one day we will experience this in a measure that will far exceed anything we have yet experienced.

As you consider all that this Psalm says to you, be at peace today, and let His goodness and mercy continue to follow you. May you experience this reality today and all the days of your life.

JANUARY 23

GENERATIONAL BLESSING

Today would have been my grandfather's 108th birthday. He has been gone from us almost 24 years now, yet the impact on our families' lives has not diminished. I am sitting writing this devotional thought in a house that he built. My grandmother still lives in this house, although we did add an addition to it twelve years ago to better accommodate her needs so she could stay with us. But every day I can see the work of my grandfather's hands in providing for his family, and now, his extended family. Members of five generations have lived in this home at some time or another, being blessed because of the setting of a foundation by one generation.

Of course, there has been some remodeling that has had to go on through the years to update or maintain this family home, but the undergirding structure that was built 60 years ago is what carries the weight and allows for the more decorative expressions to be demonstrated from one generation to another.

Surely, in this model, we can glean from what the Lord teaches us in the scriptures. A wise man builds his house on the rock: "*And the rain descended, the floods came, and the winds blew and beat on that house; and it did not fall, for it was founded on the rock*" (Matthew 7:24-25).

Who was the wise man? "*Whoever hears these sayings of Mine [*Jesus' teachings*], and does them.*"

My grandfather left us much more than just a home. We learned much from the character and instruction of his life. We all can learn from this example. Each of us is building something. Whether what we build will be a blessing is dependent on what law and whose words we follow.

If you raise your eyes beyond your own generation, you might understand what I am saying. Build well, future generations are depending on the content, care and character you display as you do your work today.

JANUARY 24

GOD'S FAITHFULNESS

Today, our church will participate in a memorial service for a dear sister in the Lord. As I ponder some of the scriptures that might be shared, I am drawn to one particular this morning. It was written by the prophet Jeremiah in a very difficult time of his own country's history. He could have focused on his difficulties, his countrymen's failure to live right. Instead he began to think about his God, the Lord of all the earth. Here are his thoughts:

"Through the Lord's mercies we are not consumed, because His compassions fail not. They are new every morning; Great is Your faithfulness. "The Lord is my portion," says my soul, "Therefore I hope in Him!" The Lord is good to those who wait for Him, to the soul who seeks Him. It is good that one should hope and wait quietly for the salvation of the Lord." Lamentations 3:22-26

Jeremiah describes God's mercies, love and faithfulness. He proclaims the fact that each day we can begin again with a new clean slate because we can find forgiveness for the previous day's failures. It makes us need to ponder some questions: Apart from God's mercies, where would we be? Without God's loving-kindness, to whom would we go? Unless God's faithfulness kept us, how would we progress? Therefore, waiting for Him is paramount. Seeking Him is rewarded. Hoping in Him is our salvation.

Great is God's faithfulness to His people. It just makes me want to break out in worship and praise.

Thank you, Lord, for leading me. Thank you, Lord, for caring for me. Thank you, Lord, for forgiving and loving me. I have been given a fresh start today. May I glorify You in all that I do.

How about you? Will you do the same? Take some time to give Him thanks. Make it personal. Make it real.

JANUARY 25

DISCOVER THE CITY'S JOY

Isaiah spoke the word of the Lord when saying:

"Be glad and rejoice forever in what I create; For behold, I create Jerusalem as a rejoicing, And her people a joy." Isaiah 65:18

Of course, we take these scriptures and others like, "*Pray for the peace of Jerusalem.*" And restrict them to one physical place, but fail to see in these scriptures principles that God wants us to grasp. Like the prophet Jeremiah, when he instructed his people to seek the peace of the city to where they were exiled, we must see the relevance of what this means for us where we live.

We do not think of our city as a "City of Joy." Nor for the most part do we delight over our city. Just read the commentaries that people post in the local papers for example. But God wants us to delight in the city, and He wants His people to find joy in the city, as well.

The church, which is comprised of you and I, is called to be a cheerleader (encourager/ enabler) to the city. We are called to name all that is evil and dark, particularly to confront the city's systems and structures when they act in exploitive and oppressive ways.

In order to truly be effective in the city, however, we cannot allow ourselves to be overwhelmed by the city's evil. We must take delight in our city, in the people surrounding our churches, and in each other, in the community of faith. It is time to start being joyful! We can delight in what God has made. He specializes in making something out of nothing.

Do it again Lord in New England. Even in my city!

JANUARY 26

FAITHFUL AND WISE SERVANT

Idleness is not a welcomed activity in the Kingdom of God. Industry, faithfulness, serving others, providing for our families are all looked upon as characteristics of Kingdom people. Jesus said:

"Who then is a faithful and wise servant, whom his master made ruler over his household, to give them food in due season? Blessed is that servant whom his master, when he comes, will find him doing. Assuredly I say to you that he will make him ruler over all his goods." Matthew 24:45-47

I remember one of my grandchildren instead of asking "What are you doing?", she used an abbreviated question, "Doing?" But in that question was really the key idea: the fact that I was "doing" something!

The purpose of doing is to be faithful to those with whom you have been entrusted. We have been trusted with the care of our immediate families, extended families, neighbors, and those who are in need around us. Our diligence will mean the difference in whether there is a supply in the needed season.

Today in the Northeast of America, we are preparing for a severe forecasted snow storm. Those who are wise will prepare. Those prepared will be in a better position to help others who might be in need.

Know who your neighbors are. If there are elderly, or others nearby that may be alone, look in on them. See if they have any needs. When the storm is over, help clear their walkways. Of course, we do not need storms to meet pressing needs to those around us. Your diligence and faithfulness can make the difference to those around you. Your Heavenly Father will be seen through your caring actions.

May He lead you in all you do today.

JANUARY 27

MY REFUGE AND FORTRESS

Waking and spending time with the Lord before the morning light, I have been listening to the sounds of the day. I can hear the howling of the wind, which seems from time to time to try and penetrate through the doors. Usually snow tends to deaden the sound, but not today. There is the pelting against the glass of the snow being driven horizontally. Occasionally I hear the rumbling of equipment that is being used to plow the snow.

I am also thinking about what sounds would have been heard in Noah's ark when the door finally shut and the storm began. Or when it rained fire and brimstone on that dreadful day in Sodom. What about the evening in Egypt when the death angel passed over? What sounds would have been heard when Jerusalem was destroyed as Jesus predicted? I can't even imagine. Can you? In each situation there was a preferred place to be. There was a place of judgment and there was a place of refuge.

The psalmist writes:

"He who dwells in the secret place of the Most High shall abide under the shadow of the Almighty. I will surely say of the Lord, 'He is my refuge and my fortress; My God, in Him I will trust.'" Psalm 91:1-2

When the storms of life come, and they will, where is your shelter? Is it in a place? Or, is it in a person? Or is the place the Person? Thankfully, a place for our sheltering is available. Jesus calls us to Himself; those who come, He shelters.

Look and learn from history. It's not time to look for shelter in a storm, but to make your residence secure before the storm. Find this place for dwelling. Stay there. You will find refuge. God is trustworthy.

JANUARY 28

THE NEED FOR REPEATED ACTIVITY

This morning when I looked outside, I could see that the wind and snow had once again covered the walks and driveways that I had cleared several times before. With the sun shining and the winds now subsided, I will have to go out and do it again.

It kind of reminds me of my need to be continually cleansed by God. I know that I have received the forgiveness of sins by Christ's great work on the cross, yet my daily dealings and walk are affected by choices, conditions, storms and heart issues. That is why the psalmist asks the question:

"How can a young man cleanse his way?" Psalm 119:9

I am glad that he answers this question, and that it is equally fitting for older men and women also. His answer is, "*By taking heed according to Your word.*"

While I might be bemoaning having to go out and shovel snow again, I am reminded of how Jesus continues to provide forgiveness for me each and every day. If I continue to read and heed His instruction for my life, I am able to keep the path clear. That is why the psalmist continued to say:

"With my whole heart I have sought You: Oh, let me not wander from Your commandments! Your word I have hidden in my heart, that I might not sin against You." Psalm 119:10-11

So, like the walks, driveways and cars we must be clear off, let the Word of God clear our pathways today. God's Word is something we must continually seek and apply, to keep our way clear to the Father. Happy digging!

HIS FAVOR IS FOR LIFE...

After reading through the Scriptures this morning, I went back to the first reading, a psalm, and reread it again. One particular verse is standing out to me. The psalmist wrote:

"Sing praise to the Lord, you saints of His, and give thanks at the remembrance of His holy name. For His anger is but for a moment, His favor is for life; Weeping may endure for a night, but joy comes in the morning." Psalm 30:4-5

We know that God loves us; included in that love is His directives, even His corrections. When we read of His anger, it is God's judgment brought forth, but it is not a lashing out like we might expect from someone who has not bridled his anger. It is God's great mercy applied in our lives to bring about what is needed to change. While none of us like this, it is what is necessary to mature us and shape us in His image. If we refuse this work of God, we can become bitter, even staying deformed in our growth.

But that is only one reason to rejoice and give God praise. The corrective aspect is like a moment compared to His favor which is for life. God's favor is forever. Think about that for a moment, you and I are living with the favor of God! Therefore, any difficulty which causes us pain is momentary. It may cause us to weep. But know that it will be followed by rejoicing. "*Weeping may endure for a night, but joy comes in the morning.*"

This is enough reason to give Him praise today. You and I can have, and do have if we belong to Him, the favor of God. It is not fleeting; it is forever! So even if we might experience some corrective action, a difficult situation, an unexpected hardship, we can look to the Lord who gives us His favor for life. Our weeping will be turned to joy. For resurrection follows the cross. It did then and it does now.

May His joy fill you completely.

JANUARY 30

REVELATION THAT CHANGES LIVES...

Many years ago, I constructed a sub-division and called it "Bethel Estates." A good friend still lives on one of these plots of land. The name came from a story that I was rereading this morning. Jacob, while traveling from Beersheba to Haran, paused in his journey to rest, and God revealed Himself to Jacob in a dream and promised Jacob that He would lead him and protect him in his journey. God would cause him to prosper and inherit the blessing promised to Abraham, his grandfather and Isaac, his father. This blessing was not only for himself but for all his descendants as well. When Jacob awoke from this very vivid dream, it caused him to declare: "*Surely the Lord is in this place and I did not know it.*" (Genesis 28:16). He called the place of this encounter "Bethel" meaning the house of God.

In the same sub-division the streets were named, “Emmaus" and "Damascus". What they have in common with "Bethel" is that each location was significant in that God revealed Himself to those chosen in such a way that He would change their lives for time and eternity. On the road to Emmaus His disciples saw the risen Lord and encouraged their brothers. On the road to Damascus, a zealous Jew named Saul, who had been persecuting the Christians, was thrown from His horse and encountered Jesus. This eventually led to a change of name from Saul to Paul, along with a change of purpose and direction for his life.

For all of these, the revelation meant a promise, protection, and purpose. Each needed to continue on a journey by faith, many times difficult, but with the full knowledge that God would be with them.

As God revealed Himself to those chosen, He continues to reveal Himself to us today. We have the privilege in our day to be able to read the Word of God and allow His Holy Spirit to give us revelation knowledge in all it contains. We can spend time in prayer and trust that the same Holy Spirit will reveal the will and purpose of God in our lives. These are the encounters that sustain us and give us the vision to move forward. May we all have such encounters.

JANUARY 31

WHEN SECULAR REASON GIVES WAY TO RELIGIOUS NON-REASON

We are instructed to be subject to governing authorities and pray for them because they are God's instrument for order and are appointed and given authority from God (see Romans 13 and 1 Timothy 2:1-4). We are also to hold them accountable for using their authority within the bounds that have been prescribed by God. But what happens when those subject to them are not reasonable, but gather together in mob fashion to bring about forced change through a wrong process and world-view?

In Luke 23, we read the account of Jesus being brought up on charges before Pilate, Herod, and back to Pilate. While Jesus was arrested and held without a rightful charge, and declared innocent by the governing authorities, the religious leaders persisted. The scripture says, "*They were urgent, demanding with loud cries that he [Jesus] should be crucified. And their voices prevailed. So Pilate decided that their demand should be granted. He released the man who had been thrown into prison for insurrection and murder, for whom they asked, but he delivered Jesus over to their will*" (Luke 23:23-25 ESV).

The authorities were swayed by popular opinion, swayed by envy and lies, not truth. The results let an innocent man be put to death and a criminal be set free. We understand that Jesus' death became the means for our salvation, but I am looking at another principle here. If we allow popular non-reason to prevail, we will not walk in the blessing of God in our neighborhoods and nations.

If we do not influence our neighbors with proper living and a biblical worldview, but let them subscribe to the popular non-reason of our day, we will see other unreasonable things sanctioned by those in authority. Influence must be properly exerted to change both those in authority and those governed. Kingdom change works from the bottom up, from the inside out, from local to trans-local. You and I can really make a difference if we are willing to stand up and be the voice of reason in our day. It is not too late. We can still make a difference!

FEBRUARY 1

NO GREATER LOVE

Reading Luke's account of the crucifixion this morning, I am pausing at Jesus' words while suspended on the cross:

"Father, forgive them, for they do not know what they do." Luke 23:34

In agony, riddled with pain, hearing religious leaders, soldiers and even criminals mocking Him, Jesus turns to the Father, and with great compassion for those for whom He came, mutters this prayer in intercession for them and us.

As a pastor for many years, I have seen the results of people who are slow to, or refuse to forgive something that has been done to them, or they have perceived has been done to them. It causes pain that often encapsulates them into wrong actions, bitterness of heart, separation from others, isolation from God, and even disease of body. The example of Jesus' action on the cross can help us put some perspective on what others have done to us. Surely we have not suffered in the same way that He did. However, because of His example and life-giving Spirit in our lives, we can forgive as He did and does.

The Scriptures tell us that Jesus' example was that of no greater love… a love that was willing to sacrifice even His life for not just His friends, but those who were even enemies of the cross. All of us were in this camp at some point of our lives. We, who have trusted in Him, have received the forgiveness of sins. Knowing how much we have been forgiven should compel us to be slow to anger and willing to forgive those who wrong us. We too can show this kind of love. We must show this kind of love. Only by God's help can we.

Consider if there is any long-standing issue or issues that are unresolved in your life. Is there a possibility to go to the individual or individuals that might have caused you pain and seek resolution? Is there someone that you need to forgive? Is there someone that you need to ask for forgiveness? If you look to Jesus as your example and enablement, you can find new freedom for your life.

FEBRUARY 2

AT WHAT POINT IS IT IDOLATRY?

I don't know if I am alone in my thoughts this morning. I want to be cautious about what I am about to say. I do not intend to condemn what some people might be celebrating in our New England region and beyond, only how important some have elevated this competitive sport. Please do not get me wrong, each morning I put on my favorite sweatshirt hoodie, with a sport team emblem on it, to warm me while I read Scripture, pray and write some devotional thought.

I, too, enjoy the competition and was joyful that our local team was victorious. But my joy was tempered by the over emphasis of all the news coverage and importance that people seem to put on the matter. When I watched the celebration and a trophy being handled like it was the golden calf, my spirit was vexed. By grace the victor prevailed, even though it could have easily been the opposite. Winners should be humble and losers gracious. But the trash talking continues. Does anyone agree that we might have moved toward idolatry in modern day sports?

The psalmist says,

"I will bless the Lord at all times; His praise shall continually be in my mouth. My soul shall make its boast in the Lord; the humble shall hear of it and be glad. Oh, magnify the Lord with me, and let us exalt His name together" (Psalm 34:1-3).

I pray that I communicate more about my Lord than the local sports channel. He is the sustainer of my soul, whether my team wins or doesn't. He is the One in whom I want to boast. I can't get Him out of my mind. I want my energies directed toward His purposes.

May I congratulate both teams who fought hard to get where they are and to accomplish what they did. Now, today, life goes on, and there are many that need us to point them in the direction that will bring them peace and a vision for life. We have something, even Someone, to introduce them to, that will not be temporary, but everlasting; a hope that will not fade, a glory that will be revealed. Can you join me today, and turn your attention and declaration to the One who deserves all our adoration? He makes us all winners.

FEBRUARY 3

WALKING WITH A LIMP...

It is amazing the encounters that Jacob has in his journeys. Leaving from his home to seek a wife, he encounters, in a dream, angels and the voice of God giving him a promise that He would be with him. Twenty years later, in his return trip home, Jacob meets up with angels again. He called this place "Mahanaim" meaning "This is God's camp" (Genesis 32:2). Jacob is about to meet up with his brother Esau soon and is afraid of what that encounter will be like. But God promises him to be his protection.

After developing a strategy of how he will approach his brother, he is alone and finds himself wrestling with an angel through the evening, and will not let go, unless blessed. The angel touched the hip of Jacob which left him with a limp, a reminder of his encounter. This incident makes me wonder about the dealings of God. We can be left with a limp because we do not heed His correction (Heb. 12:13), but this is not what happened here.

The limp was a reminder of the grace and purpose of God that needed to be remembered. As we get older in our faith, we recognize that God has been gracious to us. He has shaped us, not just in the mountain top experiences, but also in the very difficult times of life. His dealings with us may leave us with a limp, but we have learned to rely on the strength of the Lord and not in ourselves. When Paul cried out to the Lord for deliverance, God said, "*My grace is sufficient for you, for My strength is made perfect in weakness*" (2 Corinthians 12:9).

So with maturity, a greater measure of grace and humility should be our clothing. Recognizing that the promises of the Lord are sure, we endure with patience even the presumptive responses of those who oppose us. We can recognize in ourselves the dealings of God. We bear the marks of the Gospel we have preached (see 2 Corinthians 11:23-28). The limp of our own step reminds us of our own humanness, but at the same time we rejoice in God's great guidance. He promises to journey with us. He is faithful to His promises. So, lean on His staff. Continue your journey. Trust that He who began a good work in you will complete it until the day of Christ Jesus.

FEBRUARY 4

CONCERN AND PRAYER FOR MY UKRAINIAN FRIENDS AND NATION

It is easy to live our lives insulated from everything that goes on around us. But we are called of God to pray for the nations of the world. One such nation on my heart this morning is the nation of Ukraine. I have had the privilege of ministering in this nation numerous times beginning 11 years ago. I have had the opportunity to get to know so many fine people of God who are serving Him with great faithfulness, often with meager resources. What they are not short of is hospitality, love, and great sacrificial care. I have a great love for many there and continue to enjoy communicating and encouraging to the best of my ability.

As you read the news, you understand the great conflict that continues to plague the well-being of this country. Many people have died in the continued battles, with rebel forces that are unwilling to give up ground through employing an antagonistic armed force. Much of this armed force seems to be supplied from a neighboring country seeking greater power and control.

Today, Lord, I pray for this nation. I pray for Your mercy, faithfulness, righteousness and sure judgements. The psalmists declared: "*Your mercy, O Lord, is in the heavens; Your faithfulness reaches to the clouds. Your righteousness is like the great mountains; Your judgements are a great deep; O Lord, You preserve man and beast*" (Psalm 36:5-6).

May You hide Your people under Your wing of protection. May You cause them to be salt and light in this nation to present Your Kingdom to all to whom they are called to minister. May Your peace encompass this country, so that Your Word may be carried to the nations of the world through Your servants. Put the enemy to confusion and flight. Exalt the humble and put down the proud, so that You may be glorified. Comfort those who are mourning the family members that have perished in the process. May they lift up their eyes and receive Your great care. Let Your Kingdom come on earth as it is in Heaven.

THIRTY YEARS AGO TODAY....

A precious baby girl was added to our family. From a very young age she set her heart on the Lord and has never wavered in her devotion to Him. Joy of heart, kindness, and a willingness to serve and work with and for others, distinguishes her from her peers. She has brought much love and joy to those whom are close to her and to our home. This has not been without testing. But in the journey of life, the Lord has strengthened and shaped her faith and witness. It is a joy to watch her love her husband, raise her daughter, interact with her mother, love her extended family and minister to children and adults alike. As a father, I could not be more proud.

The psalmists wrote:

"Behold, children are a heritage from the Lord, the fruit of the womb is a reward. Like arrows in the hand of a warrior, so are the children of one's youth. Happy is the man who has his quiver full of them; they shall not be ashamed, but shall speak with their enemies in the gate." Psalm 127:3-5

I have been most blessed with two children, and many spiritual children. Today, I want to commend my daughter Andrea. Happy Birthday Andrea! May the Lord bless you with His most choice blessing. You are much loved. You have grown up to be a beautiful woman of God. Even so, you will always be my little girl.

FEBRUARY 6

PROGRESS REPORT

Our school report cards went out this week. Periodically we also send out progress reports to let parents, students and administrators know what the development looks like in the life of the student at a particular time. Luke also gives progress reports. When you study the Book of Acts, you can see at least six such progress reports in Luke's account. The progress reports seek to bridge what accomplishment or development has been attained, while at the same time creating a bridge for a new development or direction he will unfold to us. One in particular was part of my reading this morning.

In Acts 6 we read of seven chosen to serve in the distribution of bread to the Hellenists widows. The fact that there was some complaint between the Hellenists against the Hebrews signified a need that was not being properly addressed. The apostles did not brush this off, nor did they simply add more to their already great responsibilities. What they did was seek to expand their administrative support by selecting others who could assist them.

Criteria are set for their selection and a decision was made by the apostles to broaden their base of ministry without compromising, or taking them away from their specific calling. They realized that they could not do everything. And if they tried to, the ministry of the Word and prayer would suffer. Building a greater team would enable the church to be healthier and see that the needs of the saints would be met. It also created the opportunity for others to advance in their own callings. Luke closes this section with this progress report:

"Then the word of God spread, and the number of the disciples multiplied greatly in Jerusalem, and a great many of the priests were obedient to the faith." Luke 6:7

This is instructive to us today. We can only expand in our effectiveness of ministry to others to the degree that we include others to work along with us. Consider how we can join with others or have them join us in effective service to others. we cannot do it all alone.

FEBRUARY 7

STEPHEN'S CLIMATIC CONCLUSION

One of the longer sermons recorded in the book of Acts is one spoken by Stephen (Acts 7:1-60). He was a man attested to be full of faith and power, who did great wonders and signs among the people. He had been chosen as one of the seven who administered to the needs of the Hellenists widows. Now he addresses the council, having been falsely accused, but the Word of God says, as those in the council looked steadfastly at him, they saw his face as the face of an angel. When others had disputed with Stephen, the Bible records: "*They were not able to resist the wisdom and the Spirit by which he spoke*" (Acts 7:10). Therefore, they stirred up people to seize him, speak falsely about Stephen and bring him before the Jewish council.

What is particularly significant is his ability to clearly articulate the history of Israel, from the call of Abraham through the period of Solomon and relate it to the faithfulness of God and the unfaithfulness of His people. From his historical account, he is able to bring them to the present date and address their own unwillingness to follow the Lord, His prophets, and His law. They have set up their own systems, customs and temple to a greater significance than the truth. In fact, they are willing to destroy truth, and Christ, in order to preserve their false ideas in the name of religion. Here are Stephen's concluding remarks:

"You stiff-necked and uncircumcised in heart and ears! You always resist the Holy Spirit; as your father's did, so do you. Which of the prophets did your father's not persecute? And they killed those who foretold the coming of the Just One, of whom you now have become the betrayers and murderers, who have received the law by the direction of angels and have not kept it" (Acts 7:51-53).

This sermon did not win Stephen a popularity contest. In fact, they became so angry that they rose up and stoned him to death. Stephen died a martyr's death. A significant witness stood by, his name was Saul. Stephen's witness would become a significant seed planted in Saul's life to germinate at a later time, teaching us that even though death works in us, life can be produced in another.

FEBRUARY 8

A NEW SONG

One of my favorite psalms is Psalm 40. It speaks of the faithfulness of God to raise us out from the muck and mire of this world. Stuck in our human condition, God's arm is not too short. By His grace and mercy, He lifts us up. He answers our cry and secures our standing. No longer tossed about with every wind and doctrine our steps are established, and here is the amazing thing:

"He has put a new song in my mouth - Praise to our God: Many will see it and fear, and will trust in the Lord." Psalm 40:3

It seems that some people seem to sing the same old song, complaining about life, ever grasping for meaning and purpose; ungrateful, unthankful and discontent in all that is around them. But, for the child of God, it should not be so. For we have been showered with the greatest grace and mercy we could ever encounter: forgiveness that is beyond measure; a love that cannot be compared; a future that is hopeful and secured by the very precious blood of the Lamb of God. If that doesn't change your song, nothing will. But that is not all!

When we begin to sing this new song, others take notice. They see the change that encompasses our lives. They hear the melody and harmony of the music of our lives. The cadence is different; the key signature has been raised from a minor key to a major key. There is something significantly catchy. Something about the melody stays with you. You can't shake it out of your mind. You begin to hum the tune in your mind, and even break out in song because this song causes others to take notice and to trust in the Lord for themselves.

Let this new song emanate from your life. Like water that bubbles forth from your innermost being, let it flow, let it go, let it be heard. Proclaim it from the mountain tops, and sing it in the congregation; sing it in the busses, and the corridors of your work. Be the music that others see and hear. Let your life be the melody that warms others to smile, be warmed and changed. Let the new song come forth!

FEBRUARY 9

I DO NOT RESTRAIN MY LIPS...

We have heard it said that "actions speak louder than words." There is a great truth to this saying. But does that mean that words are not needed? Obviously if there is not a corresponding action that would cause the words spoken to be verified or established, we could say that the words are empty, or even hypocritical. But again I ask, "Does this invalidate the need for words"?

In continuing to reflect on Psalm 40, the psalmists wrote:

"I delight to do Your will, O my God, and Your law is within my heart." Psalm 40:8

So, we see that the psalmist (ascribed to David) is speaking of his right standing and the desires of his heart. This is his walk, or his way of life. Yet there is more, he continues to write:

"I have proclaimed the good news of righteousness in the great assembly; I do not restrain my lips, O Lord, You Yourself know. I have not hidden Your righteousness within my heart; I have declared Your faithfulness and Your salvation; I have not concealed Your loving kindness and Your truth from the great assembly." Psalm 40:9-10

If we are people who hide righteousness in our heart, but do not proclaim it with our lips, how will people come to the knowledge of the truth? Perhaps they will observe in us that we are nice people, but being nice people will not change others.

Unless we share our faith (and faith comes by hearing the Word of God), real change will not happen to others. We then must ask ourselves an important question: Have we restrained our lips and privatized our faith? Until we open up and let others know of the hope that is within us, they can only guess. We do not want to stop living and doing good to others by being good examples, but in our doing, let us also proclaim the Good News of righteousness to those we meet. Words are powerful! Let us use them for God's glory!

FEBRUARY 10

ICE DAMS

With all the snow we have been having in New England, the shallow pitched roofs are covered and the thawing and freezing continues to produce ice along the edges of the roof. Perhaps you have witnessed the icicles hanging from the edges if the roofs. When this condition occurs, and other areas of the roof begin to melt, the water has no place to escape. Water therefore finds its way behind roofing material and can cause leaks in a building structure. All because the ice dam hardened and caused a physical obstruction not allowing normal drainage to occur.

This physical condition has me thinking about other hardened obstructions. The Bible refers to heart conditions of individuals as having a hardened heart. One cause of a hardened heart is unbelief. The writer of Hebrews wrote:

"Beware, brethren, lest there be in any of you an evil heart of unbelief in departing from the Living God; but exhort one another daily, while it is called "Today" less any of you be hardened through the deceitfulness of sin." Hebrews 3:12-13

When hearts are hardened, it causes other damaging things to occur. Peace is loss. Relationships are broken. Rest is not entered. It causes us to walk away from God, instead of turning to Him. It is a vicious cycle that continues to perpetuate itself into greater and greater damage. Unless the ice jam is broken, the condition will continue.

If you find yourself in this never-ending cycle, you have a choice to make to get help. Let the love of the Lord melt your heart, which will allow all that has built up in your life to be released. God's mercy is much greater than His judgment. It is fresh every day. Because of His great forgiveness and grace, we can also extend forgiveness and grace to others. Go ahead, just allow the Lord to enable you to let it all go! You will be glad you did!

FEBRUARY 11

GO THEREFORE...

How hard is it for us to comprehend simple words of instruction? Why do we almost have to be compelled to respond? Many years after the Jerusalem church was started, they still struggled with the initial command of Jesus. He had told them: "*Go therefore and make disciples of all the nations, baptizing them in the name of the Father and of the Son and of the Holy Spirit, teaching them to observe all things that I have commanded you; and lo, I am with you always, even to the end of the age*" (Matthew 28:19-20).

We read of the reception of the Gospel by Cornelius and his family and friends at Caesarea, in Acts chapter 10. Then we read of all the divine intervention that it took to have Peter present that Gospel message to these Gentiles and the supernatural acceptance of God which causes Peter to accept them also. However, as soon as he returned to Jerusalem, he had to defend his actions. Those of the circumcision contended with him. Peter had to retell the story and help them understand what God's intention was from the beginning. "*When they heard these things they became silent; glorifying God, saying, 'Then God has also granted to the Gentiles repentance to life'*" (Acts 11:18).

It makes one wonder what understanding the disciples had of the Great Commission, or, did their own prejudices get in the way? This will not be the last time we see encounters of religious leaders who struggle with those who come from different cultures and experiences. Instead of building on what would unify them together, they would try to make them the same, not by substance, but by form.

I wonder how much change the Lord needs to bring in our own hearts to obey His commission? Are there prejudices in us that stop us from going and making disciples? Are we so tied to our own forms that we miss the substance of our faith? Jesus' sacrifice on the cross was for all who would believe on His name. Which of these "all" are we reluctant to share His Gospel with? If He sends us (and He has) are we going to obey? May the Lord deal with all the things that cause us to hesitate.

FEBRUARY 12

CEASE FIRE...BUT NOT PRAYER!

Anxious to see if there was any news from the multi-nation talk going on yesterday in Minsk relating to the Ukraine crises, I sought out particular articles this morning. Even though a cease fire agreement has been agreed upon, I realize that what man says and does is not always kept. A peaceful agreement is better than escalating war. However, much more needs to happen for there to be a transition where peace and opportunity can prevail in this nation again. So much damage has already been done. More than a million people have been displaced. Thousands killed, many others injured, houses and facilities bombarded and infrastructure damaged.

While we might seem to go on in life, thinking that this doesn't matter to us, we could not be more wrong. We must engage ourselves in prayer and seek just what the Lord requires of us to support our brethren. If not in this nation, where is the Lord calling us to be part of His local and global ministry? This morning I was also reading about the prophetic pronouncements that were made about the famine that would affect the then known world (Acts 11:27-28). "*The disciples, each according to his ability, determined to send relief to the brethren dwelling in Judea. This they did, and sent it to the elders by the hands of Barnabas and Saul*" (Acts 11:29-30). Interesting enough, I also had read of Pharaoh's dream that Joseph had interpreted about the famine that would come over Egypt and the need to prepare for that day.

The questions that I am pondering this morning are: (1) Do we understand that we are committed to the Kingdom of God for something bigger than our own local community or church? (2) If so, are we connected in our own local church expressions to hear the direction of the Lord and join to do something collectively, or are we just independent and doing our own thing, or simply doing nothing? (3) How can we send "relief" to those who are under a difficult yoke? How might we be practical and also encouraging? We must first and consistently pray! May God give us a heart to ask Him for the nations of the world as His inheritance, and then the resolve to answer His call to do what He calls us to do.

FEBRUARY 13

THE LORD WITH US...OUR REFUGE

My heart is drawn to the nations. Amidst the tactics and theater being played out on the world scene, there is a Theocracy!

"God is our refuge and strength. A very present help in trouble. Therefore we will not fear. Even though...." Psalm 46:1-2

The psalmists continued to speak of present and possible future difficulties. I am sure that you and I could offer our own list of difficulties. But the important thing to see is that the psalmist is reminding his readers of the greatness and superiority of God above all the circumstantial world events playing out.

The fact that God is with us, should bring us comfort. He is greater than anything we can possibly face. The psalmists wrote expanding his thoughts:

"Come, behold the works of the Lord, Who has made desolations in the earth. He makes wars cease to the end of the earth; He breaks the bow and cuts the spear in two; He burns the chariot in the fire. Be still, and know that I am God; I will be exalted among the nations, I will be exalted in the earth! The Lord of hosts is with us; The God of Jacob is our refuge." Psalm 46:8-11

Peace in any storm is found in the One who is peace. We can take refuge in being in Him no matter what the external circumstances are. If we put our trust in anything, or anyone else, we will not rest. But, true rest is found in putting our trust in the One who is trustworthy.

Let us exalt His name among the nations! Let us trust that He is with us, as He already has promised! There we will find refuge. Let us remind each other - He is with us. If He is for us, who can be against us? Be encouraged; you are not alone. Let us thank the Lord for His presence with us. He is our refuge.

FEBRUARY 14

DO JUSTICE - LIVE JUSTLY

When Micah made a statement to his people, he said:

"He has shown you, O man, what is good; and what does the Lord require of you but to do justly, to love mercy, and to walk humbly with your God?" Micah 6:8

Often times, people seem to generalize living righteously as meaning broadly, for a Christian to be obedient to God's Word, or for them to simply make a certain commitment to avoid certain egregious sins. But is this understanding adequate? We must explore just what it means to do justice.

I like one definition of justice I have read recently. Here is my recollection of it. "The righteous are willing to disadvantage themselves to advantage the community; the wicked are willing to disadvantage the community to advantage themselves."

This definition is something worth pondering. You see wickedness is not just what you see as the visible tip of the iceberg, but the very support structure which is not so visible, revealing itself in everyday actions. If we choose to live justly, then, we must see it also as an everyday activity. Living justly, we must have a constant recognition of the claims of community on us, disadvantaging ourselves in order to advantage others.

In what ways might you be willing to disadvantage yourself, in order to advantage someone else? Examples could include things like: feeding the poor when you have the power to do so; not taking so much income out of your business so that your employees are too poorly paid; even being willing to shovel the snow out of the driveway of an elderly neighbor, even though you have your own to do. Think of your own examples. Then walk justly!

FEBRUARY 15

CULTURAL SENSITIVITY AND DOCTRINAL PURITY

In reading Acts 15 this morning, an interesting conclusion is reached in the debate over salvation and how both Jew and Gentiles are to continue in their faith. Both groups believed that through the grace of the Lord Jesus Christ they would be saved. The issue was going forward, how would this continue? For some, they wanted to add a yoke of bondage, the Law as a means of continuing in the faith; in other words, Jesus plus the Law. This is a yoke that Peter declares is something that both Jew and Gentile were not able to keep in the past, nor would they be able to keep in the future. In fact, their hearts would only be purified by faith.

However, they did stipulate some things that the Gentiles should follow. And here is their reasoning for why:

"For Moses has had throughout many generations those who preach him in every city, being read in the synagogues every Sabbath." Acts 15:21

In drawing up this consensus, they not only had the Gentiles in mind, but also those whom the Gentiles might seek to reach. In other words, could they be culturally sensitive to those who had not yet turned to God, while at the same time walking in the freedom that they had found?

How about us today? Do we understand the religious makeup of our own communities? Have we considered that how we walk in our own freedom affects those brothers and sisters who might not yet know that same freedom? For their sake, are we willing to forgo some of our liberty, without letting go of our convictions, in order to reach them?

If we were more sensitive to those around us, might we have a greater means of sharing the truth of the Kingdom of God? Give it some thought! Just remember, being sensitive does not mean conforming to our cultural ideals. There is a great difference in being culturally sensitive and being culturally absorbed. The goal is cultural sensitivity while maintaining doctrinal purity.

FEBRUARY 16

MESSAGE AND MISSION - WORD AND DEED MINISTRY

When we consider justice and mercy ministries and the ideas that undergird them, we can find that the ideologies can become self-righteous. One may advocate compassionate responsibility-based solutions that can become paternalistic, patronizing and blind to many problems like poverty. The other can be orientated against system injustice, leading to anger, rancor, and division. One blames the poor for everything; the other tends to blame the rich for everything. One approach overemphasizes individual responsibility; the other under emphasizes it.

As Christians, we are called to live justly as a response to grace. It is our salvation, given by grace, that should move us to do justice. We cannot separate Word and deed ministries. An integrative ministry means weaving together Word and deed ministry as much as possible.

When Jesus raised the dead son of the widow of Nain, He spoke words of comfort (Luke 7:13). After He healed the blind man, He returned with a Gospel charge (John 9:35-38). These go hand in hand. In Acts 2, explosive growth in numbers (v. 41) leads to radical sharing with the needy (vv. 44-45). In Acts 4, economic sharing by people inside the church accompanied the preaching of the resurrection outside the church with great power (vv. 32-35). The practical actions of Christians on behalf of people in need demonstrated the truth and power of the Gospel.

Jesus calls us to both Gospel pronouncement (urging everyone to repent and believe) and Gospel demonstration (sacrificially meeting the needs of those around us). The two concerns must go together; message and mission; word and deed. God has liberated us by His grace and power. Now we are to treat all people who have less power or fewer assets as neighbors, demonstrating justice to them.

So the theological and motivational basis for doing justice is salvation by grace! Is your desire to help someone arising out of a heart touched by grace, a heart surrendered to its feelings of superiority towards any group or class of people? If so, you can live and do justly, loving mercy and walking humbly.

FEBRUARY 17

MOCKERS, PATRONIZERS AND BELIEVERS

In reading Luke's account of Paul ministering in Athens, there are a couple of verses that just seem to stay with me this morning. In the intellectual center of where Paul was preaching, there were many philosophers who loved to do nothing more than learn new things, not doing anything with it. Their lives were just filled with debate, yet the images of that place spoke of their supreme ignorance. They worshiped what they did not know. Yet, when Paul identified for them the God who is known, their reaction is telling:

"When they heard of the resurrection of the dead, some mocked, while others said, 'We will hear you again on this matter.' However, some men joined him and believed, among them Dionysius the Areopagite, a woman named Damaris, and others with them." Acts 17:32-34

I am reflecting on the work we have had in Fall River. Throughout the years how many have simply mocked the words of life; others think they have forever to live to make a decision for Christ. They would rather live their own way, so they just patronize what is said, not really listening. They are too absorbed with the cares of this world, making money, having fun, going wherever the wind takes them. But there is a third group: those who do hear and believe. They might be in the minority, but they are willing to be joined with you. They allow God's Word to penetrate their lives, change their priorities as the Lord also changes their character and motivations.

While I struggle with so many who fall into the first two categories, I must also be thankful that God is reaching those whom He can raise as salt and light in our community. Therefore, I must persevere; we must persevere, declaring the Good News of the Gospel to our generation. Even though we may be mocked or patronized, there are those whom God will call to Himself.

May we be found faithful.

FEBRUARY 18

BEHOLD MY SERVANT

Matthew records Jesus quoting from Isaiah 42:1-4 about His own ministry. Consider the words and description of Jesus. He is full of mercy and justice. A servant we can trust.

"Behold! My Servant whom I have chosen, My Beloved in whom My soul is well pleased! I will put My Spirit upon Him, and He will declare justice to the Gentiles. He will not quarrel nor cry out, nor will anyone hear His voice in the streets. A bruised reed He will not break, and smoking flax He will not quench, till He sends forth justice to victory; and in His name Gentiles will trust." Matthew 12:18-21

Matthew presents Jesus as the Ideal Servant; showing us that Jesus' concept of Messiahship was radically different from that of the conventional expectation. A remarkable aspect of the quotation is the reference to the Gentiles, extending God's grace beyond the borders of the ethnic community of Jewry. For the Gentiles in the crowds, this was a word of grace.

The Holy Spirit rests creatively upon Jesus; the hope of all nations is centered in Him; the helpfulness of grace characterizes His ministry. His work is marked by His bringing justice to all men. His modesty is seen as He will not stir up discontent among the people. His compassion is exhibited in the aspect that He will respect even the smallest element of faith, for He will not break the bruised reed nor quench the smoking flax. He opens His invitation to all.

Not only is Jesus full of mercy and justice, He sends forth victory. There are so many people (especially Christian people) declaring gloom and doom in our world today. They speak of defeat and not of victory. Let us understand that Jesus has all authority and has already won the victory. If we trust in Him, we will see this victory come to pass.

Fear not; be encouraged, we serve an awesome God.

GOVERNMENT DEPENDENCY AND SLAVERY

The story of Joseph in Egypt is amazing on so many levels. The elevation of this man in everything he put his hand to, even though so much opposition could have left him bitter. As wise management of the revelation of a dream regarding an impending famine, Joseph had Egypt store up resources in years of plenty, so that in time of scarcity, they would have what was needed. This is a principle everyone should have followed, and even one we can learn from today. But, most people just live day-to-day, not willing to forgo something today in wise planning for any difficult rainy day in the future. As a result, the borrower becomes servant to the lender. In other words, those who are in need must come under the control of those who have, if they want to survive. But their survival is not without a cost.

Here is what we see as a result in Egypt. In order to have food, the people sold to Joseph (Egypt) first their money, then their livestock, then their lands and finally their very selves. In short, the people became slaves to the state willingly (see Genesis 47:23-26).

So, not only did the people end up with no land of their own, they were also required to be taxed 20% on everything they produced. In our own day, we continue to look to the government for supply, not realizing that all we have has become subject to that same government. In addition, we are seeing taxes of all sorts being enacted on our production, reducing any potential we will have to become more financially stable to meet our own needs in the future. If we don't change our ways, bowing to government as our god, we, too, will be fully enslaved, actually doing it willingly (even though it is ill advised).

The question for us is: are we willing to look to God as our provider, and follow His direction for wise stewardship in our own lives? He is the answer to famine in our land. There are Biblical principles we can follow in our own lives. As long as we follow the god of the state, our end will be increased slavery. But, if we trust in God, He will instruct us in wise management and production to supply our every need.

FEBRUARY 20

FRAGILITY OF LIFE

Last night the overflow shelters were at capacity. With the persistent snow, and the dropping temperatures and wind chill, there were many new faces. Some were more animated than normal. They had learned that one person who had been sheltered just a couple days before had died of a brain vessel burst. He was only 41 years old. He had not been well known but considered one of their company of friends. I spent time talking to one individual who was having real difficulty with this issue.

The reality is that we don't know how the little time we have with people can be the only time we might have with them. Life is difficult at times and can become most difficult for people during some seasons of their life. As God's people we are called to share His love and offer hope to those around us. We might never know whom we have really helped. But we must not let the moment of opportunity pass. Peter exhorted us to be ready to give a defense of our faith even to those who might want to oppose:

"Sanctify the Lord God in your hearts, and always be ready to give a defense to everyone who asks you a reason for the hope that is in you, with meekness and fear; having a good conscience, that when they defame you as evildoers, those who revile your good conduct in Christ may be ashamed. For it is better, if it is the will of God, to suffer for doing good than for doing evil." 1 Peter 3:15-17

As your day unfolds today, consider the people whom you will encounter; whether they are those in your house, your job, or any you will meet along the way. Consider their eternal value. Recognize that Jesus came to provide a way to the Father for all of us who would believe in Him.

You and I are called to point people in His direction, to offer hope and eternal life. We don't know if we will have another opportunity. This does not mean that we will always be successful in changing people's hearts and minds. However, it should not stop us from our responsibility. Remember, the duty is ours, but the results belong to God.

FEBRUARY 21

WE NEED EACH OTHER

God has designed the Body of Christ so that each member contributes to the spiritual growth of other members of the Body. As Paul wrote to the Ephesians:

"...Every joint supplies, according to the effective working by which every part does its share, causes growth of the body for the edifying of itself in love." Ephesians 4:16

We are "members of one another" (Rom. 12:5) and we need each other.

As we talked among the men who had gathered for our Men's Ministry last evening, it was apparent that each one was facing his own battles. However, more often than not, the thinking was that they had to do this alone with God's help.

What seems to be missing in this kind of thinking is that since we belong to a church community, in order for God to be able to shape us for His glory, He uses individuals in the community to help us in our challenges. We do not need to go it alone. There might be an answer through the multitude of counselors for the roadblock we might be facing. There is accountability to help us in developing new habits, overcoming problems and growing in Godliness. We are not alone, and we need each other.

If these men had these thoughts of rugged individualistic warfare, perhaps others are thinking the same. How ironic that God has fashioned us for community and positioned us to be fruitful in the context of community that we would think that we are isolated and needing to face our battles alone.

Today as you are thinking about your individual situation, has this been your mindset? Are you carrying the weight of your situation on your shoulders? Have you shared this with someone you can trust? You can have a greater victory if you allow the community to come along your side.

FEBRUARY 22

GOD'S GREAT COMPASSION AND FORGIVENESS

I had a troubled sleep last night. I had heard disturbing news that broke my heart and troubled my spirit. If it wasn't for God's mercy, I would not be able to minister to those who had sought me out. In reflection of Israel's stubbornness in the wilderness, the psalmist records these words:

"For their heart was not steadfast with Him, nor were they faithful in His covenant. But He, being full of compassion, forgave their iniquity, and did not destroy them. Yes, many a time He turned His anger away, and did not stir up all His wrath; for He remembered that they were but flesh, a breath that passes away and does not come again." Psalm 78:37-39

The example we see from the Lord is that He often held back the fierceness of His anger because it was tempered by His mercy considering the humanness of people. While justice was needed, He still held back on the severity of the penalty, even later becoming the sacrifice for all the sins of mankind.

This is the same position from which we can minister. People will disappoint us. Those who should know better are still subject to the same temptations we all face. With humbleness and compassion, we, too, must seek to be a help. Justice must be served, but we allow the Lord to bring about that His way.

In everyday teaching and leading, our hope is to help people avoid the consequences of sin. Yet, when they do sin, we must ask the Lord for the grace to point them back to Him. We must help them seek His forgiveness. We must help them take accountability for their sins, whatever that may cost. We must cry out with them calling upon the Lord's mercy in their present situation.

We are thankful that we have Christ as our Intercessor. While He was tempted in all ways, as we are, He was without sin. As we hide ourselves in Him, He can give us the strength to walk in the forgiveness of sin and trust in His mercy for our future hope. By God's grace we continue.

FEBRUARY 23

FREEZING AND THAWING

I looked at the weather forecast last evening and saw that the temperature was predicted to be below freezing for another week. Some of the issues that many people have been facing are ice dams, leaks backing up on roofs, and the damage that leaking water is causing. It has me thinking that the only remedy is for the temperature to rise a few degrees. With just a little bit of warmth, the ice will melt, and we will be on our way to fixing whatever situations have been affected. But, if the temperature stays cold enough, we may incur more damage, and surely, the road to recovery is postponed.

This natural occurrence has me thinking of our spiritual existence. There are things in our lives that can cause us to be hardened, embittered, and even angry. The writer to the Hebrews says:

"Therefore, as the Holy Spirit says: '*Today, if you hear His voice, do not harden your hearts as in the rebellion.*" ..."*Beware, brethren, lest there be in any of you an evil heart of unbelief in departing from the living God; but exhort one another daily, while it is called 'Today,' lest any of you be hardened through the deceitfulness of sin.*" Again he says, "*Today, if you will hear His voice, do not harden your hearts as in the rebellion.*" Hebrews 3:7, 12, 13, 15

A heart turned cold to God's voice becomes hard. A heart that is warmed with the presence of the Lord is softened. The turning in one direction or the other has significant consequences. One way can lead to continued damage in our lives; the other, a life of fruitful service to our great God. I hope you will respond to His voice today, and be warmed and softened in His presence.

Lord, touch my heart so that I might respond properly to Your leading. If there are any hard areas, soften my heart to be more pliable before You. I want to experience Your presence. Help me clean out anything that hinders me from hearing Your voice speaking to me. Help me forgive as You have already extended forgiveness to me. Amen.

FEBRUARY 24

BEARING OTHER'S BURDENS

Maturity is something we should all want to see developed in our lives. But with maturity comes responsibility also. For instance, Paul wrote to the Romans:

"We then who are strong ought to bear with the scruples of the weak, and not please ourselves. Let each of us please his neighbor for his good, leading to edification." Romans 15:1-2

Paul also wrote to the Galatians:

"Brethren, if a man is overtaken in any trespass, you who are spiritual restore such a one in a spirit of gentleness, considering yourself lest you also be tempted. Bear one another's burdens, and so fulfill the law of Christ." Galatians 6:1-2

To be honest, it is not an easy thing to bear the weight for the weak, or take the required steps to help someone be restored. The circumstance of others and their situations can be wearing and wearying.

While the burdens of others are meant to be shared, unless we share our burdens with the Lord and others, it can be unbearable. Knowing that Jesus bore our sin and shame gives us the motivation to be able to be long-suffering with others. Casting our burdens at the cross gives us the needed relief so that we might once again help meet the needs of others.

If you find yourself a bit overwhelmed today, just call on the Lord and answer His invitation to you. He will give you true rest.

"Come to Me, all who labor and are heavy laden, and I will give you rest. Take My yoke upon you and learn from Me, for I am gentle and lowly in heart, and you will find rest for your souls. For My yoke is easy and My burden is light." Matthew 11:28-30

FEBRUARY 25

WITH LOVING KINDNESS I HAVE DRAWN YOU...

Who can understand God's love? When Jeremiah was writing to the remnant of Israel he prophesied the word of the Lord:

"Yes, I have loved you with an everlasting love; Therefore with loving kindness I have drawn you. Again I will build you, and you shall be rebuilt." Jeremiah 31:3-4

God's promise to His people is tied to His everlasting love. If we can grasp and receive the love of God we will have a greater understanding of His purpose in our lives.

Paul prayed that the Ephesian Church would be strengthened with might through God's Holy Spirit in the inner man, that Christ would dwell in their hearts through faith; that they would be rooted and grounded in love. But he goes on that they:

"...May be able to comprehend with all the saints what is the width and length and depth and height - to know the love of Christ which passes knowledge; that you may be filled with the fullness of God, exceedingly abundantly above all that we ask or think, according to the power that works in us, to Him be glory in the church by Christ Jesus to all generations, forever and ever, Amen." Ephesians 3:18-21

It is by God's love that we are drawn to Him. It is by God's love that we receive forgiveness and right standing. It is by God's love that our inner man is strengthened. It is by God's love that we are filled with the fullness of God.

God's love is beyond our comprehension but is something we must continue to receive and to go deeper in our knowledge of this love. With this knowledge, we are assured that He will build us for His habitation and purposes. Just know that His love for you is not fleeting; it is secure; it is everlasting.

May a deeper understanding of the love of God lead you in your service and love for others today.

FEBRUARY 26

YEARNING FOR THE LIVING GOD

If there is one word to describe what I am sensing this morning; it is a deep yearning; a longing for the power and presence of Almighty God to break through in this generation. In my own Spirit there is a stirring, a deep desire to understand and embrace the depths of our loving Father in a measure never reached before. Like the psalmists, I meditate:

"How lovely is Your tabernacle, O Lord of hosts! My soul longs, yes, even faints for the courts of the Lord; My heart and my flesh cry out for the living God." Psalm 84:1-2

When I read the last chapter of Acts, Paul quoted from the book of Isaiah about the response of his own people, I wondered, and thought, "things are not much different in our day." People are hearing but not hearing; seeing but not perceiving; their hearts have grown dull; their ears hard of hearing. With the eyes dimmed and ears deaf, there is a lack of understanding and repentance. Therefore, there is no healing to take place (see Acts 28:26-27). living in a dry and thirsty land where no one is looking for the water.

But in my own spirit is a yearning. There is a river that makes glad the city of God. There is a reality to the power and presence of God. And even if others won't press in, I must. I am compelled. My God lives! He is alive! And He is alive in me.

God's presence is real! He wants (yearns or longs) to tabernacle with all of us. He is our strong tower, our refuge in the midst of the storm, but most of all, our dwelling place encompassed in His love and communion.

Is your heart yearning this morning? If so, draw from the strength that He has for you. If your heart is not yearning, ask the Lord to cause a hunger in your heart to come close and commune with Him. He desires to fill you to the fullness. He will not send you away lacking.

FEBRUARY 27

ARE OUR EXCUSES VALID?

Rereading the account of Moses' call from God to go to his people in Egypt, I am confronted with Moses' reluctance to respond. Even with the great encounter he was experiencing, his view of himself caused doubt and resistance to what God was about to do. Here is his conversation with God:

"I am not eloquent, neither before not since You have spoken to Your servant; but I am slow of tongue." So the Lord said to him, "Who has made man's mouth? Or, who makes the mute, the deaf, the seeing, or the blind? Have not I, the Lord? Now therefore, go, and I will be with your mouth, and teach you what you shall say." Exodus 4:10-12

This is not the end of the conversation, for Moses continued in offering his handicap, and the Lord by His grace brought Aaron to Moses as a help in this area. But, it also angered the Lord that Moses did not simply trust that God was more than adequate to be His supply, even in his weakness.

What about you and I? Have we offered any excuse or multiple excuses as to why we cannot fulfill the call of God on our lives? I can tell you, none of them impress, nor move the Lord. He is able to bring to pass whatever is needed in our lives to accomplish His purposes.

If God calls us, He will also fashion us for that calling. In fact, He already has; we just might not know it, but the work He has begun in you and I, He will also complete. He is God! He knows all things. He is all powerful! He is everywhere! We can try to talk our way out of His call, justifying any deficiency, but He is the One who has made us. He knows us. He knows the plans He has for us. They are for certain, plans for a future and a hope. Just answer His call; give up the excuses.

By the way, the deficiencies that you see are purposeful. We are never to trust in our own strength or ability. We must always put our trust in God to be our enablement and strength. So it's not so much about us, but all about Him!

FEBRUARY 28

LEAD ME...

Some days, like today, you wake up spent, emotionally and physically. Trying to read the Scriptures this morning, my eyes keep wanting to close. Of course, there is more on the agenda for today: somethings that I can do, other things that God must do in His work in others' lives. Knowing the difference between these things is huge. But in any case, I need the Lord's enabling power. Therefore, I return to God's Word and take comfort in His truth.

The psalmist writes:

"Hear my cry, O God; Attend to my prayer. From the end of the earth I will cry to You, When my heart is overwhelmed; lead me to the rock that is higher than I. For You have been my shelter for me, a strong tower from my enemy." Psalm 61:1-3

Here is from where my strength comes. The Lord is my shelter, my rock and my abode. He is the One who brings comfort and safe keeping. He can always be trusted. No matter what kind of day I may face, or how weak I may feel, He will supply all that I need according to His riches. I do not need to be afraid, nor overwhelmed; He is my surety, my strong tower, and my supply. Because of this, I am lifted up higher than any problem, circumstance, weakness or limitation. What I am lacking He will supply. I can find real rest in this.

Let Him be your shelter today also. His covering over your life is sure. He promises to do the leading in your life. Wherever He leads you, He will always accompany you. He will also give you what is needed for that journey. He will never leave you, nor forsake you. His promise is true. He is the Rock that is higher than you. Give your day to Him

Lead us Lord to this high place! We desire to be in Your presence and see Your glory. Thank you for always being there. May Your wisdom guide our decisions today in every situation we face. Let Your name be glorified in all we do. Amen!

MARCH 1

CAN'T GIVE WHAT YOU DON'T HAVE!

If we want to pass something along, we must first be the possessors of that something. We are called to pass on our beliefs to our children, but what exactly are those beliefs? Moses articulated to the Israelites just how this is to be done:

"You shall love the Lord your God with all your heart, with all your soul, and with all your strength. And these words which I command you today shall be in your heart. You shall teach them diligently to your children..." Exodus 6:5-7

You can see from these verses that our relationship, passion and commitment in our service to the Lord, in every area of our lives, are what give us the something we have to give. There is integrity of purpose and life that is not just a head thing, but a whole being commitment. Our heart, emotions, substance and strength are directed toward the purposes of God. If so, the teaching is in line with the testimony. Only then is the testimony validated for those who are hearing. There is an integrity of belief and action that can lead to a valuable inheritance to be passed on to others.

Understanding this should have us desiring to be teachers to others in our actions in addition to our words. The outcome is important enough for us to walk in integrity. Otherwise we are not showing by our actions that we really do believe what we are saying.

We must then consider a couple of questions for our own lives. Do our children, family, friends and co-workers see in us the substance of what we believe? Is there a testimony that validates the words that we desire to proclaim and teach? It is in the everyday normal activities where we have the awesome opportunities to speak forth words of life. May our words bring life as they are backed up by our own actions.

MARCH 2

MY SOUL THIRSTS FOR YOU...

There are times when we have all experienced a real natural thirst, either when working or exerting ourselves in some sports activities, or just after not having sufficient fluids. Our entire body cries out for water, to refresh and satisfy our thirsts. That is what happens in our natural world. But, there is also a thirsting in the Spirit. Aware of the dryness all around us, our own life is in need of a fresh encounter with the Lord.

The Psalmists writes:

"O God, You are my God; Early will I seek You; My soul thirsts for You; My flesh longs for You in a dry and thirsty land where there is no water. So I have looked for You in the sanctuary, to see Your power and Your glory. Because Your lovingkindness is better than life, My lips shall praise You." Psalm 63:1-3

There are so many people that come to me when they have problems. They want quick fixes and look to God for this kind of encounter. Theirs is a relationship of convenience. However, seeking the Person of the Lord, longing for His presence, knowing His power, is far from their pursuit.

But the reality is that it is only in this pursuit of the Person of the Lord that we can know the way, live in His life, and walk in His power. I know that there is a thirst in my spirit to be in His presence. This longing is satisfied only in the Lord. The culture around us is so dry that we might not even know the reality of not being dehydrated in the presence of God anymore. But I can tell you that He promises that those who do thirst for Him will be filled.

Are you thirsty today? Only God can satisfy that thirst. Come to the waters, and be satisfied.

MARCH 3

THE BLESSING OF AN OFFERING

Yesterday, I officiated at a funeral for a woman who recently had been suffering with a form of dementia. Because she was in a nursing facility, the family sought out someone to do her funeral who was of the Christian faith. Upon speaking with the woman's daughter, I found out that in the 80's this woman had lost her husband, sold her house, and though she was not someone of great means, made a significant contribution for a children's wing to be built by her church. After more conversation, I learned that the church to which this contribution was made was the very church that I also had attended. Not only that, being a general contractor, I actually constructed that very children's educational wing. Eventually, the addition provided for Sunday School and then a Christian School.

More than that, my own children attended that school. It was there that I was called into the ministry and after serving as a Minister of Education for a number of years planted a church and school in Fall River. Now we have ministered to children for 20 years here in Fall River, while the former church is still ministering to children through Church and Sunday School for various levels.

The point I want to bring out is that this woman's gift has made such a difference in so many people's lives. . . mine included. It was wonderful to be able to let her family know what a blessing she had been. More than that, just imagine what rewards she will have in heaven.

It was a privilege for me to be able to serve this family. What is important is for us to consider how we can make such contributions that will impact future generations. This year we are celebrating 20 years as a church and school. On March 20th, East Gate Christian Academy will have our 20th Annual Banquet and Auction. If you would like to be a part, let us know. Your contribution today can make such a difference to so many. It is through ordinary people that extraordinary things happen.

March 4

How often I wanted to gather you…

This morning I am lamenting the condition of unity among church leaders. I understand that we must have substance in which to be united. That is not the question, it is the unwillingness by so many to try and find out just how we can be united in the cause of Christ. Jesus lamented over Jerusalem. He proclaimed:

"Jerusalem, Jerusalem, the one who kills the prophets and stones those who are sent to her! How often I wanted to gather your children together, as a hen gathers her brood under her wings, but you were not willing! See! Your house is left to you desolate." Luke 13:34-35

Is this not also a warning and a promise for our own times? We see the Lord's heart to gather. We see the people's heart to resist His prophets. What if we turned and repented of our ways and received His Word and His representatives? What if we tried to work together for His glory and not for our own? Shouldn't our condition of desolation change? Wouldn't we see a greater gathering of those who trust in the Lord, who come under His protection? This is the heart cry of God. Do you sense it? Can you imagine what it would be like to be a part of the solution and not part of the problem?

Lord, I pray that we would be willing to give up our own control and resistance to what You want to do in our communities, our nations, and the world. May we recognize the value in our brothers and sisters and work together for Your glory. Then we will know Your purposes. Then we will see greater fruit. Then we will find rest under the shadow of Your wings. Amen!

MARCH 5

OH IT'S SNOWING AGAIN!

There was an old expression that said, "If you can't beat them, join them." It is amazing to me how with this season of snow, so consistent and persistent that while we might bemoan the new accumulation, the shoveling and even the plow bills, we are also becoming more resilient in the process.

A morning, like this morning, with snow falling and an expected accumulation might have cause school cancellations in past years. I remember that even when the snow would begin to fall some days, parents would begin panicking and calling, asking if we would release early, and if we didn't, they would come and pick up their kids early anyway.

So where am I going with this. You know that I must have a Scripture in mind. Here it is from the book of Hebrews. The writer exhorts:

"Now no chastening seems to be joyful for the present, but painful; nevertheless, afterward it yields the peaceable fruit of righteousness to those who have been trained by it." Hebrews 12:11

There is a great race in which all of us are called to run. Our focus must be on the One who can give us the strength, endurance and motivation to complete our course. It is through the training of the Lord that we actually build endurance and stamina to continue. The things in life that offer resistance can actually make us more resilient. Instead of setting us back, we forge ahead, weather the storm, and trust God to bring us through.

So, maybe this long winter has done some productive work in us after all. I pray that as the snow has fallen, let the Spirit of God fall in our region as well. Come, Lord Jesus, Come!

MARCH 6

YOU ARE MY BELOVED SON

These are the words I am hearing in my spirit today. Twice, God spoke over His Son Jesus that we see recorded in Scripture: once at His baptism, the other at the Transfiguration. The first He spoke to Jesus personally, the second to His disciples about Jesus.

In John 3:22 He says: *"You are My beloved Son; in You I am well pleased."*

In Luke 9:35 He spoke to the disciples on the Mount of Transfiguration: *"This is My beloved Son. Hear Him!"*

In both cases God affirms the value and love that He has in His relationship to His Son Jesus. It is in that relationship that Jesus faces all the challenges to His ministry. Remember how many times He had to deal with others, even demons, saying, *"If you are the Son of God..."*

It is the same for us. We must be secure in the knowledge of who we are and to Whom we belong. Paul wrote to the Romans:

"For as many as are led by the Spirit of God, these are the sons of God. For you did not receive the spirit of bondage again to fear, but you received the Spirit of adoption by whom we cry out, 'Abba, Father.' The Spirit Himself bears witness with our spirit that we are children of God, and if children, then heirs - heirs of God and joint heirs with Christ, if indeed we suffer with Him, that we may also be glorified together." Romans 8:14-17

It is in this security of knowing who we are, and to Whom we belong, that we can progress toward the destiny that is marked out for us. We never have to question our heritage. We are the beloved of God. When we settle this issue (which God has already settled), we can minister and even face opposition knowing we will not be unsettled. Let that settle in your spirit today. Go ahead, cry out, "Abba, Father." You are loved! You are part of the beloved of God! Let peace and joy replace any fear you might have. You need not fear any longer.

MARCH 7

BOLDNESS TO SPEAK - POWER TO CONFIRM

It wasn't long before the leaders of the Early Church found themselves being threatened. A short time before Pentecost, they had been in hiding and afraid to step forward declaring the Kingdom of God. But after the Holy Spirit was poured out on them, they were no longer afraid. They spoke the Word of God and as a result, the religious leaders tried to stop their progress, even threatening them. Therefore, the disciples more earnestly prayed:

"'Now, Lord, look on their threats, and grant to Your servants that with all boldness they may speak Your Word, by stretching out Your hand to heal, and that signs and wonders may be done through the name of Your Holy Servant Jesus.' And when they had prayed, the place where they were assembled together was shaken; and they were all filled with the Holy Spirit, and they spoke the word of God with boldness." Acts 4:29-31

Why don't we pray prayers like this one? Jesus is the same! His Holy Spirit is the same! The Holy Spirit has been sent to us by Jesus, to empower us to be His witnesses. Our duty is to speak with boldness, to proclaim the Kingdom of God to our generation.

Surely, we will also face resistance. But don't we have the ability to face this resistance through our faith in Christ and the power of His Holy Spirit. When we face these types of situations, and we will, we can also pray that Jesus will extend His hand to heal. Even more than that, we will see even greater things done in His name. I don't know about you, but I feel a power surge coming.

There is no need for us to be locked up in a room hiding, nor holding back on our testimony because we fear how someone will receive us or even persecute us. We have the example of the early disciples, ordinary people like us, who were called to be witnesses. The same power that filled them and gave them boldness is at work in all of us. May we be bold and experience great things in our generation.

MARCH 8

I DO NOT SEEK YOURS BUT YOU...

There is an important principle from which all of us can learn. Paul, the apostle, had such a love for the church that he often worked in need, not to be a burden to those to whom he was called to minister. He spoke to the Corinthian church, even having to defend himself, saying: *"I ought to have been commended by you"* but instead, he had to commend himself, letting them know that they were not deficient in anything as a church because of what he had been given as an apostle. He continues to say:

"And I will not be burdensome to you: for I do not seek yours, but you. For the children ought not to lay up for the parents, but the parents for the children." 2 Corinthians 12:11, 14

While the parent is deserving of honor, it is because of the sacrifice that has been laid down. The mature must lay up for the immature; the strong for the weak. In a little over a week, we (East Gate Christian Academy) will be celebrating 20 years as a Christian school. Our annual benefit banquet is where we ask all who would help, to fund whatever is possible, to continue ministering to those children we have the opportunity to train up. I know that it is a sacrifice. But it is a much needed sacrifice. We do all that we can do so we will not be burdensome, so that more of the resources are available to go to the children. It's the right thing to do. We could sure use your help.

Contact us, if you want more information. We would love it if you can join us (www.eastgatechristianacademy.org)

What about in your own situations? Are you doing what you can so that the next generation, or the present generation can reap from what you have sown? Is there an inheritance that is being built up for others to have a greater opportunity to extend and expand the Kingdom? We have the great opportunity to serve others. But it does require a certain aspect of denying ourselves in the process. Jesus gave us this example. May we walk in His example as we lay up foundations for succeeding generations.

MARCH 9

WHERE IS THE RESET BUTTON?

Today is one of those days where I would like to push a reset button. There are various issues that I am trying to work on: a heater that is not functioning properly, a digital sign that has some of the LED lights out, a door that appears to not have accepted stain properly, an internet router that is not working properly. None of these issues have been solved yet, though they are on the agenda at various stages of process. Computers also have a refresh button that can be tried when things need to be updated or simply rebooted. Life is not always that simple.

For the Christian, we have been given a promise that is like a reset button. Peter preached his second recorded sermon after Pentecost and let people know just how they could reset their lives:

"Repent therefore and be converted, that your sins may be blotted out, so that times of refreshing may come from the presence of the Lord." Acts 3:19

Imagine the grace of God that no matter how you have lived your life, if you would turn from your sin and turn to Christ, He will forgive your sin and refresh you to walk in His presence. Of course, this does not mean that we do not need to live our lives with the responsibilities of the decisions that we have made in the past. However, we do not need to live out our lives under the condemnation and judgment of our past sins. We have the opportunity to begin living under the grace and mercy of God with the debt being paid for and the future secure.

Even if we just have a difficult day, we can continue to live in this same promise that was given to us when we started our walk and trusted in Christ. God is still there to give us fresh mercies, new every day. He promises to guide us and empower us as we put our trust in Him. As a result, we cry out to the Lord in thanksgiving saying, “Thank you Lord that your compassions never fail!”

May His love and grace help us to have a reset in His presence today and every day of our lives!

March 10

THE REST OF THE STORY...

I often hear people quote the beginning of Romans 8:1: *"There is therefore now no condemnation to those who are in Christ Jesus..."*

But in the verse there is not a period but a comma. It is not the end of the sentence or thought given by Paul. He continues: "*...Who do not walk according to the flesh, but according to the Spirit.*"

Now there is a period! You see, it is possible for someone to be a Christian and still walk according to the flesh and not the Spirit. In fact, Paul says:

"For those who live according to the flesh set their minds on the things of the flesh, but those who live according to the Spirit, the things of the Spirit. For to be carnally minded is death, but to be spiritually minded is life and peace." Romans 8:5-6

Now the reality is that if we are in Christ, we are not to live carnally, but in the Spirit Who gives us life. The same Spirit that raised Christ from the dead, lives in you and I and will give us life. "*Therefore, brethren, we are debtors - not to the flesh, to live according to the flesh. For if you live according to the flesh you will die; but if by the Spirit you put to death the deeds of the body you will live. For as many as are led by the Spirit of God, these are the sons of God*" (Romans 8:12-14).

This is a choice we have. What and to whom we put our attention, will determine, for the most part where we are dwelling. Is it the Spirit or the flesh? In the flesh we cannot please God, nor will we find life or peace. But if we live according to the Spirit and are led by the Spirit, the law of the Spirit of life in Christ Jesus makes us free from the law of sin and death.

Today, on what is your mind set? It is a choice you have. Just let me remind you Who bought you with a price. You do not belong to you. You belong to Him!

March 11

If God is for us...

Who can be against us? Paul the apostle has been carefully expounding to the Romans just what it means to be a son or daughter of God; how to walk in that sonship, according to the Spirit of God and not according to the flesh. He reminds his readers that sufferings in this present time are not worthy to be compared with the glory which shall be revealed in us. Now he centers on just how much we are loved by God. So much so, that if "*He did not spare His own Son, but delivered Him up for us all, how shall He not with Him also freely give us all things*" (Romans 8:32-33).

Do you see what this is saying? Do you see the length to which God went to secure our redemption? Paul tries to put dimension on the love of God using height, depth, also length and width in Ephesians 3:18. It includes the hope to which we have been called; the riches of His inheritance of the saints; the fact that we are seated together with Christ in heavenly places, far above principalities and powers; and the living death out of which God has called us.

Knowing just what a price was paid for our union, we must also know the depths to which Christ will go to make that union secure. Yes, no one and nothing can separate us from the love of Christ. For Paul writes:

"I am persuaded that neither death nor life, nor angels nor principalities nor powers, nor things present nor things to come, nor height nor depth, nor any created thing, shall be able to separate us from the love of God which is in Christ Jesus our Lord." Romans 8:38-39

The reality is that you and I must be persuaded also! Whether we are or not does not change just how much we are loved. However, when we get this revelation settled in our spirit, we will understand what it means to be more than conquerors through Him who loves us.

If you didn't hear it yet today - You are loved! It is a matchless love. Walk in that love. Remain in His love.

MARCH 12

BURDEN TURNED TO BLESSING

In conversations with different ministers, I could say there has been a holy dissatisfaction with the way things presently are, so much indifference among the people of God. In the name of grace, people have been walking in ways that do not bring glory to God, but, in fact, judgment. We see it manifested in how people show little care to join with, or assemble together in the church in exhorting each other in the things of God. If they do, they have a mechanical observance of ritualistic meetings. What the father of the bride in "My Big Fat Greek Wedding" called "dry toast."

Yesterday in our pastors' prayer, we had real prayer, gut wrenching, heart felt, passionate intercession over situations and people's lives. We prayed for God to move, to move through us, to move His people, to manifest for this generation what we have seen in our own. Jesus is the same, yesterday, today and forever. His Spirit is present. We do not need to live in dryness, but can expect the river to flow again, even in a greater measure. The needs we all face and the pressure each leader carries is small in comparison to what our God is able to supply.

We continued that same conversation in our elder's meeting and really sensed that we need to trust God to interrupt our ritual and planned meeting. We want to be open to His move and empowering for this generation. Even as we moved into our various Bible Study groups in the evening, we scrapped our individual teaching programs and sought the Lord in prayer and worship. We simply asked Him to lead us. What we experienced was that we went from burden to blessing. The Lord led us in worship, prayer for specific needs, and exhortation over individuals and instruction on how to prepare and enter into worship.

It was only the beginning of what the Lord wants to do. We are only scratching the surface of what could be a significant outpouring of His Spirit in our community. All I know is that there is a real hunger and thirst in some of God's ministers. If we are all hungry and thirsty for His righteousness, His promise is to fill us. It's time. Prepare yourself! It's time!

MARCH 13

DO ALL WHO HEAR BELIEVE?

In reading Romans 10 this morning, Paul addressed the interplay of the Gospel being proclaimed and the rejection of that very Gospel by Israel. We read of the value of those sent to proclaim the Gospel:

"How beautiful are the feet of those who preach the gospel of peace. Who bring glad tidings of good things!" Romans 10:15

Paul also wrote:

"So then faith comes by hearing, and hearing by the word of God." Romans 10:17

So it would seem that if the Gospel is preached, people will hear it and grow in faith. But is that always the case?

Here is where Paul asks a question: *"Have they not heard?"* Then answers it by quoting Isaiah: "*Yes indeed: Their sound has gone out to all the earth, and their words to the ends of the world.*" Romans 10:18

So just what is the problem? Looking back at verse 16 we find the answer: "*But they have not all obeyed the gospel. For Isaiah says, "Lord, who has believed our report.*"

Therefore, for faith to come, one must first believe. One must act on the very Gospel being presented. It is not only the seed of faith, but continued faith, that enables one to grow. Each time we hear the Gospel preached, we must respond by obedience, and thereby grow in faith.

So, we might have heard the Gospel preached all our lives and yet not have grown in faith. Or, we might not be in the faith at all. However, if we have an open heart, and respond to what has been proclaimed, we are the recipients of glad tidings of the Good News, and will continue to grow thereby!

Are your ears open today?

MARCH 14

MEMBERS OF ONE BODY

There are many things that I am thinking through this morning. Yesterday, Pastor Adelson and I traveled to New Hampshire for a meeting of the KCA pastors. Part of the agenda was the planning of our joint Youth Leadership Conference that will be hosted in Fall River in May. While what we seek to do is so important, the very fact that we can gather and encourage each other in the work of God is also so much valued. Each one, with their diverse gifts and concern for the body of Christ, both locally and globally, ministered life and helped us individually and continued to be a blessing to our group of churches.

I was thinking also about Romans 12, in reflecting on how we worship God, presenting our bodies a living sacrifice, holy, acceptable to God, which is our reasonable service. Paul writes: *"And do not be conformed to this world, but be transformed by the renewing of your mind, that you might prove what is that good and acceptable and perfect will of God" (Romans 12:2)*

Parts of our conversation yesterday centered on people who claim they worship God, but do so without submitting to the authority of His Word. In that case they can come up with any range of ideas and call it what they want, even operate with an independent spirit. But is this the purpose of a surrendered life?

The next few verses have something to say about that: "*For I say, through the grace given to me, to everyone who is among you, not to think of himself more highly than he ought to think, but to think soberly, as God has dealt to each one a measure of faith. For as we have many members in one body, but all the members do not have the same function, so we, being many, are one body in Christ, and individual members of one another*" (Romans 12:3-5).

So the important thing is not doing our thing, but using whatever gifting you and I might have to be the body of Christ expressed to others. Of course, this requires humility and an appreciation and value of others. It is in this setting of community that we are all shaped for His glory and grow in His purposes.

MARCH 15

CAN YOU HEAR THE WIND?

When Jesus was speaking to Nicodemus, He said:

"The wind blows where it wishes, and you hear the sound of it, but cannot tell where it comes from and where it goes. So is everyone who is born of the Spirit." John 3:8

I sense that there is something happening in our day that might just be stirring. The wind is beginning to blow. I don't mean by this that we haven't walked faithfully to the call of God before. But, even so, each season in God is not the same. If you have walked long enough as a Christian, you can probably relate to what I am saying. It is not about the work we do, but just how God breathes on that work that makes the difference.

The important thing is to distinguish just what season we are in. And if we haven't experienced different seasons, we might not be ready to discern what is about to happen around us. I believe that the Holy Spirit is about to visit us in a refreshing way. He has a mission for us, but we also must be prepared to receive His instruction. How we prepare to listen will make a great difference in whether we will respond correctly.

When and where the wind of the Spirit comes we cannot control. We can, however, prepare and cultivate an anticipation of His coming in a fresh way into our lives, churches and the community. The issue is for our mind and heart to be willing to respond to His leading, staying centered in the authority of His Word and walking in His covenant community.

We need the power of the Spirit to complete His mission! Are you ready? Listen for the wind. There was a change of sound today in our church service. Could you hear it? The season is changing!

MARCH 16

POWER TO WITNESS

Reading the last letter of Paul, he makes a summary statement to Timothy that is very revealing. With so many experiences in his life as an apostle, he wants to assure his disciple of the Lord's great faithfulness. When Jesus commissioned His disciples, He promised them the power to be His witnesses through His Holy Spirit (see Acts 1:8). Now reflecting back on his own ministry, Paul acknowledges that even though he had been abandoned by others, the Lord was and is faithful. He writes:

"But the Lord stood with me and strengthened me, so that the message might be preached fully through me, and that all the Gentiles might hear. Also I was delivered out of the mouth of the lion. And the Lord will deliver me from every evil work and preserve me for His heavenly kingdom. To Him be glory forever and ever. Amen!" 2 Timothy 4:17-18

A major mission of the Holy Spirit is to give us power for ministry, the power to be witnesses for the Lord. Many people confuse just what this power is for. They might think it is for self-promotion. But, we never see that in the Scriptures.

God gives us power to overcome the enemy and do the very thing He calls us to do - advance His kingdom. That does not mean that it is something easy. We will need to persevere and trust in the Lord through many situations, some most difficult. However, we can trust that when we do meet these difficulties, we are not to proceed in our own power, or according to our own understanding. We must put our full trust in the Lord and the power of His might, trusting Him to reveal to us His ways.

He who has called us is faithful! Let our trust be in Him today. Let us thank the Lord for the value of His covenant community who also encourages us according to His Word. May His word guide our hearts and minds today, as we trust the Lord to continue to stand with us and strengthen us for His glory.

MARCH 17

PUT ON HOLD

Yesterday, I began reading a book called "*Saul of Tarsus*." In part of Paul's life, after receiving his call from God and visiting Peter and James, he spent a considerable time in obscurity in His own home town, possibly as much as nine years. This makes me also think of Patrick of Ireland, in whose honor we celebrate today. Patrick also had a great time period in which he had to wait on his calling before he was released to move forward. Obviously, there is a time of development necessary for the servant of God to go through.

People who have been truly called by God understand the necessity of being "put on hold" before beginning their ministry. While it is a most painful time of frustration and uncertainty, it is a time of preparation for God's servants. Dr. Richard Booker writes:

"There is a time gap between when God calls a person and when He sends them out. We call this time period, 'waiting on God.' God calls it 'waiting on us.' It is a time when God works the necessary patience and character in His servants before He sends them out with His important mission to accomplish through their lives. This is not pleasant but it is a normal part of spiritual development."

While one is waiting, God is working even in the place one will be sent. This waiting does not mean that one is not working, but instead, being developed under God's hand of authority so that the shaping process is brought to a maturity needed for the call. This was true in Paul's life. It was true in Patrick's life. It is also true in our lives.

May we allow the Potter to shape the clay for His purposes. When our vessel is ready, He will accomplish His will in our lives and receive the glory for all that is accomplished.

MARCH 18

"STILL WATER" OR A "BUBBLY BROOK"?

In reading a section of a book written by Gene A. Getz, I am reminded, and in full agreement, that one must not judge a person's maturity by the degree to which they project an outgoing personality. "Still water" runs deep, whereas a "bubbly brook" can be shallow. Gene writes, "people who appear to have it all together in public are sometimes very different in private. Conversely, others who may be quiet and appear reserved can have enduring qualities that represent a true measure of maturity."

He goes on to say, "this, of course, is not always true. But when it is true, bubbly people don't wear well on the long haul. The people who are more real - although perhaps more quiet - may be the people you truly want to have as close friends. They do wear well. The more time you spend with these people, the more you'll realize what quality people they are."

This idea is also extended into leadership. When the Church faced its first organizational problem in Jerusalem, the apostles recommended that "*seven men of good reputation*" be selected to help solve the problem of food distribution among the Grecian widows (see Acts 6:3). The Apostles knew that they would only make the problem worse if they delegated this task to men who were not respected in the Christian community. Having a good reputation meant that they had been proven in being responsible and faithful. Obviously, this would take time, where one was observed growing and maturing in harmony with Christian principles in community.

I thank the Lord for those of you who have been "still water" in my life, people with whom I can share the depths of my heart with, those that I can trust that go the distance to work through any relationship strain. They are always willing to seek the truth and care more about the relationship than any position or advantage the relationship might give them. So many people come to mind as I am writing this note. For you, I am eternally grateful. You have my greatest love and respect. You are true builders in the Kingdom of God! May the Lord bless you greatly today.

MARCH 19

RECOGNIZING PRUDENCE

Prudence is not a word that we use frequently in our day, but it an important character trait that we must understand, embrace and demonstrate as God's people. The Bible says, "*The wise in heart shall be called prudent*" (Proverbs 16:21, KJV). One passage Paul wrote to the Romans helps to explain what he had in mind when he used the word "prudent" to demonstrate maturity.

"For through the grace given to me I say to everyone among you not to think more highly of himself than he ought to think; but to think so as to have sound judgment [to think soberly, sensibly or prudently], as God has allotted to each a measure of faith." Romans 12:3

Paul was concerned that we have a proper view of ourselves in relationship to God and to other Christians (Rom. 12:4-8). Evidently, some believers in Rome as well as in Corinth (1 Cor. 12:14-27), had an overly exalted view of their positions in the Body of Christ. Some thought they were God's "special gift" to the church. Consequently, Paul exhorted them to "*be devoted to one another in brotherly love; giving preference to one another in honor*" (Rom. 12:10), rather than put each other down while they built themselves up. We see him address the issue again in his letter to the Philippian church"

"Do nothing from selfishness or conceit, but with humility of mind regard one another more important than yourselves; do not merely look out for your own personal interest, but also for the interest of others." Philippians 2:3-4

Those who are prudent have a proper view of the grace of God and grow in sound judgment; going to their knees in humble and prayerful adoration, and then rising to new levels of righteous and holy living. I can say that I have been so blessed to walk with such wonderful people who have servant's hearts. They are willing to go to whatever extent to help each other. Never looking for any credit, but doing whatever it takes to get the job done well, all to the praise and glory of God. Thank you all for your expressions of love and maturity. You are the ones who truly make the difference.

March 20

Going for the "Win"

Charles Stanley's son Andy teaches in his leadership exhortations that the "win" must be defined in everything we do. If we are not clear in just what the target is, how will we know if we hit the target? For that matter, just what exactly will we shoot at? Tonight we will celebrate our 20th Annual Fundraiser Banquet for East Gate Christian Academy. I can tell you that there is much anticipation for this event.

But just what is the "win"? We have defined this, as in past years, as (1) increasing the awareness in our community of our Christian educational program and the value that it is to the future of our community; (2) encouraging each other who do have children and grandchildren to stay the course, run the race and be diligent in the training of our children; and (3) to raise support from family, friends and businesses to undergird the ability to help fund all aspects of this endeavor.

I can tell you that a by-product is not just the end result, but the process we go through. There are so many individuals that have been so faithful throughout the years to participate in ways that involve much sacrifice of time and resources. The love and service that is demonstrated makes me so proud to be a part of the team.

Some will be assembling in just one short hour to begin the process of carrying everything to White's and getting everything set-up. So many people have worked on so many fronts to make this evening a success.

I think beyond the three things that were mentioned above; this is a real "win." In the Lord's eyes He rewards the diligent service of His people. So, for the many of you who continue to work behind the scenes, you are all winners! I say that in the most sincere way. Thank you in advance. You are precious.

May all of us continue to invest whatever talent, time and treasure that we have, for the building up of the Kingdom of God to bring glory to His name!

MARCH 21

MOUNTAINS CAN BE MOVED!

As I reflect on our EGCA 20th Annual Fundraising Banquet, I am considering the theme of the evening: "For nothing is impossible with God." Within a few days of the banquet, I have heard of two different people just diagnosed with cancer, another who was in a car accident and got a concussion, another family that someone knew who was hit by a drunk driver, and our Portuguese pastor's wife fracturing her ankle. There are people all around us who have difficult mountains to face in their lives. This is true for all of us as well. It seems that some mountains are more difficult to move than others, but this should not discourage us in our faith. We must simply be more intense in acting by faith, turning earnestly to God, asking for His divine assistance in our lives and the lives of others.

We have been blessed to have been ministering as a school and church to children and adults for 20 years. We do not presume on our history, but recognize more readily today than in our first years just how dependent we must be on our Lord. The mission is as important today as when we began. While we all encounter difficulties and will face difficulties, we do not want these difficulties to rob us of our focus. Surely, we must not ignore them, but face them. And all of us will face challenges. What we do want to focus on is a God who makes the impossible possible.

Whatever obstacles you might be facing today, I can assure

you that God is faithful and more than capable to empower you to speak to your mountain and see it removed. When we truly understand Who the moving force is, we can't help but give Him glory for all He has done.

We all have a great work yet ahead. May His grace cause us to be unwavering and cause us to take bold steps of faith to accomplish His purpose for our generation. Thank you to all who have continued to show their love, through prayers, selfless service, and generous support. May God pour out His abundant blessing on all of your lives. May the generations to come sing God's praises because of your great faithfulness.

Let's continue to press in and see great things!

MARCH 22

PURE OIL OF PRESSED OLIVES

In reading about the instructions Moses gave the children of Israel about how they were to worship God, one such instruction stands out this morning. The Lord's instruction to Moses said:

"You shall command the children of Israel that they bring the pure oil of pressed (beaten, ESV) olives for the light, to cause the lamp to burn continually." Exodus 27:20

There was no way for the olive oil to be gathered without a pressing. Olives have a difficult texture and do not give up the oil as readily as a grape is squeezed. No there needed to be a special press where great pressure was exerted on the olives. They were even beaten down to produce the pure oil.

All of this points to our very lives. We, too, can be thick skinned. Without pressure, we would not see the oil produced in our lives that could produce the life and light of Christ. Many people refused to be squeezed, pressed, or even beaten into shape by the work of the Lord. But, if they yield to His work in their lives, He can produce such pure oil for His glory. Jesus said:

"You are the light of the world. A city that is set on a hill cannot be hidden. Nor do they light a lamp and put it under a basket, but on a lamp stand, and it gives light to all who are in the house. Let your light so shine before men, that they may see your good works and glorify your Father in heaven." Matthew 5:14-16

There is a connection between the press and the light. No press, no oil, and therefore no light. How many want the anointing (oil) without the press that produces that very oil? Any counterfeit oil will not produce the light of the Lord.

May we submit to the Lord's press in our lives and allow the process to produce pure oils that allow His light to be seen by all to whom we have the opportunity to minister.

MARCH 23

CHRIST THE POWER AND WISDOM OF GOD

After encountering the intellectual but spiritually bankrupt center of Athens, Paul traveled to Corinth. There he was determined to preach the message of the cross. He had tried debating the intellectuals who just wanted to debate but not learn truth. In fact, they could not learn the things of the Spirit, being in the flesh. Therefore, Paul addresses the Corinthians with this experience fresh in his mind:

"When I came to you, I did not come with excellence of speech or of wisdom declaring to you the testimony of God. For I determined not to know anything among you except Jesus Christ and Him crucified. I was with you in weakness, in fear, and in much trembling. And my speech and my preaching were not with persuasive words of human wisdom, but in demonstration of the Spirit and of power, that your faith should not be in the wisdom of men but in the power of God." 1 Corinthians 2:1-3

Paul wasn't saying that he had no wisdom to share. In fact later he says that he did have wisdom for those who were mature. But, the wisdom from above is not discerned by those who are not spiritual. So in presenting the Gospel, it is more important that the Gospel is presented in power and demonstration. Jesus said that signs and wonders would accompany those who believed. The Gospel message is attested to by the Lord through the power of His Spirit. For us, we need to get out of the way and allow the Holy Spirit to use us as His conduit of blessing to those to whom we are sent.

This is the same power the disciples received on the day of Pentecost that is available for those who would seek it. What you have freely received, freely give. Jesus promised you and I could do greater works than He, if we believed. In fact, if we had the faith of a mustard seed, we could speak to the mountains in our lives and see them removed. And nothing will be impossible for you.

Lord, let Your wisdom and power work through us today. May we reveal Your truth in word and deed. Amen.

MARCH 24

WORK THAT ENDURES

So much of what we do is temporary. Yet, even in the temporary we can be doing something that is enduring. When we begin to see our work as not just what needs to be done for the provision of our family, but that we have a life work that is much greater, we can ascribe value to what might be just regular and even at times mundane. It can change the way we go about our daily activities.

Paul instructed the Corinthians that there can be no other foundation than that which is laid, which is Christ Jesus:

"Now if anyone builds on this foundation with gold, silver, precious stones, wood, hay, straw, each one's work will become clear; for the Day will declare it, because it will be revealed by fire; and the fire will test each one's work, of what sort it is. If anyone's work which he has built on it endures, he will receive a reward." 1 Corinthians 3:12-14

What we need to see is that there are eternal moments that happen in the midst of everyday activity. You might be doing the task that you do every day, but the conversation, example, or advice that you give, might stir someone into the plan of God for their lives. Your contribution can make such a difference in meeting a particular need that it changes the outcome for a family. Even in the ordinary there can be something so extraordinary.

Ask the Lord to help you see the ways you can build that which is enduring, even while you are doing what seems so ordinary. Ask Him for the discernment to know how to use your time so that it is being redeemed and productive.

Lord, give us an ability to be a part of Your plan, even in the midst of our normal lives. Let what we do have eternal significance. Help us focus on things that will have permanence - that will change people for all of eternity. Give us discernment between that which is good and that which is best. Lord, may You be glorified in the work of our hands as You establish the work of our hands. Amen.

MARCH 25

HAPPY 99H BIRTHDAY MEMERE

What a blessing to have a grandmother that has lived well for these many years. The lessons she has taught all of us are innumerable. For so many years, her hospitality has kept her family together and made room for so many others. She gladly served, gave, loved, cooked, cared for those in her circle of influence and responsibility. She has been our intercessor and continues to pray for the needs of our family and all the needs of which she hears. She has made us laugh, made us consider how we can do good and be a peacemaker with those around us. God has blessed her with a long life, a joyous heart, and many friends.

I am thinking of a psalm that is written in the masculine. But it does not limit gender as it is spoken. As you read it, don't just think it was written for men, but for men and women alike. Consider the blessing that flows because one has walked righteously in their generation. The psalmist says:

"The steps of a good man (woman) are ordered by the Lord, and He delights in his (her) way. Though he (she) fall, he (she) shall not be utterly cast down; for the Lord upholds him (her) with His hand. I have been young, and now am old; Yet I have not seen the righteous forsaken, nor his (her) descendants begging bread. He (she) is ever merciful, and lends; and his (her) descendants are blessed." Psalm 37:23-26

We have been blessed as descendants because of the life of grandparents and parents who have loved the Lord and have been willing to do good to others. Our children and their children are also reaping the blessing of this heritage.

May we, our children, and their children continue to walk in these steps and continue to draw on Godly blessings for many succeeding generations. Happy Birthday Mem!

Consider your own life and the heritage that you can build through your own faithfulness. May the Lord enlarge your circle of influence as you serve Him faithfully.

MARCH 26

GOD'S PRESENCE - A MARK OF HIS GRACE

Reading the Exodus story, one can see the development of Moses' intimacy and desire to know the Lord and His glory. God promised Moses a sign of His grace by saying: "*My Presence will go with you, and I will give you rest*" (Exodus 33:14). Moses responds by saying:

"If Your Presence does not go with us, do not bring us up from here. For how then will it be known that Your people and I have found grace in Your sight, except You go with us? So we shall be separate, Your people and I, from all the people who are upon the face of the earth." Exodus 33:15-16

God responded to this request by saying, "*I will do this thing that you have spoken; for you have found grace in My sight, and I know you by name*" (Exodus 33:17).

The Israelites were on their way to inheriting a promise and the sign authenticating them as a people was the very Presence of God to be manifested in their midst. All of us who have believed in the saving work of Christ also have entered into that same grace. When the disciples were commissioned, they, and by extension, all of us, were given a promise. Jesus said, "*All authority has been given Me in heaven and on earth. Go therefore and make disciples of all the nations, baptizing them in the name of the Father and of the Son and of the Holy Spirit, teaching them to observe all things that I have commanded you; and lo, I am with you always, even to the end of the age*" (Matthew 28:17-20).

This is the mark of separation of those who are the disciples of the Lord from all others. It is the very Presence of the Lord. The Holy Spirit is the abiding Presence of the Lord in our lives. Without Him we can do nothing. With Him we are more than conquerors. Our hearts should burn like Moses' heart to say, "if Your Presence does not lead me, I do not want to move from here." Lead us Lord. May Your Presence continue to be the mark of Your grace on our lives. May we remember that we have been made separate to seek Your glory and find rest in You. Lord, show us Your glory!

MARCH 27

PRAYER IN DISTRESS

Fairy tales begin with "Once upon a time" and usually end in "They lived happily ever after." But we don't live out fairy tales. We live in the real world. Sometimes circumstances can be difficult and for some more than others. I am glad that the Bible doesn't read like a fairy tale. There are real people, living real lives, thinking deeply, and even expressing their reality to the Lord in the only way they can, as they are living out their lives. This morning, I am encountering one such person as I read Psalm 88, a contemplation of Herman the Ezrahite. I encourage you to read this Psalm for yourself.

What strikes me is that while Herman is praying to the Lord for deliverance from his situation, the psalm doesn't shift and close with the answer to that prayer. I can only imagine just what condition that Herman is in. It seems that he is suffering in such a degree that his very life is slipping out from him. In his condition, he is having difficulty sensing that the Lord is with him, even feeling like he is under some form of judgment. He is reasoning that if he dies and is buried, no longer will he be able to declare the wonders and majesty of God through praise. Being a psalmist, this is so much a part of his life. And he wants to use his breath to bring praise to God's mighty works. He knows where his redemption comes from for he begins his psalm by saying, "*O Lord, God of my salvation*."

I wondered when I finished this psalm, where is the uplifting part, the answer to the prayer, the hope that we walk away with? But, in my life and in yours, don't we have seasons of enduring, where we might not have answers, but must simply trust in an all-powerful, knowing God to act in His own wisdom, in His own timing, according to His own purposes? This part I do know, He is faithful! He can be trusted! He does care for those who are His own.

Whatever place you find yourself in this morning, know that turning to the Lord is the right thing to do. Thank God for a psalm that helps us to identify with real, even difficult situations that might be hard to accept. Do not be overcome with your circumstance, turn to the Rock that will sustain and strengthen you as you wait on Him.

MARCH 28

GUIDANCE VS. RESTRICTION (LESSON FROM A LEAKY PIPE)

This morning, I am heading back to my office to meet a plumber. Over the past week or so, I have noticed a peculiar odor in my office the first thing in the morning when I open my door. With all the different situations this winter, I wondered if something had leaked and was drying. But yesterday, I found the culprit. It was a return heating pipe that was leaking. After moving some shelving units so access could be made, I realized that the part that was meant to be a guide to support the pipe had been pinched. Therefore, whenever the pipe heated and cooled, expanded and contracted, it didn't have the freedom of movement to slide, but over time it has worn out the pipe to the point of causing a leak. It will need to be cut and a new section installed today. It will bear the scars of this radical experience but will once again carry out its purpose.

This episode has me thinking about how we nurture, instruct, and enable people to mature into their purpose. Paul gave instruction to the Ephesian church in relation to their families:

"Fathers do not provoke your children to wrath, but bring them up in the training and admonition of the Lord." Ephesians 6:4

See, this training and admonition is meant to be that guidance that will support them to be able to be productive. When it becomes just a punitive, provoking, restrictive relationship, harm will come. It does not mean that through the Lord's radical surgery, someone can get back on course, but surely, there will be a mark of this kind of experience left on the individual.

Perhaps something to ponder is: "Do I help set guidance for others, or just restrictions?" Also, "Am I teaching by principles opening someone's future boundaries, or just enforcing rules which will confine their borders?" Let this leaky pipe be instructive to us today.

MARCH 29

HOW LONG?

I so much want to see God move in our day, to be a part of His demonstration to our generation. For two days in a row, I have read this question "How long?" in a psalm that I have read. Ethan the Ezrahite asked this question in Psalm 89 and Moses asked this question in Psalm 90.

"How long, Lord? Will You hide Yourself forever? Will Your wrath burn like fire?" Psalm 89:46

"Return, O Lord! How long? And have compassion on Your servants." Psalm 90:13

These are not the only verses where this question is asked of God. I quickly did a search of these words to see how many other writers of the Old and New Testament asked this question of God. To my surprise, I found God asking the question to His people just as often.

While we might focus on our impatience with God moving a certain way in our lives, He is also waiting for us to move a certain way in our response to Him. What I find is that His patience and long-suffering far exceeds ours.

Maybe, instead of focusing on what we might think of as deficiency on God's part, we should instead focus on His ability to move us out of our own deficiency in responding to Him.

Lord, help us respond to your instruction and movement in our lives. You have been patient, but we do not presume on Your grace. Lead us to fulfill all You desire. Come, return, let Your glory be seen in our generation. Satisfy us early with Your mercy, that we may rejoice and be glad all our days! And let the beauty of the Lord our God be upon us and establish the work of our hands for us; yes, establish the work of our hands. Amen!

March 30

You Can't Play It Safe!

I am reading the book of Esther this morning. We often hear people quote a portion of this book to encourage each other saying, "*who knows whether you have come to the kingdom for such a time as this?"* (Esther 4:14). But, often we do not look at the full context of the verse that we want to claim for ourselves or others.

Esther and the Jews find themselves in a life and death struggle. With a decree already proclaimed for their impending death, a fast is proclaimed, and Mordecai instructs Esther, that because of her position as queen in the kingdom, she could have influence in petitioning the king on their behalf. For her to do so could mean her own death. But her uncle reminds her not to think that she can hide from this threat by not acting. For if she ignores and trusts in her royal position for her safety, because she also is a Jew, the consequence will eventually befall her also.

So, you could say that if Esther doesn't speak up, she will die. If she does speak up, without the kings approval she will die. Action and inaction can both be condemning, but inaction will spell death anyway. The only possibility for life is action, trusting in God for His favor and deliverance. Do you still want to claim this verse for yourself?

We all live with the Great Commission as our assignment. Many, because of fear, do not proclaim the Good News of the Gospel, but this will spell destruction for those not reached. It will affect all of us because of the condition of the cities in which we live. We will die a slow death. What is the alternative? It is for us to proclaim the Gospel.

Yes, there might also be a consequence for doing this. You might be persecuted, shunned, imprisoned or even killed. But, this is the only possibility to see true deliverance come to the people all around you. So, who knows, whether you have come to the kingdom for such a time as this. Are you ready to stand in the gap?

MARCH 31

LESSONS FROM THE UPPER ROOM

Following the Last Supper, Jesus washed the feet of His disciples, demonstrating the virtue of humility. This virtue was to be a non-negotiable attribute of an apostle. First, they must humble themselves constantly before Jesus and His cleansing work of the cross (John 13:8). Second, Jesus also taught them that they needed a non-negotiable attitude of service. In the same humility that they rendered to Christ, they must wash one another's feet, willing to abandon their theological and ministry egos and serve one another.

"If I then, your Lord and Teacher, have washed your feet, you also ought to wash one another's feet." John 13:14

Jesus knew that soon these disciples would be facing extreme opposition. He wanted them to know ahead of time what degree they will need to support one another. Jesus also knew that in His absence each of these leaders at times would disagree on some of the details of His Word and strategy for building His church, for which they would soon be commissioned. So Jesus insisted that these leaders follow His example and not let pride get in the way in order to maintain a spirit of like-mindedness. Jesus was insisting that the world see his leaders having a remarkable reputation of serving each other instead of competing with each other.

"For I have given you an example, that you should do as I have done to you. Most assuredly, I say to you, a servant is not greater than he who sent him. If you know these things, blessed are you if you do them." John 13:15-17

If they did - if we would, communities would be turned upside down with blessing. If our community can see a demonstration of humility and oneness in spirit, where our service is seen complementing each other instead of competing with each other - think of the possibilities.

Living in our day, consider in what ways we can better demonstrate what Jesus was teaching His disciples. In what way might we humble ourselves and be His example to those around us? In what way can we wash each other's feet?

April 1

Jesus' Prayer for Us before His Betrayal and Arrest

John's Gospel lets us into the content of some of Jesus' prayer just prior to Gethsemane. Jesus prayed for Himself, His disciples, and also all who would believe. That includes you and me. In that part of the prayer He petitioned the Father that we would be one. Listen carefully as you read His words:

"I do not pray for these alone, but also for those who will believe in Me through their word; that they may be one, as You, Father, are in Me, and I in You; that they also may be one in Us, that the world may believe that You sent Me. And the glory which You gave Me I have given them, that they may be one just as We are one; I in them, and You in Me, that they may be made perfect in one, and the world may know that You have sent Me, and have loved them as You have loved Me. John 17:20-23

Jesus continued in that prayer to include His desire that we be with Him and that we may behold His glory. From this prayer we can see the great desire of the Lord for unity among His people.

This unity would produce two things:

It would be a visible demonstration to the world of the reality of, and existence of Christ;

It would also provide the context for our maturity.

We are to be made perfect (mature) through working together with each other. If we want to experience the fruit of this prayer, we need to also submit ourselves to the content of this prayer. Not my will Lord, but Yours!

APRIL 2

UNITY IN DIVERSITY

Yesterday, we looked at Jesus' desire and prayer for His disciples to be a visible, demonstration of the Gospel message through their lives. In Paul's letter to the Corinthians, he is also working with this theme. The church, though gifted with spiritual gifts, exhibited a lack of maturity. They have not honored each other. There were divisions reported among them. In short, they are not loving, nor united in a way that will make their witness effective. Paul gets to the root of the issue:

"There are diversity of gifts, but the same Spirit. There are differences of ministries, but the same Lord. There are diversities of activities, but it is the same God who works all in all . . .But one and the same Spirit works all these things, distributing to each one individually as He wills. For as the body is one and has many members, but all the members of that one body, being many, are one body, so also is Christ. . . But now God has set the members, each one of them, in the body just as He pleased. And if they were all one member, where would the body be? But now indeed there are many members, yet one body." 1 Corinthians 12:4-7, 11-12, 18-20

It is not in being the same that makes us united. In fact, our diversity is so much needed for us to function in a healthy way. What must happen is for us to appreciate the other functioning parts of the body. When we esteem and honor each other for what the Lord has called us to, and where the Lord has placed each one, we can grow in maturity together. The issue is, will we have the same mind toward the progress of the Gospel? Are we willing to allow those He puts in our path to challenge us in our thinking?

Gifts are meant to build. Use whatever gift the Lord has given you. But love and honor must also be present. Otherwise, we will be divided instead of being united. Unity does not mean sameness. We must work to build unity, while also embracing diversity. True maturity cannot be reached without embracing the diversity of the Lord's body, as He has given it to us for the good of all! Is there someone the Lord has put in your path or life that you need to appreciate today? Let us love in truth and deed.

APRIL 3

ONE MORE ILLUSTRATION

Today is Good Friday. Even in His death, Jesus, the Master Teacher, left an illustration for us. I see a great illustration in the three crosses of Calvary (Luke 23:39-43); two criminals and Jesus; one criminal unrepentant another one repentant. You could say that the unrepentant criminal died in sin. Sin was in and upon Him. Jesus had no sin in Him, but He did have sin placed upon Him, as the sin offering. The repentant criminal died to sin and thus represents all the repentant and believing that accept Christ and the work of the cross and enter the kingdom of God. We see in the three crosses, condemnation, justification and sanctification.

The illustration shows how God deals with sin in relation to the believer's sanctification. Sin and self-life are dealt with at the cross. Atonement is made and so is the provision for our sanctification. Christ died for sin and thus substitution, justification and sanctification were legally provided for us. Justification deals with our deeds, what we have done, while sanctification deals with our character, what we are.

Paul writes: "*Now may the God of peace Himself sanctify you completely; and may your whole spirit, soul, and body be preserved blameless at the coming of our Lord Jesus Christ. He who calls you is faithful, who also will do it*" (1 Thessalonians 5:23-24). It is the Holy Spirit that does in us experientially what Christ has done for us legally.

In walking a sanctified life, we recognize the work of the cross being applied by the power of faith and the indwelling Holy Spirit. Therefore we agree with Paul: "*There is therefore now no condemnation to those who are in Christ Jesus, who do not walk according to the flesh, but according to the Spirit*" (Rom. 8:1). And to the Galatians: "*I have been crucified with Christ; it is no longer I who live, but Christ lives in me; and the life which I now live in the flesh I live by faith in the Son of God who loved me and gave Himself for me*" (Gal. 2:20). May we look back to these crosses and recognize all that Jesus has done for us. May it not just fill us with knowledge but cause us to experience life in a new and dynamic way.

APRIL 4

THE DAY THERE IS NO VOICE

I have been up since early this morning. I am seeking the Lord's direction for tomorrow's message. But while I read the Scriptures and pray, there is a strange silence. I am thinking of that day between the crucifixion and the resurrection. What was that day like - when hope was confused? Heartbreak felt and shared. Perhaps gathered together, did the disciples have anything to say? Were they far off in their thoughts?

I am reminded of another morning. I was twenty years old. My dad had just been pronounced dead. Slowly family gathered in the very room I am now sitting. I can remember where I was sitting. My fiancée, now my wife, was with me. We did what families do. We gathered to be with one another. I can't remember if there was much conversation going on. Each person saddened beyond belief because we had suffered such a great loss. I can only remember the silence the deep dismay we all needed to experience and deal with, ourselves and together. Yet, being gathered together, we knew that we were loved. Somehow we would be able to go on. By God's grace and guidance, we would receive the comfort needed and the strength to continue.

I can only imagine what it was like for the disciples. Pondering what they had witnessed. Trying to recapture the words Jesus had told them about what would happen. I am sure there was great silence. But there was also comfort in their gathering together.

I wonder if they pondered the promises Jesus told them, if there was still a glimmer of hope. But then, on the next morning, a report came from the women that will change all this quiet brooding. They hear, "*He is alive*!"

The astonishment of the statement is beyond comprehension. Peter and John burst out of the room and go to the grave site. With an empty tomb before them, they are not sure what to make of it. But one thing is for sure. Things will never be the same.

APRIL 5

THE MIRACLE OF SUNDAY

Sometimes when life challenges us, we can choose despair. Paul writes about this saying: "*How can some of you say that there is no resurrection of the dead?*" (1 Corinthians 15:12). In other words, apparently some people said, "There is never going to be a Sunday. It's Friday. Get used to it. Do disappointment management, because that is as good as it is going to get".

Some people – silently, secretly, live here. You can choose denial, simplistic explanation, impatience, easy answers and artificial pleasantness. You can skip right over humanity, forced optimism, clichéd formulas, even false triumphalism.

Paul wrote to Timothy that some "*say that the resurrection has already taken place, and they destroy the faith of some.*" In other words, apparently some said, "It's already Sunday. The resurrection has already happened for all of us, so if you are having any problems, if you are still sick, if your prayers aren't being answered, you just don't have enough faith. Get with the program."

Or, there is another option (Isaiah 40:28-31): You can wait. Work with God even when He feels far away; rest, ask, whine, complain and trust. Oddly, the most common psalm is the psalm of complaint; the Saturday psalm – "God, why are you not listening?"

The miracle of Sunday is that a dead man lives. The miracle of Saturday is that the eternal Son of God lies dead. So Jesus Christ defeats our great enemy death not by proclaiming His invincibility over it but by submitting to it. If you can find Jesus in a grave, if you can find Him in death, if you can find Him in hell (see Ephesians 4:8-10), where can you not find Him?

Jesus' silence in your life doesn't mean that He doesn't care. In fact, He is settling eternal things in the midst of your waiting on Him. Hold on for your Sunday miracle!

APRIL 6

WHAT DOES FAITH HAVE TO DO WITH REST?

This morning, I have been singing in my spirit, "It is Well with My Soul." I was contemplating on Saturday just what it means to hear the Lord's voice. The children of Israel, when they had the opportunity told Moses to hear the voice of God for them and tell them what they needed to do. Then they would do all that He said. Well, you know how that turned out. The writer of Hebrews also refers to this time period as something that should bring us instruction. Listen to what he has to say:

"Therefore, as the Holy Spirit says: 'Today, if you hear His voice, do not harden your hearts as in the rebellion, in the day of trial in the wilderness, where your father's tested Me, tried Me, and saw My works forty years.' Therefore I was angry with that generation, and said, 'They always go astray in their heart, and they have not known My ways. So I swore in My wrath, they shall enter My rest.'" Hebrews 3:7-11

Last week, and even prior to that, I have been preparing, planning and trying to figure out to the best of my ability just how we can manage all that is before us as a church. There are so many moving parts, and anyone in leadership knows the great weight that that puts on an individual. You have that weight in leading your family, perhaps in a position you also hold. But on Friday, as I was worshipping the Lord, I gave up my own struggle in this and released the outcome to Him. He is the one with the right plan. He has always proved faithful. All I need to do is repent of my own intellect and abilities and allow Him to move things in place as He desires. Only then can the Lord receive the glory that He deserves. Also, only then, by releasing this burden to Him, can I really find rest.

This can be the same for you. Of course, this does not take away our responsibility for faithful service. It just orders things in the right way. When He leads, we just need to listen and then obey. Today, it is well with my soul. Is it well with yours? Yoke yourself with Jesus, you can find rest there as you learn from Him!

APRIL 7

WE ALL NEED TO BE COMFORTED

This morning I am reading Paul's Second Letter to the Corinthians. He begins early on dealing with the issue of suffering, something that is all too familiar to each one of us. Each one of us has our own wounds from the warfare of the kingdom. But wounds need to also be healed if we are to be able to continue advancing. Paul first gives glory to God as the One we must all trust. Then he shows the need we all have for other people to help us gain perspective and healing, and for us to be those people to others. Paul writes:

"Blessed be the God and Father of our Lord Jesus Christ, the Father of mercies and God of comfort, who comforts us in all our tribulation, that we may be able to comfort those who are in any trouble, with the comfort with which we ourselves are comforted by God. For as the sufferings of Christ abound in us, so our consolation also abounds through Christ." 2 Corinthians 1:3-5

The experiences we have all had can be used for God's glory to help others also heal. But I am also thinking about how when we have never dealt with some of our loss, our grief, our hurts, we struggle with being able to identify with others and therefore help them heal. We might, in fact, display anger, impatience, intolerance, and walk in a prideful spirit. I am thinking of times in my life where in trying to do the right thing, others might have been hurt or misunderstood. Their pain was and can still be real. How can I take steps to help bring comfort to those situations? Only God can lead in these endeavors.

How about when you do try to comfort or be reconciled with someone, and they will not receive your help. Again, we let God be the One who works in a person's heart and mind. Suffering is part of life. The question we all have to answer is whether we allow, even our suffering, to have its perfect work in us. If we do, it can enable us to come along side of others and comfort them, as we also have found comfort. Is there someone you can trust? Seek them out, open up for the things you are carrying silently. Allow yourself to be comforted. May the God of all comfort be with you and strengthen you.

APRIL 8

FAITH, THE SUBSTANCE OF THINGS HOPED FOR...

Today, I will be serving at my fourth funeral this year. As a Christian, we do not live in despair like those who have no hope. Our hope is fully fixed on Christ and His resurrection. Being just days following our own celebration of the Resurrection, we are reminded that Jesus did, and does, what He promised. With Jesus having overcome the grave and death, we who believe in Him, who put our faith in Him, will be joined with Him in not only His death, but also resurrection life.

The writer to the Hebrews said:

"Let us draw near with a true heart in full assurance of faith, having our hearts sprinkled from an evil conscience and our bodies washed with pure water. Let us hold fast the confession of our hope without wavering, for He who promised is faithful." Hebrews 10:22-23

In living our lives we can go through difficulty; sometimes that difficulty can cause us to doubt whether God is there at all. We might be tempted to even give up altogether, or doubt that His promises will come to pass in our own lives. But it is necessary that we must always remember the promise of God and trust His ability to keep us on His proper path. He is not only able; He is faithful to complete the work He begins in us.

The writer to the Hebrews continues his exhortation:

"Therefore do not cast away your confidence, which has a great reward. For you have need of endurance, so that after you have done the will of God, you may receive His promise." Hebrews 10:35-36

If we hold on with confidence to the promises that have been given to us, we will grow in our ability to persevere. Our endurance will increase as we exercise the faith that He has given us.

May the Lord strengthen us today to continue to trust Him to complete all that He has promised for us, until He receives us to Himself.

APRIL 9

DO YOU LOVE ME?

I can't fully imagine all that was going through the Apostle Peter's mind following the resurrection of Jesus. You would have thought that after seeing Him already two times that he would be back on track. But something lingered. There was that prideful declaration that he would go to his death in defending His Lord that did not materialize. In fact, he had denied Jesus three times just like Jesus said he would. Now, he reverts to doing what he always knew to do, go fishing. Something still needed to be healed in him.

There was one day he must have remembered when he went fishing. Jesus had instructed him to go and launch out into the deep. He had argued that he had been fishing all night and caught nothing. But at the command of Jesus, he went. What he experienced was a great catch of fish that was so great the nets were breaking, and he needed partners to help him with the catch. That day he was humbled and felt unworthy to be called.

This night which turns into day, he experiences another empty net. With a question from the shore and a quick instruction to cast their nets on the right side of the boat, everything changes. They realize it is the Lord. Peter quickly abandons the boat and moves toward Jesus.

Jesus provided breakfast for His disciples and asked Peter three penetrating questions: (1) "Do you love Me more than these?" (2) "Do you love Me?" (3) "Do you love Me?" These questions were not directed to the group but to Peter. Jesus wants to know just what Peter's relationship to Him is. With each response, Jesus affirms Peter's calling. He has him focus not on what He called others to do, but that Peter simply needed to follow the Lord for His purpose in Peter's life.

I guess for us, the Lord is asking the same question, "Do you love Me? If so, "Follow Me!" It is an individual question that only we can answer. If we answer "yes", then we must be ready to follow just what He tells us. Don't expect it will be the same for everyone. Just follow Jesus!

APRIL 10

DO NOT WORRY?

This is one of Jesus' sayings that is so easy to say, but in many ways so difficult to do.

"No one can serve two masters; for either he will hate the one and love the other, or else he will be loyal to the one and despise the other. You cannot serve God and mammon. Therefore I say to you, do not worry about your life, what you will eat or what your will drink, not about your body, what you will put on it. Is not life more than food and the body more than clothing?" Matthew 6:24-25

All of us have concerns that often preoccupy our minds. If you are an administrative person, you must always be looking to the future: planning, managing resources and people, determining opportunities and threats. In doing these exercises, it is hard not to worry at times. But Jesus doesn't gloss over the fact that we might have legitimate needs; in fact He instructs us to go to Him so that these needs may be met.

He even speaks of how His Father takes care of the birds of the air and the lilies of the field and emphasizes that we are of much more value to Him than these. So, how can we deal with this preoccupation to worry about what we will eat, what we will drink, what we will wear - since it does not help anyway? Jesus said:

"Seek first the kingdom of God and His righteousness, and all these things shall be added to you." Matthew 6:33

In other words, if we keep our eyes on Jesus, and not be led by other priorities or desires, He will lead us in the way where we will know His provision and peace. Note that He doesn't take away our responsibility to plan, manage or work. Just that we recognize that our supply does not come from ourselves, but from the Lord who cares for us. He has answers for our tomorrow. His provisions are to meet His providence in our lives. He provides for what He plans.

Let's trust Him for our future as we keep our eyes focused on Jesus and allow Him to lead us there!

APRIL 11

WORK REST OR REST WORK?

After the death and resurrection of Jesus, the church began worshipping on the first day of the week. Is this just coincidence or is it significant? In reading the book of Hebrews this morning the writer says:

"If Joshua had given them rest, then He would not afterward have spoken of another day. There remains therefore a rest for the people of God. For he who has entered His rest has himself also ceased from his works as God did from His." Hebrews 4:8-10

We read early of God working and resting on the seventh day. The work, rest cycle was demonstrated by One who was perfect and without sin. While Israel was called to live by faith, they could not keep the law, nor had the abiding ability to do so. The law taught them that they could not be perfected in self effort.

Without Christ's sacrifice on the cross, we, too, would still be trying to work out our salvation. But with His sacrifice on our behalf, our sins can be forgiven and therefore we do not live out our days trying to work to earn it. There is a rest for the people of God. The cycle changes - we begin with faith in what He has done for us, and then our works follow.

We begin in rest and move out to works; not works to earn our salvation, but works in the demonstration of our salvation. "*Good works that God prepared beforehand that we should walk in them*" (Ephesians 2:10). Therefore everything starts with our faith in Christ. If we start by devoting our worship to Him, the works we need to do will follow. These works will testify of God's glory.

So what do we learn from this? Give God what belongs to Him FIRST (this includes worship, offerings and our very lives), then we will experience true rest and the work that follows will be satisfying, productive, enduring and glorifying to our Lord and Savior.

APRIL 12

HEARING GOD'S VOICE

When Samuel was a boy, serving and being discipled by Eli the priest, he woke up one night thinking he had heard Eli calling him. After going to Eli, he found out that Eli hadn't called him. This he did again up to a third time. On the third time Eli perceived that it must be the Lord who wanted to speak to Samuel, so he gave Samuel this instruction:

"Go, lie down; and it shall be, if He calls you, that you must say, 'Speak, Lord, for Your servant hears' So Samuel went and lay down in his place. Then the Lord came and stood and called as at other times, 'Samuel! Samuel!" And Samuel answered, "Speak, for Your servant hears." 1 Samuel 3:9-10

So began the life of Samuel as a prophet of God.

Like Samuel, we need to learn how to discern the Lord's voice from among other voices. Jesus said, "*My sheep hear my voice and follow after Me."* But it does just take listening for His voice. We need to quiet ourselves and listen with our innermost spirit to be able to hear the voice of God. Of course, we must want to hear His voice in the first place. And His voice will not contradict His Word.

The big question we must first answer though is, "Do we want to hear His voice?" Israel chose to let someone else listen to God's voice and relay it to them. Somehow, this exercise did not have the same impact on them; for they could have selective hearing. Hearing, they did not hear.

What about us? Do we expect someone to hear for us? Then, when they do, do we brush it off as just another voice among the many? Do we choose the options we prefer? Or, do we really want to hear God's voice?

God desires to commune with us. Take the time to commune with Him. Don't just talk. Take the time to listen!

APRIL 13

BLESSINGS OF COMMUNITY LIFE - HEALING AND FORGIVENESS

James wrote to the Jewish Christians about some very specific needs that they had and ones that we all face. Let's take a look at this instruction and exhortation:

"Is anyone among you sick? Let him call for the elders of the church, and let them pray over him, anointing him with oil in the name of the Lord. And the prayer of faith will save the sick, and the Lord will raise him up. And if he has committed sins, he will be forgiven. Confess your trespasses to one another, and pray for one another, that you may be healed. The effective prayer of the righteous avails much." James 5:14-16

Both healing and forgiveness are mentioned in these verses. Both come by submitting to the community of faith, calling for the elders. Note that the elders are mentioned in the plural. Leadership in the churches was always plural. There is an agreement of faith. Not just one person praying, but a community of people praying in faith.

There is power in our corporate gathering. Wherever two or three are gathered in the name of Jesus, He promised He is present. It is the same for forgiveness, as we confess one to another, and pray for one another. This not only builds up the unity of the saints, but also guards the unity of the saints. It adds a dimension of accountability that we have for one another.

If you are struggling with one of these issues today, would you consider the value of the church community? None of us were meant to live out our faith walk alone. When we were baptized into Christ, we were also baptized into his community, the church.

May the Lord stretch out His hand to heal us as we gather together in His name and allow Him to do the work necessary in our lives. Lord, manifest Yourself today through Your servants, we pray.

APRIL 14

THE OLD RUGGED CROSS

This is the song that I am singing in my spirit. I was thinking how so many flocked to churches last week to celebrate the fact that the tomb is empty. This week, however, many of the churches that were full last week were empty this week. The reality is that the tomb is still empty. Our Lord reigns. Shouldn't we be just as excited? Does not this reality carry us from week to week?

It makes me wonder just what effect the cross of Christ has on those who claim to be His followers. In considering some of the words of the hymn "The Old Rugged Cross" one can't help but be struck with the great work of Calvary that the writer has experienced, and what it means to live an exchanged life. In this identification with the cross of Christ, the writer comes back to this simple declaration:

"So I'll cherish the old rugged cross, till my trophies at last I lay down; I will cling to the old rugged cross, and exchange it someday for a crown."

This is what it is all about. Laying our trophies down, dying of ourselves, identifying with Jesus, clinging to the cross, with the promise that one day we will once again have an exchange, being rewarded for what we have laid down in this life. Ponder further the refrains from this song:

"On a hill far away stood an old rugged cross, the emblem of suffering and shame; and I love that old cross where the dearest and best for a world of lost sinners was slain."

"O that old rugged cross, so despised by the world, has a wondrous attraction for me; for the dear Lamb of God left His glory above to bear it to dark Calvary."

"In that old rugged cross, stained with blood so divine, a wondrous beauty I see, for 'twas on that old cross Jesus suffered and died, to pardon and sanctify me."

"To the old cross I will ever be true, its shame and reproach gladly bear; then He'll call me some day to my home far away, where His glory forever I'll share."

APRIL 15

GOD WILL MAKE A WAY

There is a song we sing whose chorus says, "God will make a way, where there seems to be no way...' In 2 Samuel 31, the Bible records:

"As for God, His way is perfect; the word of the Lord is proven; He is a shield to all who trust in Him."

The issue for us is discerning just what that way is.

- For some of you, you need additional finances, but when you are asked to work an extra day, you choose not to, saying, "God will make a way."
- For others you are looking for additional income, but God is asking you to reduce your expenses. You choose not to, saying, "God will make a way."
- Maybe what you desire is a better or more meaningful relationship, and the Lord is asking you to invest in more honest communication, but you ignore doing this saying, "God will make a way."

Often, what we do not see is that the way is right before us, but we are choosing a different way. Sometimes we even get pious about the whole thing, of course, always claiming that "God will make a way."

Perhaps, we need to ask the Lord for a discerning heart, to be able to move in the small directions in which He leads us in, trusting that in these small moves, He will reveal to us an even greater means.

I am not saying that we exchange faith for works. What I am saying is that in order to walk by faith, we must actually walk one step at a time. Let us be obedient in the small things and see God open up greater avenues of blessing in the process.

God will make a way! Perhaps the beginning of that way is right in front of you. You just need to recognize it and step out in faith.

APRIL 16

GUARD WHAT WAS COMMITTED TO YOUR TRUST!

This is Paul's admonition to Timothy, his beloved son in the faith (see 1 Timothy 6:20). He had received the deposit of faith, was instructed to pass on that deposit to faithful men who also would be able to pass it on (see 2 Timothy 2:2). But along the way, he must guard what was committed to his trust. As a faithful steward, he and other leaders must be careful to keep, protect, and even "*contend earnestly for the faith which was once for all delivered to the saints*" (Jude 3).

Like a soldier, he and others need to endure hardship, be ready to stand and fight a good warfare (1 Timothy 1:18). For the "*Spirit expressly says that in latter times some will depart from the faith, giving heed to deceiving spirits and doctrines of demons...*(1 Timothy 4:1). Paul exhorts Timothy:

"Hold fast the pattern of sound words which you have heard from me, in faith and love which are in Christ Jesus. That good thing which was committed to you, keep by the Holy Spirit who dwells in you." 2 Timothy 1:13-14

We also are called to run our race. It is important that we know for what exactly we are running. What deposit has the Lord given us for which we must contend?

I fear that many Christians are fighting and contending for things that are not worthy of contending; all the while, missing out on the deposit that has been given to them in Christ and His Word.

God's Word, and His principles communicated through His Apostles, are the faith deposit! It must be guarded, contended for and passed on in our generation and to future generations. Here is where we need people to enlist in the service of the King!

Lord, help us to be servants that keep what has been entrusted to us. May we also be faithful to pass on to succeeding generations the faithful deposit that we have received. Help us contend earnestly for the faith. Amen.

April 17

But God...

I never tire of knowing how significant the work of God has been and is in our lives. Rereading the second chapter of Ephesians, Paul contrasts the flesh walk and its futility, with the work of God in Christ for those of us who have believed. Verses 1-3 describe how we walked in darkness and deadness, with a significant transition in verse 4 which begins "But God." Look what it says:

"But God, who is rich in mercy, because of His great love with which He loved us, even when we were dead in trespasses, made us alive together with Christ (by grace you have been saved), and raised us up together in the heavenly places in Christ Jesus, that in the ages to come He might show the exceeding riches of His grace in His kindness toward us in Christ Jesus." Ephesians 2:4-7

But it is not just for eternity that this promise is made. Paul continues to teach:

"For by grace you have been saved through faith, and that not of yourselves; it is a gift of God, not of works, lest anyone should boast. For we are His workmanship, created in Christ Jesus for good works, which God prepared beforehand that we should walk in them." Ephesians 2:8-10

Not only did God give us eternal value and position, He prepared for us to serve Him here and now, through that same power. He has fashioned us for His glory, but also in a very practical way. If we walk according to His Spirit, we will accomplish works which He has destined, which while meeting very practical needs here on the earth, will also be very much a part of accomplishing God's plan for eternity.

So let us be heavenly minded, but as we are, be also earthly good.

Lord, help us to use our time, talents and treasure which you have graciously given us, to help others, to build the Kingdom of God and to accomplish things that can change time and eternity. May you weave us into your great cosmic plan. Amen.

APRIL 18

ONCE WERE NOT, BUT NOW ARE...

I thank God that Jesus is the Cornerstone of our faith. Peter exhorts us by saying:

"You are a chosen generation, a royal priesthood, a holy nation, His own special people, that you may proclaim the praises of Him who called you out of darkness into His marvelous light; who once were not a people but are now the people of God, who had not obtained mercy but now have obtained mercy." 1 Peter 2:9-10

Wow! There is enough here to make us shout with joy, even dance a bit if you like. What we were, we no longer are! Once we were under judgment, but now we have received mercy. God has called us and transferred even our placement. Once were we not, but now we are the people of God. Not just that, we are a chosen generation - a royal priesthood - a holy nation - His own special people!

Why has this happened? What should we do now that it has? Proclaim His praises of course! He is worthy to be praised! This is exciting! There is more power here than in your morning coffee.

Can you stop and let this truth sink in for just a minute? The God of the universe has chosen you and I and called us to Himself. No longer are we in a domain of darkness. No longer are we under any kind of judgment. Instead, we have obtained mercy and have been given such a great heritage.

As a result it is only proper that we praise Him today and always. Let us tell everyone about His marvelous works. Let His life energize us today. Let us arise! Arise! Arise! Because what we were not, but now we are His own special people!

Thank you, Lord, for your marvelous works. Only You can transform our very beings from the estrangement we once experienced to being called by You. May Your light and love be seen in our declaration and demonstration of Your great Name. Amen.

APRIL 19

THAT THE GENERATION TO COME MIGHT KNOW...

Today is a special day for our family. Our youngest grandchild, Eva, is being dedicated to the Lord by her parents. Four generations will travel and be present to witness this event. The fifth of the generation will be with us in spirit. I am considering the contemplation of Asaph as he penned the 78th Psalm. Here are a few of the verses:

"Give ear, O my people, to my law; incline your ears to the words of my mouth, I will open my mouth in a parable; I will utter dark sayings of old, which we have heard and known, and our fathers have told us. We will not hide them from their children, telling to the generation to come the praises of the Lord, and His strength and His wonderful works that He has done. For He established a testimony in Jacob, and appointed a law in Israel, which He commanded our fathers, that they should make them known to their children; that the generation to come might know them, the children who would be born, that they may arise and declare them to their children, that they may set their hope in God, and not forget the works of God, but keep His commandments." Psalm 78:1-7

God's vision is for generations. While we do good to receive the grace of God in our lives by faith, the admonition is that we train successive generations in that faith. It is the same idea that Paul passes on to Timothy: *"You therefore, my son, be strong in the grace that is in Christ Jesus. And the things you have heard from me among many witnesses, commit to faithful men who will be able to teach others also"* (2 Timothy 2:2). Here again we see the pattern of at least four generations of faithful leaders - Paul, Timothy, faithful men and others.

As we witness the dedication of precious Eva, we do so with a mind and prayer that she, one day, may stand like her great-great-grandmother Eva and witness a fifth generation that has proceeded from her, being dedicated to the Lord. This is the true blessing of the generations. May God continue to be glorified. May He give us all the strength and grace to be His witnesses in Word and deed to see this come to pass.

APRIL 20

HOLD FAST THE PATTERN OF SOUND WORDS...

In Paul's final letter to Timothy he shared those things that were most dear to his heart. He was concerned that he had not only run his race, but that Timothy and those to follow would also run theirs. We have such an individualistic, one generational type of thinking in our present culture, that much of what is being done in the church is for the present. We have not realized how much our cultural framework has influenced us.

But that is not the way of Christ and the Apostles! Success is defined by succession. Each generation must prepare the next generation to not just make it, but to reproduce themselves. Look at what Paul instructs Timothy in:

"Hold fast the pattern of sound words which you have heard from me, in faith and love which are in Christ Jesus. That good thing which was committed to you, keep by the Holy Spirit who dwells in us" . . . "You therefore, my son, be strong in the grace that is in Christ Jesus. And the things that you have heard from me among many witnesses, commit these to faithful men who will be able to teach others also." 2 Timothy 1:13-14; 2:1-2

We are all called to be builders. But what we are building should endure. First, we must cherish what we have been given, that which has been entrusted to us. You can't leave for someone else what you have not taken care of in the first place. This is our stewardship. Then, if we value what we have been given, then we care also about to whom we can entrust this valuable deposit. Those who will follow us will need to be prepared to not only be able to care for this deposit, but also to be able to entrust it to others in the future who will do the same.

Let us be patient as we build, using the proper foundation, materials, procedures, and trust that Christ will enable us to build what endures. Ask God to lift up your eyes beyond yourself, and even this immediate generation, to see the generations yet to be born. Start preparing an inheritance for their lives. With God's help, we can and will make a difference!

April 21

Ready in Season!

Living in New England requires that we remain flexible. The weather can change quickly, even from what was predicted the night before. I have my day planned, but just before heading out the door, a thunder storm rolled in. I checked back on the weather forecast and instead of it being clear for the day, rain is now predicted till early afternoon. Obviously, I will now need to adjust how the work I had planned to accomplish will be done, and the order in which to do it.

Paul instructed his disciple Timothy:

"I charge you therefore before God and the Lord Jesus Christ, who will judge the living and the dead at His appearing and His kingdom: Preach the word! Be ready in season and out of season. Convince, rebuke, exhort, with all longsuffering and teaching." 2 Timothy 4:1-2

It is one thing to be prepared for a particular season. It is another thing to be ready in any season. For this to happen, one must always be alert and preparing, even for the situations that one may encounter. Now, I know that we can't anticipate every situation we might go through in life, but we can cultivate our love and relationship with our Lord and Savior Jesus Christ. We do this through our prayers, the reading of Scripture and the meditation on and obedience to what that Word implies. In doing so, we learn of Him. He is known to us as we are known by Him.

Through our everyday walk of obedience, we gain experience that helps us in challenging times. We learn to walk by faith, trusting that the Lord will supply us with what we will need in each season. Having walked this way - we are ready!

Are you ready today - if the Lord calls you to respond? Getting ready for any season begins by responding to His voice today. Cultivating a life dependent on the Lord's guidance trains us in preparation.

Let's be prepared to answer His call - even on a moment's notice.

APRIL 22

YIELDING IS FAITH!

When Jesus prayed in the Garden, a place called Gethsemane (the press), He did not surrender faith to purpose, but, in fact, accepted purpose by faith. Here are the words Mark records of Jesus' prayer:

"Abba, Father, all things are possible for You. Take this cup away from Me; nevertheless, not what I will, but what You will." Mark 14:36

It seems in our lives that we misunderstand faith at times. When we go through suffering, some might say we do so because we lack faith. But is that the real issue? Does it take any faith to have life easy? Do you need faith when there are no obstacles? Jesus affirms the fact that with the Father all things are possible. He is not denying this fact. He is, in fact, declaring this truth.

What is the real issue in this case? As God's trusted servant, will Jesus surrender fully to the path chosen from the foundation of the world for Him to walk? Will He complete the calling to be the sacrificial Lamb of God? Will He be our supreme sacrifice? This is the will to which Jesus must surrender to.

How about in your life and mine? What is the plan and purpose of God for our lives? As we wrestle with purpose, faith and submission, are we willing to see in our Father an absolute sovereign God who knows all things? Surely, He will be with us and strengthen us for His purpose. We do not need to fear. Just trust Him and yield to His leading.

How we respond to our Father's purpose and plans for our lives will make the great difference for how we and others will relate to God in time and eternity.

Maybe you are dealing with some challenge today. You have the option of doing things in your own understanding and strength (which is limited and incomplete) or trusting in God's sovereign purpose (which is infinite and wise). What will you choose, your way or His? This is where destinies are made or hindered. Let me encourage you to walk by faith and choose His will! There is no better place to be.

APRIL 23

LET THE LITTLE CHILDREN COME TO ME.

This week my wife and I have had the privilege of having some of our grandchildren staying over at our house, two for three days, and now we have one for the rest of the week. Of course, the morning routine that I am accustomed to has changed. I still get up early to seek the Lord, read the Bible, and write a devotional thought. However, the quietness of the morning has changed to activity from other little ones who also like to get up early and seek my attention. In fact, when they arise, they just expect that everyone else should arise to be with them.

I have a choice; I can embrace them and alter my schedule, or try to keep them at bay until I am finished. What would Jesus do? We find out in Matthew 19:

"Then little children were brought to [Jesus] that He might put His hands on them and pray, but the disciples rebuked them. But Jesus said, 'Let the little children come to Me, and do not forbid them; for of such is the kingdom of heaven.' And He laid His hands on them and departed from there." Matthew 19:13:-15

The disciples thought that Jesus' schedule was too important to have little children interrupt Him. Jesus thought differently. He taught that these little children, and others like them, were the very substance of the kingdom.

Oftentimes, we miss seeing, right before our eyes, what is truly important, while thinking our agenda is more so. If you have children cross your path today, don't be afraid to embrace them and bless them. You are the representative of Jesus to them.

Of course, children are not the only ones to whom we should pay attention. People are important. Whether it be other members of our family, work or social relationships, do not be so caught up with the urgent, that you miss the important. You might not have the opportunity before you like you have today. Do not miss this opportunity. You will have enough time to get back to your other work. Lord, give us your eyes and heart today. Amen.

April 24

The Endurance of Faith

This morning I woke up with this idea: faith endures. I was thinking of the hall of faith we read in Hebrews 11. Here we find so many examples of people who by faith did something. And what is so impressive is that "*these all died in faith, not having received the promises, but having seen them afar off were assured of them, embraced them and confessed that they were strangers and pilgrims on the earth. For those who say such things declare plainly that they seek a homeland*" (Hebrews 11:13-14).

The next verse says that if they had placed in their mind out of which country they had come, they still had opportunity to turn back. But they did not turn back. They hung on the promise, embraced the promise, and set their sights on something better, the place destined to them by God. Because of this "*God is not ashamed to be called their God, for He has prepared a city for them*" (Hebrews 11:16).

What a great cloud of witnesses. "*And all of these, having a good testimony through faith, did not receive the promise, God having provided something better for us, that they should not be made perfect apart from us*" (Hebrews 11:39-40). But now in Christ Jesus, all have attained the promise; they, because of looking toward the fulfillment of the promise; we, by believing in that same fulfillment of the promise; their walk is completed; our walk in process.

"Therefore we also, since we are surrounded by so great a cloud of witnesses, let us lay aside every weight, and the sin which so easily ensnares us, and let us run with endurance the race that is set before us - looking unto Jesus, the author and finisher of our faith, who for the joy that was set before Him endured the cross, despising the shame, and has sat down at the right hand of God." Hebrews 12:1-2

We have been given their examples; may we also embrace the promise, complete our journey, never looking back, but trusting in God's strength to bring us to our heavenly destination.

APRIL 25

TRUE FAITH

The heroes of faith displayed in Hebrews 11 have one thing in common: they put their undivided confidence in God. In spite of all their trials and difficult circumstances, they triumphed because of their trust in God. For the author, faith is adhering to the promises of God, depending on the Word of God, and remaining faithful to the Son of God.

Looking at the context of Hebrews 11, the author's design to contrast faith with the sin of unbelief (Heb. 3:12, 19; 4:2; 10:38-39) becomes clear: over against the sin of falling away from the living God, the writer squarely places the virtue of faith. Those people who shrink from putting their trust in God are destroyed, but those who believe are saved (Hebrews 10:39).

But what is true faith? In 1563 a German theology professor, Zacharias Ursinus, formulated his personal faith: "True faith created in me by the Holy Spirit thought the Gospel is not only a knowledge and conviction that everything that God reveals in His Word is true, but also a deep-rooted assurance that not only others, but I too, have had my sins forgiven, have been made forever right with God, and have been granted salvation. These are gifts of sheer grace earned for us by Christ."

The author of Hebrews expresses that same assurance in much more concise wording: "*Faith is being sure of what we hope for.*" In short, assurance is balanced by certainty. The things we do not see are those that pertain to the future, which in time will become the present. Faith, therefore, radiates from man's inner being where hope resides to riches that are beyond his purview. Faith demonstrates itself in confident assurance and convicting certainty.

What do we conclude at this point? Hope relies on faith and looks to the future. Hope holds fast the confession of our faith. Our faith is, therefore, placed in God alone Who is able to fulfill the promises He has made, for God is faithful. True faith is commended by God. May we walk with Him demonstrating our faith in Him. This is pleasing in His sight.

APRIL 26

DO NOT CAST AWAY YOUR CONFIDENCE....

I keep returning to the book of Hebrews. The author continued to exhort the Christians of his day, and us by implication, to keep moving toward the promises of God. One must run with an aim to finish well. It is not a sprint, but a marathon. He wrote:

"Do not cast away your confidence, which has great reward. For you have need of endurance, so that after you have done the will of God, you may receive the promise." Hebrews 10:35-36

For the heroes of faith and us, it is impossible to separate faith and vision. As we look at the examples that are before us, we can see four things that were exemplified in their lives and must be seen in ours.

1. **Vision:** they saw the promises a far off. They had power for today because they had a vision for tomorrow.
2. **Confidence:** They were assured of the promise. They remained optimistic because they wanted to make a legacy more than a living.
3. **Hunger:** They embraced the promises. They had ownership of what only their descendants would enjoy.
4. **Resolve:** They confessed they were strangers and pilgrims. They made up their minds, their dreams or their memories did not consume them.

Let all of us who have been justified - live by faith. Lift up our eyes. Keep the promises of God ever before us. It will give us the necessary perspective for any obstacles or difficulties along the way. Keeping our eyes on Jesus, the Author and Finisher of our faith, will give us all the confidence we need and the endurance to keep running the race set before us.

You and I can make it! By God's grace we will make it! Let's keep running!

APRIL 27

WALK WORTHY - ENDEAVOR TO KEEP THE UNITY OF THE SPIRIT...

Like many of Paul's epistles, the letter to the Ephesians begins with doctrinal teaching followed by more practical teaching that can be applied to one's life. Having already established position and purpose, Paul now exhorts the Christians to walk in a manner that is worthy of all to which Christ has called us. Knowing that He is the One who has called us should constrain us to be people who exemplify His calling and character. Paul writes:

"I, therefore, the prisoner of the Lord, beseech you to walk worthy of the calling with which you were called, with all lowliness and gentleness, with longsuffering, bearing with one another in love, endeavoring to keep the unity of the Spirit in the bond of peace." Ephesians 4:1-3

You can see in these verses that our attitude and concern for each other is important as we seek to maintain the standard and structure that the Lord is building through His church and family. If we do not esteem each other, we will not exemplify the oneness necessary to display God's manifold wisdom to the world. As we allow the Lord's grace to work through us and others, we can grow into what He has purposed. These are the qualities that the Lord has demonstrated toward us. These are to be the qualities that we should demonstrate to one another.

May God's love and peace be evident in our lives today as we trust the Holy Spirit to work His character in us. In this way we will walk worthy of our calling.

APRIL 28

PUT OFF - PUT ON...

To walk worthy of the Gospel requires that we no longer walk as we did in the past, "as the rest of the Gentiles walk, in the futility of their mind, having their understanding darkened, being alienated from the life of God, because of the ignorance that is in them, because of the blindness of their heart; who being past feeling, have given themselves over to lewdness, to work all uncleanness with greediness" (Ephesians 4:17-20).

This is a description of the old man nature - an unregenerated man, the man or woman who does not know Christ. But, this is no longer who we are, or how we should be if we have given our lives to Him. Christ has done a recreated work in our spirit, and we must now submit to His leading in our lives. Therefore, Paul exhorts the Ephesians and us by implication to: "Put off, concerning your former conduct, the old man that grows corrupt according to the deceitful lusts, and be renewed in the spirit of your mind, and that you put on the new man which was created according to God, in true righteousness and holiness."

This putting off and putting on is something of which we must constantly be aware. If we allow Christ to rule in our hearts and minds, we will not allow the old man to reign. He must die, so that the new nature may be evident. The reality is if we sow to the flesh, of the flesh we will reap. But, if we sow to the Spirit, we will see the fruit of the Spirit expressed and demonstrated in our lives. May we allow God's Word to inform our minds and transform our thinking, so that we might choose to live in the new humanity created in Christ Jesus and discern what to put off and put on. May we be clothed in His righteousness.

How might this cause you to respond to the Lord's leading today? Be ready; I am sure you will have need as to how to respond to some situation in your life today. Will you walk in the old or in the new? You have to choose!

April 29

Walking in Wisdom

Paul has a lot to say about our walk of faith. We are to walk, not like the Gentiles walk, or how we once did when we were estranged from God. We are to walk as the new man created in Christ Jesus. We are to endeavor to walk in unity, worthy of the calling with which we are called, and that requires lowliness, gentleness, longsuffering and bearing with one another in love. We are to walk using the measure of the grace of God given to us - working to build up the body of Christ for which we are all members. We are to walk in love, being imitators of Christ. Walk in light, having no fellowship with darkness. In addition, Paul says we are to walk in wisdom.

"See then that you walk circumspectly (carefully), not as fools but as wise, redeeming the time, because the days are evil. Therefore do not be unwise, but understand what the will of the Lord is, and do not be drunk with wine, in which is dissipation; but be filled with the Spirit..." Ephesians 5:15-18

In order to walk in wisdom there are two things that pop right out in these verses: (1) we need to discern the will of the Lord, and (2) we must be filled with the Spirit. In fact, you can't really do the first without the second. Walking in wisdom requires that we know what the Lord is saying. God's voice will never contradict His Word. He is consistent. He never changes. But, our natural mind can war against the things of the Spirit. Therefore, we must submit to the Spirit of God and the Word of God, if we are to walk in wisdom.

Paul is careful to point out that living in the Spirit is contrary to drunkenness. Living in the Spirit will cause us to speak to one another in psalms, hymns and spiritual songs. We will sing and make melody in our hearts to the Lord. We will give thanks for all things to God our Father in the name of our Lord Jesus Christ (see Ephesians 5:19-20). In short, we will use the time and energies we have been given for His purpose. He will direct us in His path if we allow Him to. May the wisdom of the Lord guide you today in all you do. May He fill you with His Spirit and song in whatever situation you must face.

APRIL 30

MYSTERY REVEALED THROUGH PROPER ORDERING.

Paul gets real practical in Ephesians about how families and roles in families are to operate: each one serving a specific function, each one important in these roles. As the function is accomplished according to God's Word, something even greater is happening. The administration of the church and Christ is being revealed. Paul says in speaking about Godly marriage, "*This is a great mystery, but I speak concerning Christ and the church*" (Ephesians 5:32).

When we walk as Christ has designed us to walk, we are part of the revelation of Christ's wisdom being expressed to the world in which we live. Look what Paul wrote in the third chapter of Ephesians:

"To me, who am less than the least of all the saints, this grace was given, that I should preach among the Gentiles the unsearchable riches of Christ, and to make all see what is the fellowship (administration) of the mystery, which from the beginning of the ages has been hidden in God who created all things through Christ Jesus; to the intent that now the manifold wisdom of God might be made known by the church to the principalities and powers in heavenly places, according to the eternal purpose which He accomplished in Christ Jesus our Lord, in whom we have boldness and access with confidence through faith in Him." Ephesians 3:8-12

Why is it a big deal to order our families as Christ has taught us? Because it reveals God's wisdom to the world. If we change His order, we do not end up with the same results or revelation. When we order ourselves according to His design, even the principalities and powers have to acknowledge the wisdom of God. It is important we are not deceived when people are trying to redefine marriage and relationships according to their own design. We must recognize in this an attempt to nullify the outworking and revelation of God's design. Only in keeping true to His Word can we truly stand in the day of battle and be properly equipped to continue to stand. May God give you His grace to recover in your life, His order and purpose.

MAY 1

STANDING IN THE DAY OF BATTLE

In winding down his letter to the Ephesians, Paul adds:

"Finally, my brethren, be strong in the Lord and in the power of His might. Put on the whole armor of God, that you may be able to stand against the wiles of the devil. For we do not wrestle against flesh and blood, but against principalities, against powers, against the rulers of the darkness of this age, against spiritual hosts of wickedness in the heavenly places. Therefore take up the whole armor of God, that you may be able to withstand in the evil day, and having done all, to stand" (Ephesians 6:10-13).

There is a connection between the entire letter's instruction and these concluding exhortations. It is not the beginning of a new teaching on the armor of God, but a continuation of using the armor of God as another way to say that all Paul has taught up to now needs to be applied. In that way, the Ephesians would be putting on the proper armor, trusting that this is God's revealed wisdom being displayed to even the principalities and powers of this age. It is not a choosing of what to obey from the Word of God, but a total surrendering to the authority of God's Word in our lives.

Having identified the enemy, we are not distracted to focus on those around us, but seeing that behind every action lurks a systemic opposing force that can be battled against. In order to do so, we must embrace God's ways (all of them) and trust in His wisdom and the power of His might. Only in this way can we stand. And stand we must.

In our day, so many pick and choose just what they like from the teaching of the Bible. This even includes preachers who are unwilling to speak the hard things. But unless we become students and disciples of our Master, and seek to embrace all the truth, we will be weak and not prepared for the day of battle. Let today be a turning point in your life. Make a resolution in your heart and mind to embrace the totality of God's Word. Then when it confronts you in some area of your life, confess it as sin, and then allow God's strength and grace the room to help you change. It's time to get up and get dressed!

MAY 2

THANK YOU NOTES!

In the age of electronics, it is not often that one gets a written note. However, getting a personal note from someone, either expressing thanks or sharing some kindness in words is something that I think most of us appreciate. I know that I do. These expressions of love and appreciation are the kind of things that we hold on to, even referring back to them, when perhaps, we are discouraged or needing encouragement.

In Paul's letter to the Philippians, he writes a thank you note to the believers at Philippi for their help in his times of need and uses this opportunity to encourage them in their unity of purpose to see the Gospel continue to progress. After thanking them for their fellowship from the first day up until the present time, he makes this statement: "*being confident of this very thing, that He who has begun a good work in you will complete it until the day of Christ Jesus*" (Philippians 1:6).

Here is where we must put our trust. Jesus is able to transform us and mature us completely. Much of the rest of the letter focuses on just what kind of attitude and focus we must have to see the gospel continue to progress. If we can keep our eyes on Jesus, His example, and those who have demonstrated the same, we will grow in unity and Christ-likeness and push out the borders of the Kingdom of God.

We cannot simply do this alone. We need partners in the Gospel. We must esteem each other better than ourselves. May we learn to say thank you to those who are laboring and have labored with us. May we grow in our unity, like-mindedness, being of one accord, doing nothing out of selfish ambition or conceit, but in lowliness of mind let us each esteem others better than ourselves. Looking out, not only for our own interest, but also for the interests of others. In short, let joy be fulfilled through our united purpose. Jesus is able to do all of this through us. Stop communicating that it is not possible. All things are possible. Let's learn to express our thank you more to Jesus our Lord and to each other.

AIM TO FINISH WELL

The writer to the Hebrews wrote:

"Therefore do not cast away your confidence, which has great reward. For you have need of endurance, so that after you have done the will of God, you may receive the promise" (Hebrews 10:35-36).

Every Christian and Christian leader should aim to finish well. We are exhorted to persevere because:

- Confidence will be rewarded
- Obedience will be recognized
- Shrinking back will be regretted, and
- Christ's return will be celebrated.

Our journey is not a sprint, but a marathon. We must pace ourselves and endure to the end. The goal is in sight. Keep your eyes on Jesus, and you will finish well.

JUST BEGIN

It's another Monday, the beginning of another week, the first full week of another month. Time rolls on by; what work we have done is behind us, what work is calling out for our attention is before us. We at times want to pause and celebrate what has been accomplished; however, the pressing needs keep us ever moving.

For some, though, getting started is difficult. Sometimes the energy to just begin again is not there. Maybe it has been a difficult time period for you. You are saying to yourself, "Where do I begin?" "The work before me is too much; I do not even know where to start." In fact the longer you wait, the more difficult it seems to begin.

When I was growing up, my mom would say, "Just start in a corner and work out from there." In other words, just begin. The hardest part of any job is just beginning. But once something is begun, it is much easier to keep going. The progress seen has enough of a motivation to keep you going.

The Apostle Paul said to the Philippians:

"Brethren, I do not count myself to have apprehended; but one thing I do, forgetting those things which are behind and reaching forward to those things which are ahead, I press toward the goal for the prize of the upward call of God in Christ Jesus." Philippians 3:13-14

It was the same Apostle who said:

"I can do all things through Christ who strengthens me." Philippians 4:13

Today, if you are struggling with motivation, may I just suggest that you start in a corner and work your way out. Just begin. Trust that God will give you the strength to continue forward. In fact, invite Him to work right alongside of you. He has already invited us to work alongside of Him.

MAY 5

REJOICING, GENTLENESS, PRAYER AND PEACE

Everyone ultimately wants to experience peace in their lives. However, how they go about achieving peace often does not give them lasting peace at all. Paul encourages the Philippians in a way where they can have lasting peace. Even a peace that will keep them protected to walking in future peace. Give some thought to his exhortation:

"Rejoice in the Lord always. Again I will say rejoice! Let your gentleness be known to all men. The Lord is at hand. Be anxious for nothing, but in everything by prayer and supplication, with thanksgiving, let your requests be made known to God; and the peace of God, which surpasses all understanding, will guard your hearts and minds through Christ Jesus" (Philippians 4:4-7).

It all starts with from where we get our joy. We rejoice in the abundant mercy and grace that has already been afforded us through Christ. Knowing that we can trust Him, we bring our needs and concerns to Him. We are not overcome with anxiety, for we know that He loves us and as our Father, wants to provide for our needs. This helps us to be gentle. We do not need to fear; we can be patient, we can have proper perspective, and we can bear each other's burdens.

We communicate our prayer needs always in a spirit of thankfulness, knowing that all good things come from above, and that God is wise in His disbursement of the timing and substance of what we need. This abiding peace transcends all circumstances.

What a prescription for peace. Rejoicing in the Lord - demonstrating gentleness - bringing any anxiety to the Lord in prayer, supplication with thanksgiving. Then live in that wonderful peace of God, beyond understanding, not only for the moment, but proactively, protecting us to keep His peace in the future.

Let His peace flow like a river in your life today. Let it guard your mind and heart. The rejoicing that you begin with will continue as you experience His peace.

May 6

Building with the Lord

One of my readings this morning was Psalm 127. For many, the beginning of the psalm is quite familiar:

"Unless the Lord builds the house, they labor in vain who build it; Unless the Lord guards the city, the watchman stays awake in vain. It is vain for you to rise up early, to sit up late, to eat the bread of sorrows; For so He gives His beloved sleep." Psalm 127:1-2

It is quite clear that we are to trust in God as the builder and submit to His plans and process. Only joining Him, building His way, will give us the peace and assurance that we are progressing according to His will. Perhaps what is not so clear in this Psalm is the connection from this first section to the next. I don't believe that they are disconnected thoughts. The psalmist writes:

"Behold, children are a heritage from the Lord, the fruit of the womb is a reward. Like arrows in the hand of a warrior, so are the children of one's youth. Happy is the man who has his quiver full of them; they shall not be ashamed, but shall speak with their enemies in the gate." Psalm 127:3-5

What needs to be connected here is that God has a vision of continuance, one of many generations. It is not one of building for one generation, but instead building in such a way that there is a deposit and growth from one generation to another generation. This is both in the physical and the spiritual.

What God is building will last, endure, and not be ashamed even in enemy territory. Whatever He builds will carry with it an ever-increasing spiritual family that is united in vision and purpose. The joining of the generations builds in intensity and strength as the years progress. If we build His way, there will be a legacy that will testify to what has been built. Otherwise, anything done our own way will not accomplish His purposes and will have been built in vain. Let's find out His work, and join in it!

MAY 7

WHY WE MUST PRAY FOR OUR NATION!

In America, today is a National Day of Prayer. For many, even though they are aware, they will treat this like any other day. Even though we are all being affected by the times in which we live, there seems to be no realization that we can make a difference through our persistent prayers. When Paul charged Timothy to do his ministry, he exhorted him to wage the good warfare, having faith and a good conscience. In light of this he gave him instructions that were a priority:

"Therefore I exhort first of all that supplications, prayers, intercessions, and giving of thanks be made for all men, for kings and all who are in authority, that we may lead a quiet and peaceable life in all godliness and reverence. For this is good and acceptable in the sight of God our Savior, who desires all men to be saved and to come to the knowledge of the truth." 1 Timothy 2:1-4

Prayer is to be first of all. Its direction is for all in authority so we can lead peaceable lives, not to just enjoy prosperity, or recreation, but to make a way for the Gospel of the Good News of Christ Jesus to go and be spread so that people may be saved. Not only that, but also for people to grow in maturity to the knowledge of the truth. These prayers are not self-serving, but others centered. As we pray for our leaders and our nation, we pray that God will enable us to be at peace in such a way that our witness may continue to abound and the sharing of the Gospel be unhindered.

This is our first ministry responsibility. This is something we must do daily. When there are special calls to prayer, may we join with the brethren and seek the Lord together, interceding for those in authority, and trusting that God who is above all, will open up the avenues we need to shine His light in our communities.

Many communities today will have special times of prayer. In Fall River, we will gather at the City Hall at 7 PM to do just that. You are welcome!

MAY 8

PRAYER FOR OUR NATION

Last night we gathered in the lobby that connects the City Hall with the council chambers to pray for our nation. We lifted petitions to the Lord, interceding for our government leaders, military, business, education, churches and family. We know that this is not something we should do just one special day for the year, but persisting in ongoing *ekklisia* type prayers.

The peaceable existence we seek is that the Gospel can go forth and change people and systems. On the brochure for the *National Day of Prayer* is a prayer written by Dr. Jack Graham. I will add it at the end of this devotional thought. Perhaps you can use this prayer as a guide in your own praying for our country. Please remember, it is our privilege and duty as Christians to stand in the gap where there is a breech. May we stand, with a posture of prayer, and see the hand of God move in our generation.

"We come to You in the Name that is above every name - Jesus Christ our Lord and Savior. Our hearts cry out to You. Knowing that You are a prayer-answering, faithful God - the One we trust in times like these - we ask that You renew our spirits, revive our churches, and heal our land.

We repent of our sins and ask for Your grace and power to save us. Hear our cry, oh God, and pour out Your Spirit upon us that we may walk in obedience to Your Word.

We are desperate for Your tender mercies. We are broken and humbled before You. Forgive us, and in the power of Your great love, build us up to live in Your righteousness.

We pray for our beloved nation. May we repent and return to You and be a light to the nations. And we pray for our leaders and ask that You give them wisdom and faith to follow You.

Preserve us and protect us, for You are our refuge and only hope. Deliver us from all fears except to fear You, and may we courageously stand in the Truth that sets us free. We pray with expectant faith and grateful hearts. In Jesus' name, our Savior. Amen."

May 9

Treasure Hunt

Today we will be celebrating the birthday of one of our grandchildren. As part of the festivities, we will have a treasure hunt. I am in charge of providing the clues. Paul lets the Colossians in on this treasure hunt also when he wrote to them that their "*hearts may be encouraged, being knit together in love, and attaining to all riches of the full assurance of understanding, to the knowledge of the mystery of God, both of the Father and of Christ, in whom are hidden all the treasures of wisdom and knowledge*" (Colossians 2:2-3).

Of course they were to seek this treasure in Christ that they might grow, mature and be able to stand in their faith, not being easily deterred. Paul explained why he is saying what he did:

"Now this I say lest anyone should deceive you with persuasive words. For though I am absent in the flesh, yet I am with you in spirit, rejoicing to see your good order and the steadfastness of your faith in Christ. As therefore you have received Christ Jesus the Lord, so walk in Him, rooted and built up in Him and established in the faith, as you have been taught, abounding in it with thanksgiving." Colossians 2:4-7

See the terms to growing - rooted, built up and established. You can just imagine a tree. First, a seed that goes down, the shoot that grows up, but it takes years to fully establish. That is why it is important to continue in what we have first been rooted.

You and I have a wonderful treasure in Christ. Only as we appreciate this and continue to value what we have can we grow. There are seasons in our lives that are more difficult than others. However, each season helps our foundation to go down deeper and our lives to be established stronger. We will need the work of past seasons to help us in future seasons.

Join me in a treasure hunt today! When you find Him, don't let Him go!

MAY 10

THE BLESSINGS OF A MOTHER

It was a blessing to be able to share a church service today with my grandmother, mother, wife, daughter and grandchildren. Five generations looking to God for our strength, wisdom, endurance, and life. Without Him we would not be complete, nor could we exhibit the kind of love necessary to be a family, work in His kingdom, and have energy to pour out in others' lives.

I have been so blessed to see the kind of sacrificial service that was exhibited through my grandmother and mother, and continue to see in them. My wife is also the kind of mother and grandmother that continues to give of herself, make special meals, getting up early, staying up late, whatever is needed to be of help to her children and grandchildren.

God knew what He was doing when He designed family. Any attempts to change His plan distort the lessons and security that family was meant to give. It is His wisdom to which we must turn, when we do not know the way. Honoring our fathers and mothers was His instruction.

"Children, obey your parents in the Lord, for this is right. 'Honor your father and mother,' which is the first command with promise: 'that it may be well with you and you may live long on the earth.'" Ephesians 6"1-3

May we learn to return to this instruction and receive the blessing that He has promised.

I want to wish my mother, grandmother, wife, daughter, daughter-in law and all the precious mothers a very Happy Mother's Day! You are all so much appreciated.

WHEN THE FLOWERS FADE - HONOR CONTINUES

It is a wonderful thing to celebrate special days that bring back to mind something special. The idea is that this reminder is not just for a one-time remembrance, but to bring to our minds principles that are good and needful to our everyday existence. *Mother's Day* and *Father's Day* are such special days. They remind us that God's Word has commanded us to honor our fathers and mothers. This is more than a passing platitude, but a lifelong orientation.

To honor someone is to ascribe weight to them because of the position that they have carried. They may or may not have exercised that position of authority to the best, but then have we in our following?

The idea of weight is that we ascribe value because God has deemed it so. Even when that person is not able to perhaps do what they did in the past, they are still ascribed value because of God's creative order, unlike evolutionary thought which discards those who are not able to produce, only ascribing to them a utilitarian value.

Honor is something that should be a way of life for us. If flowers are all we give, they will shortly die. But honor will continue to manifest itself in the everyday things that you do for others - praying, serving, loving, caring for, and just doing the simple things that bring joy and care to others.

Our attitudes must match our service for true honor to be given. Perhaps today we can consider how we might make honoring our parents or other authority figures in our lives a practice, not just an event. May God pour out His grace in our lives so this will be true.

MAY 12

GLIMPSE OF REFRESHING

This morning, I paused near one window and took time to take in the freshness of the breeze following an early morning shower. The air seems so clean that it makes one appreciate the stillness and crispness of the moment. Somehow the rain brings a cleansing that is evident even to the senses.

The experience made me think back to words that Peter preached to his own countrymen. He was referring to the promises that are found in Jesus. After pointing to Jesus, he instructed those listening how they could benefit from His sacrifice on the cross. Listen to what Peter said:

"Those things which God foretold by the mouth of all His prophets, that the Christ would suffer, He has thus fulfilled. Repent therefore and be converted, that your sins may be blotted out, so that times of refreshing may come from the presence of the Lord, and He may send Jesus Christ, who was preached to you before, whom Heaven must receive until the times of restoration of all things, which God has spoken by the mouth of all His holy prophets since the world began." Acts 3:18-21

The refreshing that I experienced from the early morning rain was just temporary. However, the refreshing that I received, because of the cleansing that Jesus brought to my life as I have trusted in Him, is forever. Not only that, but each time that I seek His presence and turn from my own sin, I can experience renewed refreshing in His presence.

That same refreshing is available for you. What a great promise Peter preached. Maybe look to the Lord for renewed cleansing and be refreshed by His Spirit. Open your spiritual window. Can you smell the freshness?

May 13

Run with Endurance

I am preparing for today, thinking that ministry is not for sissies. Paul exhorted Timothy to:

"Wage the good warfare." 1 Tim. 1:18

The writer to the Hebrews tells us to:

"Run our race with endurance." Heb. 12:1

These scriptures make me think that I can't let yesterday take up too much of my time today, if I plan on moving forward.

Three quick thoughts I can share about this today:

1. First, we need to get in the race. You can't run the race until you first enter it. Procrastination will never get you anywhere.
2. Second, once you are in, you can't quit. Giving up is cowardly. You entered the race to finish. You are not running for fame or fortune, but for God's glory. Paul was able to declare "*I have finished my race...*" (2 Timothy 4:7-8).
3. The third thought is that we must stay on the course. We must not get distracted. We are to look to Jesus - the author and finisher of our faith.

We don't get to choose our own course; it is laid out for us. We must simply stay the course, run correctly, keep focused on Jesus, and FINISH the race!

May we draw on the Spirit's power to stay on track today and always.

MAY 14

EQUIPPING SAINTS FOR THE WORK OF MINISTRY...

In about an hour from now, young adult leaders and their leaders will be arriving to take part in our 24th Annual Youth Leadership Conference. Participants will be coming from four different states, representing six different churches or church schools, to spend the next two days being exhorted and exhorting themselves in the theme: "*Endeavoring to keep the unity of the Spirit.*"

These young adults are not only here to learn, they are here to impart to their own generation what they are learning as they walk by faith. The role of the builders (five-fold ministry) is to equip the saints for the work of ministry, for the edifying of the body of Christ.

"And He Himself gave some to be apostles, some prophets, some evangelists, and some pastors and teachers, for the equipping of the saints for the work of ministry, for the edifying of the body of Christ, till we all come to the unity of the faith and of the knowledge of the Son of God, to a perfect man, to the measure of the stature of the fullness of Christ; that we should no longer be children tossed to and fro and carried about with every wind of doctrine, by the trickery of men, in cunning craftiness of deceitful plotting, but speaking the truth in love, may grow up in all things into Him who is the head – Christ – from whom the whole body, joined and knit together by what every joint supplies, according to the effective working by which every part does its share, causes growth of the body for the edifying of itself in love." Ephesians 4:11-16

In other words, all Christians are to partake, serve and be involved in the work of ministry and the building up of the body. This is what we are seeking to do, joining generations to walk worthy together in fulfilling the call of God in our lives personally and corporately.

Please pray that the Lord will accomplish in all our lives what He has purposed for this season. May fruit abound from seeds sown in fertile ground and bring glory to His Name.

MAY 15

WALKING TO PLEASE GOD

So many times the apostle Paul speaks of a believer's walk. In his first letter to the Thessalonians he writes:

"Finally then, brethren, we urge you and exhort in the Lord Jesus that you should abound more and more, just as you received from us how you ought to walk and to please God; for you know what commandments we have through the Lord Jesus." 1 Thessalonians 4:1-2

First, I want to point out that Paul is not just giving the Thessalonians suggestions to live by, but the commandments of the Lord. If they are to please God, there is a specific way in which they need to walk. This is not some return to legalism or the law, for Paul was adamant when he taught by "*grace you [we] you have been saved through faith, and that not of yourselves; It is a gift of God*" (Ephesians 2:8). This has to do with our justification and right standing before God. Yet there is a work of sanctification that Paul was also speaking of.

We are to grow and mature and represent who Christ is to the world. To do so, there are definite instructions we are called to follow. In fact, he teaches that "*he who rejects this does not reject man, but God, who has also given us His Holy Spirit*" (1 Thessalonians 4:8). You see, "*God did not call us to uncleanliness, but in holiness*" (1 Thessalonians 4:7). This holiness is not just for its own sake, but as a witness to those watching. Paul writes:

"But we urge you brethren, that you increase more and more [in the demonstration of brotherly love]; that you also aspire to lead a quiet life, to mind your own business, and to work with your own hands, as we command you, that you may walk properly toward those who are outside, many that you may lack nothing." 1 Thessalonians 4:10-12

Again, we see the word command. Paul is saying that the instructions given by Christ through His builders are meant to be followed. In doing so, we agree with the Spirit of God, pleasing Him and being a visible demonstration to the world around us. May we receive this revelation and walk in this manner - pleasing God and reaching our neighbors.

MAY 16

TO EACH ONE OF US - GRACE GIVEN

This week has been like a whirlwind. It seemed like there were so many things on my to-do list that I did not know just how it could all be done. We have kept our grandchildren a few days, attended a baseball game to support our students who were being recognized for their accomplishments, hosted a Student Leadership Conference for two days, taught at a Men's ministry last night, wrote a forward for a book this morning, besides all the other normal things and challenges. Life is like that sometimes, and we cannot do more that is humanly possible: however, the scripture does tell us that we can do all things through Christ who strengthens us.

That is the key. While it will take our utmost concentration and effort, there is something even more important that is also at work. It is the abiding presence and help that we get from the Lord. Paul wrote to the Ephesians:

"To each one of us grace was given according to the measure of Christ's gift." Ephesians 4:7

In reflecting on this scripture, I am focused on this idea of God's grace. His grace has been poured out in all of our lives in order to accomplish just what He has gifted us to do. It is His Spirit at work in us that makes it possible for all of our "to-do" lists.

I am overwhelmed right now with God's great grace, His grace to receive His gift. May we all humbly receive His grace gift to be and do all He has purposed us to do in us and through us. Apart from this we have no chance. With His grace the sky's the limit.

MAY 17

ESTABLISH THE WORK OF OUR HANDS

Psalm 90 has been attributed to a prayer of Moses. There is surely a comparison between the eternity of God and the frailty of man. Life on this earth is short compared to eternity, and therefore we must make the best use of the time that we do have. The psalmist writes:

"So teach us to number our days, that we might gain a heart of wisdom." Psalm 90:12

The apostle Paul wrote something similar:

"See then that you walk circumspectly, not as fools but as wise, redeeming the time, because the days are evil." Ephesians 5:15-16

There also is the idea that life can be difficult. The psalmist cries out, "*have compassion on Your servants, Oh satisfy us early with Your mercy, that we may rejoice and be glad all our days!*" (Psalm 90:13-14). Only God can bring satisfaction to our work and our lives. His mercy is fresh each morning. His steadfast love is abounding. His purpose is worthy of our attention.

One more request is prayed for: "*Let the beauty of the Lord our God be upon us, and establish the work of our hands for us; Yes, establish the work of our hands*" (Psalm 90:17-18). Since God has a purpose for us to accomplish, and we know that life can be tough and even at odds with the very work we are called to do, we pray for His sovereign hand upon our lives.

Lord, let the works of our hands, the very works to which You have called us, be established; let them endure, being tried in the fire, let them remain and bring glory to Your name! Today Lord we pray for Your favor. Amen.

MAY 18

LOVE, OR DO NOT LOVE, THE WORLD?

The same author wrote two phrases that seem to contradict themselves. In John 3:16, John wrote:

"God so loved the world..." John 3:16

In 1 John 2:15, John wrote:

"Do not love the world..." 1 John 2:15

How do we interpret these instructions? Is what God loved the same as what John is writing for us not to love? Hardly! We can see in the context of these verses important truth. God's love is centered on people who are in need of the saving knowledge of Jesus Christ, so that they (we also) might be restored to a rightful relationship with Him.

The love of the world that John is saying we should not have is "the lust of the flesh, the lust of the eyes, and the pride of life." He is talking about the temporal things that pertain to our fleshly existence, those things we long for that we are willing to scrape and claw to get. What pleases our flesh or satisfies the temptation of what we see, the power that we want to obtain, all of which is short lived and never brings satisfaction.

What John is saying is do not put your affections, or your strongest ambitions, on the temporal things that do not satisfy, or measure up with the purposes of God. Set your mind and affections on that which is eternal. So, even though we need to eat and have homes to live in, etc., we have been created for so much more destiny than that.

Therefore, let us lift up our eyes. See what the plan of God is for our lives. Invest in His purposes. Then we will be a demonstration of the love that is in God. For "*the world is passing away, and the lust of it; but he who does the will of God abides forever*" (1 John 2:17).

MAY 19

IS SEEING BELIEVING?

Today, I am thinking about a story found in the 9th chapter of John's Gospel. It is a story of a man born blind that Jesus heals. This, in and of itself, is a marvelous display of the grace and power of God. But as the story unfolds, there is an interplay of sight and blindness that continues. Presented to us are the facts that one could be physically blind and see; and another seeing but blind.

The student (the blind man) teaches the teachers (the religious leaders), "If this Man were not from God, He could do nothing" (John 9:33), but the teachers in their pride do not appreciate these words of wisdom and say, "'*You were completely born in sins, and are you teaching us?' and they cast him out*" (John 9:34). The reality is that they were blinded spiritually.

They later asked Jesus, "*Are we blind also*" to which He answered, "*If you were blind, you would have no sin; but now you say, 'We see.' Therefore your sin remains*" (John 9:41). Here is the lesson: we might be blinded in many ways, but if light is brought into the situation and we choose to continue in our ways, we carry the weight of that choice. We remain blind. The alternative is that we can choose the light and receive sight. This requires us to put off pride and embrace humility.

In Jesus is life and His life is the light of men and women. It is Jesus who shines in the darkness. As you and I have found Christ, then we should walk in Him, allowing Him to continue to be our Light in every given circumstance.

Lord, help us see as You see today. Remove areas of blindness and allow the brightness of Your Word to penetrate our hearts, so we might reflect the wisdom and glory of God in our lives. Amen!

MAY 20

GOD'S KINGDOM IS NOT SHAKEN!

Yesterday [May 19, 2015], I was overjoyed to see the pictures posted from Kiev, Ukraine of the new Doctors of Ministry. I remember, many years ago when having a discussion with Dr. Paul Shotsberger, who was a missionary in Ukraine and the acting director of The Institute for the Development of Christian Leaders there, of the need for such a program. He had already developed a Master's program, training pastors and leaders through a church-based network of Bible Colleges, and with a Doctoral program, it would allow the Ukrainian Church leadership to be able to train their own leaders in the future.

I have lost count of how many Master's student cohorts that have now been completed. I believe at least eight in Ukraine, but they are also being done now in other countries. This was the second cohort of Doctoral students to complete the program. I have to say, looking at that visible picture of the graduates and their professors yesterday, gave me such a hope for this nation. Under the able leadership of Dr. Paul Shotsberger, and the present director Valentina Grenchuk and the Doctoral Student Mentor, Dr. Siarhei Padniuk, much has been accomplished to establish in Ukraine a great foundation for the future.

As I think of the pastors and teachers and all the new graduates and professors that I have had the privilege to know, I am reminded of what Paul wrote to the Philippians:

"I thank God upon every remembrance of you, always in every prayer of mine making request for you all with joy, for your fellowship in the gospel from the first day until now, being confident of this very thing, that He who has begun a good work in you will complete it until the day of Jesus Christ." Philippians 1:3-6

No one knew ten years ago what you as a nation would need to go through. However, God knew. He prepared a people who will continue His witness, not just in Ukraine, but to the ends of the earth. Congratulations and God's riches blessings on all of you.

We can all trust in God's wise plans for our lives!

MAY 21

WE CAN ONLY BE PART OF THE SOLUTION IF WE ARE NOT PART OF THE PROBLEM!

We live in serious days. While much is in upheaval around us, we do not need to despair, but we must be serious and watchful. Joel addressed his generation in a call to repentance. If there is ever a time to heed that call it is now. Here are his words:

"Now, therefore," says the Lord, "Turn to Me with all your heart, with fasting, with weeping, and with mourning." So rend your heart, and not your garments; return to the Lord your God, for He is gracious and merciful, slow to anger, and of great kindness; And He relents from doing harm. Who knows if He will turn and relent, and leave a blessing behind Him" (Joel 2:12-14).

Notice what this text says. The prophet exhorted his own people to turn to the Lord with all of their hearts. Judgment had already been pronounced and was being seen in their present culture. Yet, if the people would turn to the Lord with a sincerity of heart, not just external religious activity, perhaps the Lord would relent from the judgment that He had already determined. Instead of looking at the severity of the Lord, they were to see His mercy and grace, knowing that the Lord desires to show forth His kindness and bless His people.

We, too, must seek the Lord in our own day. Recognizing the signs of judgment that we see all around us, we can have hope in the mercy of God. He desires us to turn to Him, not only for ourselves, but for the people of our land.

If we as God's people would stand in the gap for our communities, we may see and experience the blessing, and not the judgment of the Lord in the same communities. It is not just about the outward show of our deeds, though they are important, but the inward, humble turning to God, looking for His great mercy that can and will make the difference. May we heed His call today.

MAY 22

REMEMBER NOW YOUR CREATOR...

Life has cycles. One is born and another dies. Solomon in writing Ecclesiastes reflects on such things as this and tries to bring some conclusion to the matter. He writes:

"Remember now your Creator in the days of your youth, before the difficult days come, and the years draw near when you say, I have no pleasure in them." Ecclesiastes 12:1

As one continues to read the rest of chapter 12, Solomon is writing about the issues associated with getting older, the difficulties of what this process presents and the fact that some things need to be acted on when younger, not when it is too late.

Many people look back with regrets on their life choices. Aging will happen to all of us. The challenges of this can be very difficult for most, but looking back on your life and having regrets for where you find yourself can be even more painful. But, this does not need to be. You can make choices that will change this. At least you can face the challenges of life with hope and faith in a Sovereign God who loves you.

Solomon continues to say you must "*remember your Creator before...*" (Ecclesiastes 12:6) it is too late. In fact hearing the conclusion of the matter he writes:

"Fear God and keep His commandments. For this is man's all. For God will bring every work into judgment, including every secret thing. Whether good or evil." Ecclesiastes 12:13-14

Life will always be a challenge. Various seasons have their different challenges. What is uplifting and gives us hope is that we can face these challenges with the help of God. We do not need to be alone, nor finding ourselves living in a sea of regrets. Today, we can choose to put our past under the blood of Jesus and trust Him for our future. He will never let us down. He will be our strength and joy.

MAY 23

THE GOSPEL OF THE KINGDOM!

Jesus preached a kingdom message. His apostles did the same. Accompanying this message were great signs and wonders. Jesus promised it would be so. The records of the Gospels and Acts declare it true. In Matthew, we read one such account in the life of Jesus:

"And Jesus went about all Galilee, teaching in their synagogues, preaching the gospel of the kingdom, and healing all kinds of sickness and all kinds of disease among the people. Then His fame went throughout all Syria; and they brought Him all sick people who were afflicted with various diseases and torments, and those who were demon possessed, epileptics, and paralytics; and He healed them." Matthew 4:23-24

Considering this text and the testimony of the Early Church, we are confronted with thinking through several questions, which we must give considerable weight to.

- If we, in our day, would preach a kingdom message, is it not the same Holy Spirit that has been given to us to testify and validate the Word of God?
- Can we believe for more than what we might have experienced in the past?
- Jesus said we would do greater works because He would go to His Father. Can you believe with me for greater works?

May we preach the Gospel of the Kingdom and allow God to show Himself strong in our midst. Jesus is the same yesterday, today and forever. The same power that raised Christ from the dead is at work in those who believe.

Let us go and trust God to do what He has already promised He would do.

May 24

A Safe Inheritance

When we learn that our names are mentioned in a will, we know that we have a share in an inheritance described in that will. Often we do not know the value of that inheritance. We have to wait for the death of the testator and for legal transactions and financial settlements. After the period of waiting is over, however, the value of the inheritance often has diminished. Also, the distribution of the inheritance frequently causes jealousy and strife.

By contrast, our eternal inheritance is a constant source of happiness. From the moment of our salvation we are filled with joy. Granted that we possess our inheritance in principle now, we know that when we leave this earthly scene we receive our inheritance in full. We are unable to comprehend the value of this inheritance, for:

"The gift of God is eternal life in Christ Jesus our Lord." Romans 6:23

Furthermore, we cherish that gift in perfect harmony with all believers in the presence of our testator, Jesus Christ, who is very much alive! Peter testified about the blessed hope we have for our future when he declared:

"Blessed be the God and Father of our Lord Jesus Christ, who according to His abundant mercy has begotten us again to a living hope through the resurrection of Jesus Christ from the dead, to an inheritance incorruptible and undefiled and that does not fade away, reserved in heaven for you." 1 Peter 1:3-4

Let us walk in this hope. It is not just something that pertains to the future. Instead it is personal, living, active and part of us. This guarantee and hope keep us rejoicing even if we need to go through various trials. This testing of our faith produces life to all of us who patiently wait, with patient discipline for God's revelation of Jesus Christ.

MAY 25

STAND FAST IN LIBERTY!

In America today, we pause and remember with much reverence and grateful hearts the ultimate sacrifice that many have paid in securing our liberties against tyrants, rogue regimes, and ideologies that threatened our nation's freedom. Still others' sacrifices are also great, who bear in their bodies and emotions the scares of these wars. There are many families that carry a great price in losing their loved ones or in receiving them back broken, bruised and battered. As a nation it is fitting that we honor and reflect on this *Memorial Day* in a most serious manner.

One of the greatest ways we can show honor is to fight ourselves to preserve the liberties that we all have enjoyed as a nation and stand fast to not allow these liberties to erode. As Christians, we, too, must be concerned, to be ready to put our lives on the line in this same way. The apostle Paul wrote:

"Stand fast therefore in the liberty by which Christ has made us free, and do not be entangled again with a yoke of bondage." Galatians 5:2

You see, our own heritage is also linked with the ultimate sacrifice of a hero - Jesus Christ. He paid the ultimate sacrifice to enable all of us to receive the forgiveness of our sins and the promise of eternal life.

Jesus said, "If you abide in My word, you are My disciples indeed. And you shall know the truth, and the truth shall make you free." John 8:31-32

It is when we align ourselves with His truth that we work to preserve true liberty. We must be concerned that what others have fought to preserve our nation from outside forces has not succumbed to destruction from interior forces. May we ponder the days we are in and humbly ask God to heal us as a nation. It's not what is out there that will destroy us, but what resides within us.

May 26

An Alternative Story - The Kingdom of God

The kingdom of God is found anywhere God has operative dominion. Although the "*earth is the Lord's, and everything in it, the world, and all who live in it*" (Psalm 24:1), the kingdom of God is present in those places, spiritual or material, where God is honored as sovereign and His values are operative.

The kingdom of God has a King, and His name is Jesus. So preaching the message of the Kingdom, among other things, demands that we tell people through our words and communicate with our actions Who this King is and what He values. We tell an alternative story of what life should be, can be, and one day will be.

If the Kingdom of God is a place where God's perfect will is operative, any place where sorrow, weeping, infant mortality, hunger, premature death, or other signs of original sin's effects on the world is an affront to that Kingdom. This helps us understand why the miracles of Jesus were so significant to people.

Through His miracles, Jesus gave us a picture of what the kingdom of God is and will be like. Later, when Jesus sent His disciples out to minister, they preached the message of the coming Kingdom and did the very same things that Jesus had done to show the people in living color what the Kingdom of God looked like.

Our Father, our prayer is joined with Your will, let "Thy kingdom come on earth as it is in heaven." May we tell and show others the alternative story of what life should be, can be, and one day will be.

MAY 27

WHY DON'T WE PREACH THE KINGDOM?

I have been pondering the past few days what it will take for the church to really make a difference in our city. I don't know if anyone even gives this much thought anymore. We seem to be so fixed on our own worlds that we don't value the reality of what the Kingdom of God is like, nor do we hunger to see this kingdom come into being.

The kingdom of God is a place where worldly values are turned upside down and things are not as we expect them to be. One of the clearest places to catch a glimpse of these unexpected values is in the Sermon on the Mount (Matthew 5-7; Luke 6:17-49). Since He is King of the Kingdom, we will assume that whatever Jesus values is a Kingdom value and whatever Jesus taught is Kingdom teaching.

Look briefly at a few examples:

- Children are valued and held in high esteem (Matthew 18:1-4; Mark 10:14).
- The poor are blessed and given a place of honor (Luke 6:20).
- Servanthood is valued over power (Matthew 20:20-28).
- We love our enemies, do good to those who hate us, bless those who curse us, and pray for those who mistreat us (Luke 6:27-28).

These values, and more like them, are a sample of what is most attractive when people live together the way God intended them to live. Even those who do not know Christ know that the kingdom is a better story than the one they have.

May we live out what we have professed to believe and make His story, His kingdom, compelling for all in our community.

MAY 28

UNITY OF PURPOSE

Today I will be meeting for the fourth time with some pastors from the south coast. We have been meeting, seeking what preferable future we dream of for our community and endeavoring to see just what we might be able to do together to see progress and change.

Uniting around purpose means that the church in the city shares a common function. That common purpose is given to us by Jesus in His prayer in John 17:20-23:

"My prayer is not for them alone. I pray also for those who will believe in me through their message, that all of them may be one, Father, just as You are in Me and I in You. May they also be in us so that the world may believe that You have sent Me. I have given them the glory that You gave Me, so that they may be one as We are one: I in them and You in Me. May they be brought to complete unity to let the world know that You sent Me and have loved them even as You loved Me."

Upon first glance, it seems as though the purpose of this prayer is greater unity, but a closer look reveals that Jesus actually mentions two results that grow out of unity. The first is that our unity would communicate to the world that God sent Jesus. Second is that it would communicate to the world that God loves the world just as much as He loves Jesus. The end of our unity is not simply good relationships between fellow Christians. Instead it is the proclamation and demonstration of the Gospel to the world.

It is through verbal proclamation that people discover that Jesus was sent by God. Along with that, however, we see that it is through demonstration that people experience the truth that God loves them as much as He loves His own Son. Most people have never experienced the love of God in a tangible way.

This is the responsibility and privilege of the church, and all of us as God's people, to bring heaven a bit closer to the people in our world through defining acts of love and service. May we grow around this purpose.

MAY 29

THE WHOLE CHURCH BRINGING THE WHOLE GOSPEL TO THE WHOLE CITY!

Of course, some might take this title and substitute "city" for "world", which is the larger vision. Yet, it is a formidable task to reach our cities, and in doing so, we have such diverse nationalities that we are, in effect, reaching beyond the cities to the world also. But just what does it mean the "whole church"?

To speak of the whole church is a shorthand way of speaking about the unity of the church in a given city. The church is really only one church in a city made up of different congregations that meet at various locations and times. When Paul wrote his letters to Christians in a city, he wrote them to the church of the city - for example, "the church of God in Corinth" (1 Cor. 1:2), "the church of the Thessalonians" (1 Thess 1:1). Though there were likely multiple house churches and various groups of believers meeting at different times and locations in these cities, every city has a church.

This is a helpful concept to consider, not just as we think about the power of unity, but also as we look at how spiritual gifts are distributed within the church. Have you ever considered that while all the necessary gifts for ministry and maturity are contained within the church, they may not all reside in a particular congregation? If this is true, we really do need to work with other congregations if we want to accomplish the work that God has given His church to do in a city.

Just imagine what we could accomplish with greater unity. I believe that the transformation of our cities will occur when the church in the city is intent on becoming exactly what God wants it to be - a visible, united presence that seeks the city's good. Maybe we should each consider how we can be a part of creating greater unity, and boycott disunity.

What action could you take that will help to build in this direction?

MAY 30

HOLD FAST...

In Paul's last letter, a letter written to his beloved son in the faith, Timothy, he commits many final reminders and exhortations. One of these exhortations is to "*hold fast the pattern of sound words which you have heard from me, in faith and love which are in Christ Jesus. That good thing which was committed to you, keep by the Holy Spirit who dwells in us*" (2 Timothy 1:13-14).

These "sound words" were the deposit of faith, including the first principles of the faith that Paul wanted Timothy to keep, guard, and also pass on to those other faithful men who would continue to teach others (see 2 Tim. 2:2).

It is so important that we return to holding fast to sound words in our generation. We are to be equipped for the work of ministry, for the edifying of the body of Christ, growing toward maturity. We should no longer be tossed to and fro by every wind of doctrine (see Ephesians 4:12-14).

There is a pattern of sound words that we can apply our lives to. Through this foundation we can be secure in facing any difficulties that might confront us and also be able to discern directionally where the Holy Spirit would guide us to go.

God's Word is a lamp unto our feet and a light unto our path. It is His Spirit that illuminates His word to bring understanding in our lives. May we hold fast to the pattern of sound words committed to us, and live our lives accordingly, applying these principles to our individual, family, church, and work spheres.

MAY 31

YOU MUST ENDURE HARDSHIP...

If this was a title of a book, I don't think many of us would be drawn to pick it up. However, it is part of the instruction that Paul is leaving Timothy and any other leaders who will follow him. He had already instructed him to be strong in the grace that is in Christ Jesus. He used the imagery of a soldier (endure hardship), an athlete (run to win, but follow the rules), and a hard-working farmer (first to partake of the crops), to give Timothy, and us, a measure of what it takes to be bearers of the Gospel.

Paul reminds Timothy of the example that he set in speaking forth the Gospel:

"Suffering trouble as an evil doer, even to the point of chains; but the word of God is not chained." 2 Timothy 2:9

Now as a result of this Paul continues his exhortation:

"Therefore I endure all things for the sake of the elect, that they also may obtain the salvation which is in Christ Jesus with eternal glory." 2 Timothy 2:10

This is his motivation - that the elect of God hear the Word of God preached, and through this hearing, obtain salvation found in Jesus Christ.

This, too, must be our motivation. For whatever degree of hardness, we encounter, it is nothing compared to the knowledge and reality that others are receiving salvation through the Gospel preached and exemplified.

JUNE 1

DOING SOMETHING...

What a different message we would convey to the world if the church showed the world an alternative story of truly transformed lives, infused with kingdom values lived out through missional actions.

It's important to understand that serving others changes and transforms the very people who are doing the serving. Even though we can learn from preaching and good Bible study, we don't grow past certain points without serving others. Although we are saved by grace through faith and not by our own works (Eph. 2:8-9), we are saved so that we are free to do the good works that God has prepared in advance for us to do (Eph. 2:10).

"For by grace you have been saved through faith, and that not of yourselves; it is the gift of God, not of works, lest anyone should boast. For we are His workmanship, created in Christ Jesus for good works, which God prepared beforehand that we should walk in them." Ephesians 2:8-10

In fact, every helpful resource that God has given us point to the same goal of actually having us participate and doing something:

- Leaders to prepare us (Eph. 4:11-12)
- God's Word to equip us (2 Tim. 3:16-17)
- The body of Christ to encourage us (Heb. 10:24-25)
- Spiritual gifts to empower us (1 Peter 4:10)

The something we are to do is the something that God has already planned for us to do. Knowing what to do is discerned as we begin on the road that He has fashioned for us.

What is that something you are being called to do? Follow Jesus by listening, responding, meeting the needs that you already see and the things that touch your heart. Let the Lord continue to direct your steps. It is a day-by-day choice of following Him. Doing so will glorify the Lord.

PROCESS OF COMMUNITY TRANSFORMATION - PART 1

If God is going to use the church to bring transformation to our communities, then it is the church itself that needs to be transformed. A great picture of transformation can be seen in Isaiah 61:1-6.

"The Spirit of the Lord God is upon Me, because the Lord has anointed Me to preach good tidings to the poor; He has sent Me to heal the brokenhearted, to, to proclaim liberty to the captives, and the opening of the prison to those who are bound; to proclaim the acceptable year of the Lord, and the day of vengeance of our God; to comfort all who mourn, to console those who mourn in Zion, to give them beauty for ashes, the oil of joy for mourning, the garment of praise for the spirit of heaviness; that they may be called trees of righteousness, the planting of the Lord, that He may be glorified. And they shall rebuild the old ruins, they shall raise up the former desolations, and they shall repair the ruined cities, the desolations of many generations. Strangers shall stand and feed your flocks, and the sons of the foreigner shall be your plowmen and feed your flocks, and the sons of the foreigner shall be your plowmen and your vinedressers. But you shall be named the priests of the Lord, they shall call you the servants of our God. You shall eat the riches of the Gentiles, and in their glory you shall boast." Isaiah 61:1-6

Transformation begins with one person who is yielded to the Spirit of God. "*The Spirit of the Sovereign Lord is on me to preach good news to the poor*" (v. 1). The empowering presence of God's Spirit is where all transformation begins.

In many ways, Isaiah himself serves as a great example of this. We read in Isaiah 6:8 that when the Lord was looking for a willing, available person, Isaiah responded, "*Here am I. Send me*!" The critical mass to transform a community begins with just one person who is yielded to the Spirit of God.

Might you be that one?

JUNE 3

PROCLAIMING AND DEMONSTRATING THE GOSPEL (TRANSFORMATION PART 2)

This is how transformation comes. As you read Isaiah 61 verses 1-3, you see Isaiah describe how his message will come - through both a verbal message and a lifestyle of love and compassion. Look at the words Isaiah uses:

"The Spirit of the Lord God is upon Me, because the Lord has anointed Me to preach good tidings to the poor; He has sent Me to heal the brokenhearted, to, to proclaim liberty to the captives, and the opening of the prison to those who are bound; to proclaim the acceptable year of the Lord, and the day of vengeance of our God; to comfort all who mourn, to console those who mourn in Zion, to give them beauty for ashes, the oil of joy for mourning, the garment of praise for the spirit of heaviness; that they may be called trees of righteousness, the planting of the Lord, that He may be glorified." Isaiah 61:1-3

He is "proclaiming" a message, while at the same time he is "binding up the broken-hearted," "releasing from darkness ... the prisoners," "comforting all who mourn," and "providing for those who grieve." Transformation is the result of both compassionate deeds and passionate proclamation of the Gospel.

We need both of these (compassionate deeds and passionate proclamation of the Gospel) and must be careful that we do not avoid neglecting either one. The works verify the words, and the words clarify the deeds.

For us, the question must center on just what we are proclaiming? Is it the gospel? Then, what actions are we doing? Are they filled with compassion and service? One without the other will lead us to an extreme. Taken together we have the proper balance.

Jesus proclaimed and demonstrated what Isaiah had prophesied so many years earlier. The way of transformation is the same today. May we be instruments of transformations as we proclaim His Word and do His work.

JUNE 4

A WONDERFUL EXCHANGE

We have been looking at the idea of transformation. The last two days I have posted two different aspects of transformation. Today, we add a third. Transformation begins as people are transformed. A wonderful exchange occurs when people yield their lives to Jesus Christ.

Again, looking at Isaiah 61 we see this great exchange in verse 3. Those being transformed receive "*a crown of beauty instead of ashes, the oil of gladness instead of mourning . . . A garment of praise instead of a spirit of despair.*" Isn't that an incredible exchange?

But wait, there is even more. "*The [the formerly despairing, ash-covered mourners] will be called oaks of righteousness, a planting of the Lord for the display of His splendor.*" The small acorns grow into large oak trees. The children grow up and become strong leaders.

When people are genuinely transformed by the power of God, it is the splendor of God that is displayed to the world, and God's splendor is best seen in changed lives. The most basic reason why the "restorers" are effective is that they lead people to Jesus Christ - the source of salvation and the power of self-transformation. Restorers emphasize a transformation of the heart and a renewal of the mind. The spiritual growth they encourage is directed and spiritual. It is centered on Jesus and the Bible.

Without transformation in our lives, we lack what is necessary to be the restorers of our communities. But if we exchange our lives for His, we will display His splendor and be active participants as change agents in our own culture. With Him we can do mighty things.

Lord, I desire to be changed to become a change-agent. Renew my mind as you transform my heart. Help me spread the hope that comes from knowing You. Amen.

JUNE 5

REBUILDERS

I have been commenting the past few days on steps to transformation for us as individuals and also for our communities. Another way we could look at it is the process of community transformation. The key scriptures have been coming from Isaiah 61:1-6. Today, let us look at verse 4:

"They [the oaks of righteousness] will rebuild the ancient ruins and restore the places long devastated; they will renew the ruined cities that have been devastated for generations."

What we have in principle is that transformed people want to transform their communities. When people are transformed by God's Spirit, many are compelled to act in response. Many challenge the status quo. Though things may have been destroyed for generations, they rebuild, restore, and renew.

This is what we are called to do. To be rebuilders of our culture, we cannot rebuild by simply offering criticism. We cannot tell everyone what we do not like about our house or community to gets things changed. We must do something new to replace what we see as wrong. We build by presenting a new compelling narrative of what an alternative lifestyle and allegiance is like, one that glorifies God and serves our neighbors in love.

What do you envision? Begin to work toward that end. Allow the transformation principles of God's way and Word to direct all you undertake. There is a correct foundation to build on. If we do so, what is built will stand the test of time.

"For no other foundation can anyone lay than that which is laid, which is Jesus Christ. Now if anyone builds on this foundation with gold, silver, precious stones, wood, hay, straw, each one's work will become clear; for the Day will declare it, because it will be reveal by fire; and the fire will test each one's work, of what sort it is." 1 Corinthians 3:11-13

JUNE 6

TRANSFORMATION INVITES OTHERS TO THE WORK

We have been examining Isaiah 61:1-6 as it relates to God's idea of transformation in our communities. We see something interesting in verse 5 about how others join us in the work of transformation. "*Aliens will shepherd your flocks; foreigners will work your fields and vineyards*." The question we must answer is who are these aliens and foreigners?

One of the best tests of the sustainability of your work in transforming your community is whether it can be transferred to others, whether others can join you and continue the work that was started. People who once we're strangers to you, now come and work the same field, even taking over to produce in that field. They become the community builders, taking over and continuing the work that you began.

Someone defined success as succession. It is the continuing of the building where a foundation has been laid, but more work needs to be done. When we see ourselves as the servants to our communities, we begin the task of building greater community. There are many people who care and want to see change; they just need some means of empowerment and direction to see it come to pass. May we be bridge builders who empower others as we demonstrate kingdom building values and service.

Perhaps we need to look around us and begin to identify those whom God is calling to join with us in the work. All of us can help train a new generation of Kingdom builders. If success is succession, what is our succession plan? Look around – there are people all around us that need mentoring. May we invite them to work with us as transformers.

JUNE 7

MINISTERS OF GOD'S GRACE

For the past several days we have been looking at Isaiah 61:1-6 and considering what it has to say about our roles in our present day as change-agents and transformers of our own communities. In verse 6, we can sum up the idea that transformation is recognized by how the city identifies your role:

"And you shall be called priests of the Lord, you will be named ministers of our God." Isaiah 61:6

In this generation, the most important ministerial titles will not be those conferred by a seminary or ordination board, such as Reverend or Doctor, they will come from those in the community. In other words, what is the community saying about you? Do they call you by some title or do they recognize you for the work and way in which you work within the community? What began with a single, visionary individual in our scriptural reading (see Isaiah 61:1-6), had now culminated in a transformed community.

The highest compliment a city transformer can receive is to be known as a priest or a minister of God's grace to the community. Notice the position is not one of status but one of service. Notice also the description of service is one of grace. Here is how leaven is added to the mix. Here is how a real difference is being made.

Lord, as we consider our call to be transformers, may we also do what we have been called to do with grace and service. As we seek the welfare of our communities, may we do so for the benefit of the community in integrity, demonstrating care. May the work of renewal in our lives bring about recognition of Your sovereignty and glory through our service so those we seek to reach may rejoice under Your care. Amen.

JUNE 8

MOVING FROM CHURCH TO KINGDOM

Jesus promised to build His church (Matthew 16:18). But the church is different than the kingdom. The church is called to help build the kingdom, the embodiment of what life looks like when people are living under the reign of God. We are called to go out into the world, serving as witnesses (in practice also) to the King and kingdom.

God has placed within every human being a desire for a certain story line: the kingdom story. Isn't the story line - the narrative of the Gospel - a call to adventure, to give ourselves away to a noble and worthy cause - to follow Jesus in His redemptive and transformational work?

For many, though, we may want to keep what we have received and make our faith private and personal rather than public and transformational. We refuse to return to those in need and bless them with what we have been given.

That's the real adventure of faith. Have we co-opted God's story by making faith in Christ the end of the journey rather than the beginning of an adventure? In doing so, have we reduced the Gospel to simply a way of escaping danger, rather than embracing the compelling call to follow Christ into our broken world - a call to adventure? Are our churches growing but our communities getting worse? Perhaps we need to reevaluate our kingdom calling: proclaiming the Gospel as a call to adventure rather than simply an escape from danger.

Proclaiming the Gospel of the Kingdom of God invites others to join in an ever-advancing army of God. Settling for salvation for self-preservation turns our world on self and hinders the further advancement of our witness.

May we accept our responsibility and step forward accepting our yoke from Jesus and sharing in His adventurous journey.

JUNE 9

LEARNING TO MAINTAIN GOOD WORKS AND MEETING URGENT NEEDS

As I was reading Paul's final instructions to Titus as he was closing out his letter, he is again repositioning his men in various places for the apostolic work for which they are called. Let me just key in on a couple of verses:

"Send Zenas the lawyer and Apollos on their journey with haste, that they may lack nothing. And let our people also learn to maintain good works, to meet urgent needs, that they may not be unfruitful." Titus 3:13-14

While the brethren were to meet needs and maintain good works in their localities, they were also expected to have a view of the greater field and kingdom. In other words, they would need to have a vision for the apostolic work of the church. Sometimes the work was planned in advanced and other times it was necessary to send team members urgently to meet certain areas of need.

The important thing is that, as God's people, we have a heart to participate in the unfolding apostolic work of the kingdom. Some of that work is right before us in our own cities. But at the same time we are working at various levels in other communities and countries of the world. What must be evident in our own lives is that we are willing and able to meet urgent needs, while at the same time maintaining good works in our everyday lives. It does require planning and positioning ourselves to be able to be such a blessing.

The choices we make in our own lifestyle can either help us or hinder us in such a work. However, if we cultivate a heart for the kingdom and learn to maintain good works and meet urgent needs, Paul describes this as fruitfulness. May we be fruitful in our participation in the unfolding work of the gospel and the building of the kingdom.

JUNE 10

PRAY WITHOUT CEASING

Last night I had one of those interrupted nights. Slept well for a few hours and then up every hour from then on. What I was able to do was intercede for those the Lord put on my heart. I so want to see the manifestation of the Lord working in people's lives; to see His presence embodied filling others with joy, peace and assurance. I long to see a greater demonstration of His healing power for His body; that those who are called would understand the greatness of his power that is at work in all who believe.

Paul wrote to the Thessalonians:

"Rejoice always, pray without ceasing, in everything give thanks for this is the will of God in Christ Jesus for you." 2 Thessalonians 5:16-18

Knowing that the Lord is leading us, we can rejoice in every circumstance. Even when things do not go as planned, we can trust that the Lord will allow us to grow from that experience, to use that time for something for which we might not have planned, even touch the heart of people that might otherwise not have been in our minds or encountered on our path. In everything, we can pray to the Lord for direction, strength, even deliverance. He is ever with us, so we can thank Him for His sovereignty in our lives.

Today, I have a full schedule. There those things that I have planned, but I am sure that the Lord has His own plan. At noon I will be giving my testimony at a Full Gospel Businessman's luncheon. I would appreciate your prayers that the Lord would be glorified and His presence experienced by all who attend. I will also continue to pray for you. May God's healing be experienced in your life, and may His empowering presence fill you completely today and every day. May you be most blessed.

JUNE 11

I APPEAL TO YOU...

This morning I was touched by the greeting that Paul sent to Philemon. Actually, while the letter is addressed to him, it was also addressed to a family and a church in his house (see Philemon vs. 1-2). There are beautiful words of thanksgiving in regards to the love, faith and demonstration exhibited by Philemon that Paul addresses. Now to get to the subject for which Paul has written; as an intercessor, Paul seeks to foster reconciliation between Philemon and a runaway slave, now a Christian, Onesimus.

What stands out in this letter is the position that this apostle takes. While he had authority because of his position, he appealed to his brother in the faith rather than commanding him. Look at what Paul wrote:

"Therefore, though I might be very bold in Christ to command you what is fitting, yet for love's sake I rather appeal to you - being such a one as Paul, the aged, and now also a prisoner of Jesus Christ - I appeal to you for my son Onesimus, whom I have begotten while in my chains, who once was unprofitable to you, but now is profitable to you and me..." Philemon 8-11

Instead of Paul using his authority as an Apostle of the Lord to command, he chooses to come alongside his brother to appeal to his good sense. What can we learn from this model? Too many people use their position to strong arm others into doing what they want, instead of using their influence (which must be earned) and appealing for the change that is necessary.

When you or I appeal to others to do what is right, we leave the responsibility to do what is right to the other person who must decide to make the right choice. If they were forced to make that change, even when they were unwilling, we didn't help to have them change their hearts, only their actions.

Might we be people with enough influence and character that others would change based on our appeal, rather than force of position.

June 12

Receive Him As You Would Me...

As Paul is beginning to close out his letter to Philemon, he continues to intercede for his new brother in the Lord, Onesimus. He has appealed to Philemon to receive Onesimus back, not only as a slave being returned to his master, but as a brother in Christ. He uses words reminiscent of Jesus' own words. Like Jesus, Paul is appealing that Philemon forgive whatever offense he might have against Onesimus, even willing to charge to his own account any cost or loss that Philemon might have incurred. Paul wrote:

"If you count me as a partner, receive him as you would me. But if he has wronged you or owes anything, put that on my account." Philemon 17-18

We should note a couple of things: first, Paul is willing to absorb the cost of any past wrongdoing. Here, he demonstrates the love of Jesus who bore in His own body the payment for our sins. All forgiveness has a cost to be paid. The one forgiving absorbs the cost of the offense, unless someone else has already paid for that offense to be settled. Second, Paul reminds Philemon of the debt that he owes for his own salvation. Again, we see that because we have been forgiven much, we, too, must be willing to forgive.

Paul's expectation is that Philemon will not just obey, but abound in forgiveness, even going to great care to extend mercy and build a bridge of reconciliation with Onesimus.

How about in our lives? Do we understand and appreciate the great debt that Jesus paid for us? While we have received His great mercy, do we extend that same measure of mercy to those who have offended us? Paul's expectation was that this should be so. Jesus' expectation is the same.

May we receive forgiveness from the Lord and be just as quick to merit it out to others who wrong us also. To whom much has been forgiven, much is also required. May we be conduits of God's grace and forgiveness to those we encounter.

JUNE 13

A LATE DAY'S REFLECTION

Today had been an active day, setting up and hosting a birthday party for our oldest granddaughter. Her birthday is actually early next month, but since they will be getting ready to travel, and clear out their house, we did this a bit early. Things are a bit quieter right now. Two of the children are asleep. The youngest is out on a date with her mom and dad.

Life is precious and the simpler things of life the best. Love of God, family, friends, and walking in His purpose is exciting and fulfilling. Hope your day was blessed also.

JUNE 14

TWO IDEAS FROM PROVERBS

The writer of Proverbs shares many ideas that lead to wisdom. In chapter 11 he gives us two different verses that speak to different aspects of a similar issue:

"There is one who scatters, yet increases more; and there is one who withholds more than is right, but it leads to poverty. The generous soul will be made rich, and he who waters will also be watered himself." Proverbs 11:24-25

In the law of sowing and reaping, it is necessary that seed be sown in order for a crop to grow. One who withholds the seed will never be able to reap in a harvest. This is both in a very practical, natural circumstance (which includes hard work and providing for your family) and in spiritual circumstances (where the sowing of the Word of God, discipleship and meeting the needs of others) is considered. The first enables one to provide and have resources to share with others. The second lifts our eyes to a greater field that needs to be sown.

While we have a provision promised in the first because of diligence, we are also promised emotional and spiritual uplifting when we do the second. Whatever we do, and with what spirit we do the sowing, the reality is that God will cause others to respond to us in like manner. Not necessarily that we will reap a material benefit, but surely we will have a satisfaction of the soul.

Perhaps you might consider just what kind of seed you are sowing today. Be ready to give out of the resources you have. Also, allow God to enable you to grow in diligence, not just to build yourself a retirement home, but resource God's kingdom. All of us have something to give. It could be a simple smile, hug, a listening ear, a friendly visit, a special note of encouragement, etc.; it could also be material resources that can be used to build God's kingdom. As you consider these ideas, let the Lord lead you. You will be enriched.

JUNE 15

CAN'T MAKE PROGRESS WITHOUT SOME MESS

As I write, there are visible reminders that I can see that testify that we have hosted our family this weekend. In fact, we still have one grandchild with us who is still sleeping. As I read Proverbs one scripture caught my attention this morning:

"Where no oxen are, the trough (manger) is clean; but much increase comes by the strength of an ox." Proverbs 14:4

This scripture sheds light in so many ways. As a contractor, I understand that you can't enjoy a renovated home without going through the process in taking something apart, dealing with the temporary mess to come to a greater and more enjoyable product. The same can apply to community work, raising children, building churches and even the transformation of our lives.

While the writer of Proverbs is saying how productive an ox can be, the one who possesses the ox will have to tend to that ox. If all we want is a clean barn, we can have no productive animal. We should understand that in order to make progress, we must encounter some temporary discomfort. But only those of us willing to go through the process can gain the benefits.

You and I are called to be the rebuilders and transformers of our communities. Let us not be afraid of the mess we might need to encounter to get to accomplish all the Lord's desires for our communities. After all, what He begins, He also finishes. So must we.

JUNE 16

THANKFUL FOR GOD'S GREAT FAITHFULNESS

This morning (June 16, 2015), we will be completing 20 years of instruction as a school. EGCA was founded in 1995. That first year we had 11 full time students, 2 home school children, 2 teachers who joined along with Bernice and I to begin with very small beginnings and humble hearts what the Lord had called us to. We had years of great growth and years of financial challenges, but through it all, we have kept our faith in an awesome God who is forever faithful. We have also kept our eyes on His vision for our community and worked to be faithful to all whom He has entrusted to us.

Through these years we have been joined by so many wonderful teacher servants, who have been an extended family to us. I can't tell you just how much they have sacrificed to see these young people taught properly and given the very best we could give. I am humbled by their level of generosity and diligence in which they have executed their positions as mentors of so many.

We are proud of the graduates throughout the years who are faithfully serving their own families, communities, employers, and churches. You are all making such a difference in this world. Keep your eyes on the Lord, He will continue to be your strength and joy.

For this year's graduates, may the Lord continue His good work in you. You have demonstrated great gifting and service. As you continue to allow yourself to be mentored, may your gifts flourish as you take positions of responsibility in your calling.

As we reflect on this year and begin planning for the next, may the Lord strengthen us to continue to persevere and trust Him for even greater things. Our God is an awesome God, and nothing is impossible with Him.

"And God is able to make all grace abound toward you, that you, always having all sufficiency in all things, may have an abundance for every good work." 2 Corinthians 9:8

JUNE 17

MY BELOVED SON

It is so important that we understand who we are in the Lord. When Jesus was baptized by John the Baptist, the heavens opened and the voice of God was heard saying to Jesus:

"You are My beloved Son; in You I am well pleased." Luke 3:22

It is important to note that up to this point, Jesus had accomplished no great miracles or feats. He had simply lived in subjection to His parents, where He "*increased in wisdom and stature, and in favor with God and man*" (Luke 2:52).

But as He was beginning His public ministry, His Father assured Him of just who He was and how much He was loved. Immediately, after this time, Jesus was led by the Spirit into the wilderness where He encountered temptation from the devil. The point of attack centered on Jesus' identity:

"If you are the Son of God ..."

This is where you and I also are confronted in our own walks. When things are not as we think they should be, the devil comes and poses this question, "*If you are a son of God...*" It is in knowing and settling this issue in our own mind and spirit that we are equipped to ward of any temptation of the enemy.

You and I may not have all the answers for the difficulties that we might need to face, but we can have a great assurance if we have given our lives to Christ:

You and I are the beloved of God and He is well pleased in us. Not because of anything we have done, but for whom He has declared us to be. Nothing else in life compares to knowing this. You and I have victory, because He is, and we are His beloved.

June 18

WHY THE COMPETITION AND INSECURITY?

John the Baptist has something interesting to say. It is said in response to those who had come to him because Jesus and His disciples had come into his area of ministry, and people were joining Jesus and being baptized.

Obviously for John's disciples, this was a bit disconcerting. Perhaps they thought they would be losing their influence, and it began to produce fear in their hearts. The religious leaders who had been disputing with John's disciples were also quick to point out this aspect. People can often do the devil's work through how they edge us on and often do not speak the things that give proper perspective nor peace.

John responded to all of this by saying:

"A man can receive nothing unless it has been given to him from heaven." John 3:27

Think about what he is saying. What you have is because God has given it to you. That means no one can take that from you. Your gifts and calling are from above. In the same way, what has been given to another is his or hers, and no one should try to take what belongs to them. In fact, no one can.

If we can understand this, we can walk much more securely in our own lives and ministries. It is the Lord who gives, and it is the Lord who takes away. Blessed be the name of the Lord.

May we not be so concerned with what another of the Lord's disciples is doing, and simply do what we have been called to do. Only in doing this can we find great joy and peace in our own measure of responsibility. Only then can we truly begin working with others to accomplish greater united efforts for kingdom purposes.

Lord, help us be secure in Your call. May we be faithful to what we have received from You. Amen.

JUNE 19

CASTERS AND MENDERS

Reading the fourth chapter of Matthew's Gospel this morning, Jesus calls forth four men to follow Him. These are from two pairs. The first pair consists of two brothers Simon called Peter, and Andrew. They were casting a net into the sea. The second pair also consists of brothers, James and John, sons of Zebedee. They are mending their nets. Both pairs of brothers were called to follow Jesus, who said to them:

"Follow Me, and I will make you fishers of men." Matthew 4:19

What catches my attention this morning is the diversity of activity in which the fishermen were involved. Both were important to their success of the enterprise. Unless one casts the net, there can be no catch. But if one does cast the net, and it is not in good working order and strong, then even if there is a catch, one will not be able to bring the catch of fish into the boat.

How does this apply to our work in the Lord? We need to be concerned with both:

- Evangelism and discipleship
- Outreach and administration
- Nations and networks

If we are to be successful in building the kingdom, we must recognize the diversity of gifts necessary to release power and also sustain perseverance. In the body of Christ we need both casters and menders. It is not one or the other, but both.

Jesus recruited a diversity of leaders to accomplish His purpose. May God give us wisdom to do the same.

JUNE 20

QUICK THOUGHT ON GOOD SAMARITAN

You are probably familiar with the story of a man who is left beaten by robbers while traveling from Jerusalem to Jericho (see Luke 10:25-37). As he lies there beaten, naked, and half-dead, we see that God gives the first opportunity to respond with compassion and mercy to the people of faith, a Priest and a Levite.

But when they choose to go their own way and not engage with the need that lies in front of them (probably for very spiritual reasons, at least they think), Jesus discloses that it is the Samaritan - the person despised by the religious people of that day - who becomes the hero of the story.

"But a certain Samaritan, as he journeyed, came where he was. And when he saw him, he had compassion. So he went to him and bandaged his wounds, pouring oil and wine; and he set him on his own animal, brought him to an inn, and took care of him. On the next day, when he departed, he took out two denarii, gave them to the innkeeper, and said to him, 'Take care of him; and whatever more you spend, when I come again, I will repay you.'" Luke 10:33-35

In the same way as this Samaritan, God would love to use the church today to heal the hurts of the bruised and battered world, but when the church fails to respond or is more predisposed to counting nickels and noses, God will raise up just about anyone to carry out what He wants done - that's how much He cares for our broken world. When I say the church, I am not just talking about the institution of the church; I am talking about all of us who make up the church. It is our individual responsibility as well as our collective responsibility.

I am thankful for the many who have been telling me lately of the great opportunities they are experiencing in witnessing to those in their individual spheres of influence. Keep it up - the fields are white for the harvest – you and I are part of the answer to minister to those that are broken all around us and help them heal.

JUNE 21

KEEPING IT SHORT

Today, I just want to make a short but meaningful declaration; one we can all share if we are people of faith. It can be a declaration, or the beginning of our prayer. Jesus, in fact, modeled it for us. Here it is:

"Our Father in heaven..."

Let it sink in. Let it give you illumination. May it be your comfort, praise and thanksgiving.

You are loved, accepted and your Heavenly Father is proud of you. You are His beloved. It doesn't get any better than that.

Happy Father's Day my most Heavenly Father! You are my daddy. I am most blessed.

JUNE 22

THE KING AND HIS KINGDOM

The Church is different than the Kingdom. Jesus builds His Church (Matthew 16:18), and the Church helps to build the Kingdom, the embodiment of what life looks like when people are living under the reign of God.

To be Kingdom Christians, we must be committed to helping build the Kingdom as well as introducing people to the King. God calls us to be the Church and to live out the Kingdom - whether it builds our individual church or not. It's about God, not about us. It's about the welfare of the city, not about the well- being of our church.

As the Church, we serve to be a living proof of the Kingdom, a community where the world can see what marriage, family life, business practices, work habits, generosity, mercy, race relations - all of life - look like when lived under the rule and authority of Jesus Christ.

Faith in Christ is not the end-all of our journey. It is the beginning of real adventure. Let's not reduce our declaration of the Gospel to just escaping danger. Let's offer the compelling story of redemption and attraction of what living under the reign of the King of glory is all about. The King has a Kingdom, and we must value what He values.

JUNE 23

FINAL VICTORY

This past weekend two people I knew passed on to glory. The fragility of life is ever before us. Sometimes we expect someone's passing, and then for others it is sudden and unexpected. We never know what we might face from one day to the next. It is so important that we live our lives with expectation of the goodness of God and maintaining, to the degree possible, our esteem and honor for each other.

When the final curtain closes on someone's life it leaves those who remain at a loss for words and emptiness in our hearts. These emotions are rea, and we are justified to mourn for our loss. At the same time, for those of us who are Christians, we understand that death is not as final as some think it is. In fact, death is a transition like being born is. In being born one moves from a mother's womb to another environment where life is continued. In death, we also move from one state to another. This illustration can only serve to a point.

The apostle Paul says, "this corruption must put on incorruption, and this mortal must put on immorality. So when this corruption has put on incorruption, and this mortal has put on immortality, then shall be brought to pass the saying written: 'Death is swallowed up in victory.'" (1 Corinthians 15:53-54).

This is the hope we have when we trust in Jesus and His word. There is a transformation that awaits those who live by faith. While we don't see it with our physical eyes for those who proceed us, we can see through our eyes of faith. Therefore, in our pain and mourning we are comforted and given the oil of joy in exchange for the mourning and the garment of praise for the spirit of heaviness.

This is an exchange worth receiving. In the end we share in a great victory. May this hope fill us completely and comfort us in any loss we might experience in this life.

JUNE 24

CALM FROM THE STORM

Last night our communities were under a storm and tornado warning. At the same time I was meeting with three beautiful children of a man who we will be doing a funeral soon. We came together to discuss their wishes for the service. As we did we reminisced about their dad and their own individual stories connected to him. It was interesting the different individual perspectives that gave a fuller understanding of the man, made in the image of God, they called dad.

We laughed and cried together as our conversation was edifying and brought comfort and even healing. In the midst of the storm going on outside and the storm they had recently experienced, there grew a great calm. Peace is another way to describe it. Just like when the disciples were being tossed in the boat, Jesus "*rebuked the wind and the raging water. And they ceased, and there was a great calm*" (Luke 8:24).

Jesus promised us this kind of peace:

"Peace I leave with you, My peace I give you, not as the world gives do I give to you. Let not your hearts be troubled, neither let it be afraid" (John 14:27).

I am just so thankful that even in the midst of storms we can experience this great peace. It is a peace that surpasses understanding. It is reserved for those who trust in Jesus.

June 25

The Value of One

This morning I am praying for a funeral service that will be forth coming. While those attending need to experience comfort and some closure, I am also aware that as we go through these experiences, it reminds us of the shortness of our own lives and the decisions we have made and the ones we still will need to make. There will be some, maybe even just one, who need to turn from their own way and trust in the Lord for their life.

In looking at the three parables in Luke 15, what is so evident is the value of one; one lost sheep, one lost coin and even one lost son. While we might have our eyes on the multitudes, Jesus is telling us the importance of one. In fact, He said:

"There will be more joy in heaven over one sinner who repents than over ninety-nine just persons who need no repentance" (Luke 15:7).

Again He said:

"There is joy in the presence of the angels of God over one sinner who repents" (Luke 15:10).

That joy should not only be in heaven. The prodigal son's father told his eldest son:

"It is right that we should make merry and be glad, for your brother was dead and is alive again, and was lost and is found" (Luke 15:32).

If you can join me today, please pray for the one that the Lord needs to call to Himself. The one who is estranged from the family of God. The one that we can all rejoice with, who might be presently lost, but Jesus has found. One is valuable to the Lord. The one should also be valued by us.

JUNE 26

"I'M HAVING A BALL!"

This is what I heard out of someone that Bernice and I visited in the hospital yesterday. She is about to go into surgery this morning. If you know who I am talking about, please take a moment and say a prayer for a successful surgery and a recovery without pain. Why would she say that she was having a ball being in the hospital? You can't imagine the opportunities she was having in sharing the love of the Lord.

I teased her in a text that I sent to her that she was the hospital chaplain. But the reality is that in her room and on her floor, she is the light and love of God. There is not one person who entered her room who did not leave in a different frame of mind than when they came in. Some were coming into the room early before their shift, just to talk to her again. Another stopped in to request that she please pray for an emergency situation that was going on presently. With such joy and abandonment of her own present situation, this woman of God was looking out, giving, loving, encouraging, praying, and just being a light to those she encountered.

Jesus exhorted His disciples to be the light they were meant to be:

"You are the light of the world. A city that is set on a hill cannot be hidden. Nor do they light a lamp and put it under a basket, but on a lampstand, and it gives light to all who are in the house. Let your light so shine before men, that they may see your good works and glorify your Father in heaven" Matthew 5:14-16

Letting your light shine brings glory to the Father. This woman that I just wrote about is just one story from yesterday that I can share. There are many others. I am so proud to be a part of the lives of people who really understand mission. Our mission is all around us, wherever we are, whomever we meet. May we be a shining light to the nations, but let it begin in our homes, neighborhoods, extended families, workplaces and wherever we are sent. God only knows the difference we will be making in the lives of those we touch.

June 27

Would You Be My Father?

On Father's Day I preached a message that must have touched a particular chord in one person's heart. I was reflecting on the beginning of the Lord's Prayer "*Our Father in heaven.*" In so doing, I also said that all of us long to hear from our earthly father that we are loved, that he is proud of us, that we belong. Many who were in attendance that day, either had lost their earthly father or perhaps, for some, had never come to really know their father. However, we are still blessed because we have a Heavenly Father that does love us and care for us.

For one person, their prayer was "God I have known You as my Father since I am young. However, I have never known an earthly father. Is there someone that can be my earthly father that I can go to and be accepted into his family as his child. To receive counsel, one who will love me and say, 'I am proud of you.'" It was revealed to me that I was the one face whom God revealed in her prayer and yesterday I was approached, if I would accept her into my family as my daughter. What a touching moment of sincere request. I can tell you for sure that my family is expanding.

Paul wrote to the Corinthians:

"For though you might have ten thousand instructors in Christ, yet you do not have many fathers; for in Christ Jesus I have begotten you through the gospel. Therefore I urge you, imitate me" (1 Corinthians 4:15-16).

God promises to set the fatherless in families. We do not need to be orphaned, we can belong. That is what our Heavenly Father in heaven does in our midst. He is a Father to the fatherless. And He uses real people to walk with us, encouraging us along the way. I am thanking God for those who are natural sons and daughters, but also those whom He has joined with us our spiritual sons and daughters. They all make me proud.

June 28

IF ANYONE BUILDS ON THIS FOUNDATION...

Today our church is celebrating 20 years since it's founding. It may be a small time in comparison to the move of Christianity, but for those of us who have been together for these 20 years, we are rejoicing in the great faithfulness of our God. It is right that we give Him thanks.

When Paul was trying to give the Corinthian perspective on their calling and commission, he wrote:

"According to the grace of God given me, as a wise master builder I have laid a foundation, and another builds on it. But let each one take heed how he builds on it. For no other foundation can anyone lay than that which has been laid, which is Christ Jesus. Now if anyone builds on this foundation with gold, silver, precious stones, wood, hay, straw, each one's work will become clear; for the Day will declare it, because it will be revealed by fire; and fire will test each one's work, of what sort it is" (1 Corinthians 3:10-13).

In the shifting sands of our culture, may we be found faithful to continue to build on what we have started building: a church that is founded on Christ. Anything else will burn up and be judged. Only what is built in accordance with His purpose, plans and Person, will have any significance in the end.

If God has given us His grace to build a foundation, He will give us His grace to continue building His way for His glory. May we never veer off this course. In Christ we can do all things!

JUNE 29

IF YOU WANT TO WITHSTAND, YOU MUST STAND!

There is a reason that Paul tells the Ephesians to be strong in the Lord and the power of His might. Spiritual warfare is real, intense, and if one is not attentive, overpowering. But we can walk in victory. Paul tells the Ephesians:

"Put on the whole armor of God, that you may be able to stand against the wiles of the devil. For we do not wrestle against flesh and blood, but against principalities, against powers, against the rulers of the darkness of this age, against spiritual hosts of wickedness in the heavenly places. Therefore take up the whole armor of God, that you may be able to withstand in the evil day, and having done all, to stand" (Ephesians 6:11-13).

We have been given what we need to be victorious. Notice the exhortation on the importance of standing. Yes, we must have the proper equipment, but even if we do have the proper equipment, we need to appropriate it and it still requires us to stand. We must have a certain tenacity, perseverance, and persistence if we are to overcome the onslaughts that the enemy sends us.

Sometimes people tell me: "we do not know what else to do." Paul has an answer for us: "*having done all, to stand.*" Here is where trust in God comes in. If we trust Him we will stand. No matter what, stand. Pray standing! Fight standing! Declare the word of the Lord standing! Wield the sword of the Spirit standing! Stand! Stand! Stand!

That is the only way we can withstand is to stand. Get up! Stay Up! Take authority over the ground that you must possess! Know that the enemy must be put under your feet. Are you still sitting? Get on your feet and stand! Begin to give God praise for the victory.

JUNE 30

COME TO ME...

It seems that with continued governmental actions that move in a direction away from what we believe to be Biblical, we also must be careful in how we respond in our day. For our liberty, or what is intrinsically the worth of each individual, has never come from governmental action, but from God Himself. Therefore, in the midst of the controversy of our times, we must be wise and discerning to present our Lord, not as the One who is against our fellow neighbors, for He came for such as these.

Many people see Christians as those who are judging and taking a position of superiority rather than being loving servants of the Most High God. Anything that we are is because of Him. We do not deserve any more than anyone else; we have simply trusted in the One who has borne our sins on the cross of Calvary and therefore have received the freedom that He has purchased for us. Our job is to introduce others to the only One who can give true liberty, peace and meaning to our lives.

Jesus said:

"Come to Me, all you who labor and are heavy laden, and I will give you rest. Take My yoke upon you and learn from Me, for I am gentle and lowly of heart, and you will find rest for your souls. For My yoke is easy and My burden is light." Matthew 11:28-30

What we receive from the Lord, no one and no government can take away. May we walk in this true liberty. Only then will our message have meaning for our own generation. For when someone says to us, "I want what you have", we can respond, "you need Who I have." Let us all come to Him.

July 1

Can You Hear the Thunder?

As I am finishing my Bible readings this morning, I can hear thundering. It is already raining, and the continued rumbling of the thunder reminds me of the majesty of God and the power of His voice.

The psalmist wrote:

"The voice of the Lord is over the waters; the God of glory thunders; the Lord is over many waters. The voice of the Lord is powerful; the voice of the Lord is full of majesty." Psalm 29:3-4

He continues to speak of the strength of the Lord's voice. Therefore, as he states in the beginning of the psalm we should:

"Give unto the Lord glory and strength...the glory due to His name; worship the Lord in the beauty of holiness." Psalm 29:1-2

Whatever situation we find ourselves in this morning we must declare and believe that:

"The Lord sat enthroned at the Flood, and the Lord sits as King forever. The Lord will give strength to His people; The Lord will bless His people with peace." Psalm 29:10-11

May the thundering we hear remind us of our great God's majesty, powerful voice and everlasting Kingdom. Put your trust in Him. He will reign forever!

JULY 2

A PROPHET IS NOT WITHOUT HONOR EXCEPT...

Jesus had been talking about the kingdom of God. He taught many parables. These parables are very instructive, and it would do us good to revisit them and consider just what He was saying about the Kingdom. Then Matthew wrote that Jesus left where He was and came to His own country.

"He taught them in their synagogue, so that they were astonished and said, 'Where did this Man get this wisdom and these mighty works?" Matthew 13:54

The people continued to describe Jesus in relation to His earthly family and trade, bringing into question just what value could be coming from Him, since He originated from them.

This is an interesting thought. Those who are the closest to you may look at you and because of their own natural understanding, perhaps even pride, may not be able to receive anything that comes from God. They will receive your ability as a tradesman (Jesus was a carpenter by trade), but not give honor to your calling from God.

Jesus says something profound:

"A prophet is not without honor except in his own country and in his own house." Matthew 13:57

In Luke's Gospel, He refers to Elijah and Elisha's ministries and focuses on some of their mighty works that were not done in Israel, but instead to a widow from Zarephath and a leper who was a Syrian (see Luke 4:4:24-27). This saying did not go over very well with the religious leaders.

For us it is important to understand that some of the people who might put up the greatest resistance to our own ministries are those who might be the closest to us. This does not give us the right to not be a proper example; it just helps us to be aware that our calling comes from God, and there is where our confidence must reside also. He who calls us will also keep us for His glory.

JULY 3

IN THE FOURTH WATCH OF THE NIGHT...

It's amazing that one can read a story in the Bible over and over, and yet, the Lord can reveal different truths in various seasons. This morning, I am reading a familiar story of when Jesus walked on the sea. What caught my attention is that it was in the fourth watch of the night. The circumstances find the disciples trying to cross a sea with great head winds. They have been at it all night. The fourth watch is the last watch of the night (between 3 & 6 am). It's the time of the night when one should be getting their last stage of rest awaiting a morning rising, refreshed from the sleep they had encountered.

But this is not the case. Instead of being at rest, the disciples are in toil. They had been fighting the winds and waves all night. Perhaps tiredness, fear, anxiety are setting in. Darkness has a way of magnifying the sounds and elements of life. Now, in the midst of this toil, Jesus approaches them, but instead of being overjoyed, they do not recognize Him; they think He is a ghost, and they cried out in fear.

This makes me wonder how in the midst of our most trying times, we might actually not recognize Jesus approaching us. While He is coming to our aid, we think Him to be anything but. You see, night plays a game in our understanding of where we really are and Who is present with us. Thankfully, quickly Jesus identifies Himself and speaks:

"Be of good cheer! It is I, do not be afraid." Matthew 14:27

For me, it is often in the fourth watch of the night that I am up and already seeking the Lord. I thank God that whether it is the actual time of day, or the circumstance of life, that I can trust that Jesus will reveal Himself. It is important that when He does, that I not be fearful of the shadows of my own understanding. He is ever watching, ever present; all I have to do is trust, and He will show Himself real in the midst of the roaring seas, even in the fourth watch of the night. It is there that He bids us to come and walk with Him.

JULY 4

I DO NOT WANT TO SEND THEM AWAY HUNGRY...

Twice we see Jesus multiplying bread and fish for the consumption of the crowds that were following Him. The first time, He does so on a day He had heard of the beheading of John the Baptist. He had tried to seek a secluded place, but the people followed Him. In His own grieving of the Spirit, He turned, and having compassion for the multitude, performed a great miracle and fed five thousand men, besides women and children (see Matthew 14:13-21). A principle here teaches that in our own pain, if we will look around us and serve, we will be comforted.

The second time a great miracle of feeding occurred was after the crowds had followed Jesus for three days without eating. Jesus told His disciples:

"I have compassion on the multitude, because they have now continued with Me three days and have nothing to eat. And I do not want to send them away hungry, lest they faint on the way." Matthew 15:32

Notice that Jesus, seeing the condition of the people following Him, does not want them to return home without being fed. This is the third day without food.

This sign has me thinking of Jesus as the Bread of Life. Even after being in the grave for three days, His resurrection brought hope and sustainment for all who had followed Him. It was His compassion for us that had Him endure the cross and trust in the Father's plan. The seven loaves of bread, like the manna that was provided for the seven days of the week, came down from heaven.

We do not need to go away and faint. We can be filled and joyous. We do not need to go away hungry, for Jesus promises to fill us. If you are hungry today, know that Jesus will not send you away in this condition. His heart is moved on your behalf. His bread alone can and will fill you.

JULY 5

BEFORE I FORMED YOU...

When God speaks, it is powerful, descriptive and opens the window of destiny. In one sentence, He speaks to Jeremiah something particular to him but very instructive for us. In revealing Jeremiah's call the Lord speaks:

"Before I formed you in the womb I knew you; Before you were born I sanctified you; I ordained you a prophet to the nations." Jeremiah 1:5

While specific to Jeremiah, what it reveals is God's foreknowledge of us all. That He knows us before forming us. He already has something in mind, as we are formed in the womb. We are not born by chance but born for a purpose. He sets us apart (sanctifies) for that very purpose and has made an appointment for us to carry it out. If we can understand this revelation, it will help us to realize that we all have a destiny in God.

Here is the part that we have to play. Understanding that God has a purpose for us, we must submit to His shaping and walk out that destiny. If we give Him our life, we will see the ordered steps of a righteous man (woman) opened up for us. We will find the grace of God for the tasks set before us. It is God who has chosen us.

The fact that He knew us and has knowledge of us does not mean that we remain without the knowledge of Him. His desire is that we also know Him. It is only in knowing Him that we can even come to the revelation of knowing ourselves, made in His image. We can only truly find ourselves in relationship to finding God. It's in God where we find our true purpose.

You and I are known, formed, sanctified and appointed! Now, may we go forth understanding we are sent for this very purpose.

JULY 6

PACKING DAY

Today, my son-in-law and a few boys will be joining me as we travel to my son's house to pack all his families' belongings into a pod in preparation for their southern move. We will have to carry, wrap-up, and place each piece strategically in order for things on the other end to be undamaged and usable. When unpacking, it is sometimes a problem getting to something that you need to find, and are not always sure just where it is.

This has me thinking of a simple verse found in Psalm 119:11. Here David is describing a packing away that must be retrievable in order to have any good use in our lives. It is the very word of God. Here is what he wrote:

"Your word I have hidden in my heart, that I might not sin against You."

Can you imagine if we valued the Word of God as much, or more, than any other valuable we have? If we would carefully wrap it, place it in our hearts in order to retrieve it at a later date, intact, good as the day we put it there, useful for what we are encountering? Jesus is the Word of God; personal, ever present, and able to direct our paths daily.

We are so blessed. May we be ever so careful how we handle this most precious gift. He is life-giving and life-changing. With God and His Word, all else is put in proper perspective.

A PICTURE STIMULATES A CONVERSATION.

Yesterday we emptied my son's house to prepare for their move. Last night the family stayed over, and all the men were the first ones up this morning. My four-year-old grandson wanted to have a stained-glass picture lit over our fireplace. It is a picture of Jesus praying in the garden. This picture then stimulated a conversation about the Gospel and "our Father who is in heaven."

Earlier in my Bible reading this morning, I had read about the disciples' discussion over who was greatest in the kingdom of God:

"Jesus called a little child to Him, set Him in the midst of them, and said, 'Assuredly, I say to you, unless you are converted and become as little children, you will by no means enter the kingdom of heaven. Therefore whoever humbles himself as this little child is the greatest in the kingdom of heaven. Whoever receives one little child like this in My name receives Me.'" Matthew 18:2-5

Jesus continued to warn His disciples that no one should cause one of these little ones who believed in Him to sin. There is a high price for our example. It is meant to lead and cause others to come to Jesus, not walk away from Him.

I am glad that in the presence of our little ones, we can talk openly and show by example in Whom we trust. It is not just found in a picture, but even more importantly in how we live our everyday lives.

CHILDREN OF GOD

John begins his Gospel with Christ as the Eternal Word, come down from heaven. In Him was light and life, shining in the darkness. Yet for those who are in darkness they cannot understand His coming. But there is still good news:

"He came to His own, and His own did not receive Him. But as many as received Him, to them He gave the right to become children of God, to those who believe in His name: who were born, not of blood, nor of the will of the flesh, nor of the will of man, but of God." John 1:11-13

What an awesome reality it is to know God as our Father through Christ. We have been given the privilege of being part of His family. This transcends everything we can even imagine about family. We have such love for our earthly family. Can you even imagine how much love the Father has for His children, of which we are.

If you have not received the work of Christ on the cross, give consideration to the great demonstration of love He has shown. He gave Himself so we could be a part of His family. No greater love can be shown than for one to lay down his life, not just for friends, but even those far off. His love is perfect. Give this your thoughts and meditations today. He is worthy! You are His child!

JULY 9

YOU WOULD ACT DIFFERENTLY IF IT WAS YOUR INHERITANCE.

Today, we begin painting and repairing some space that was leased from our ministry. There is a marked difference in the cleanliness and overall appearance between their room and a comparable room that our ministry is using. Both were constructed at the same time. It begs the question why one, even though it has been used as much, maybe even more, is in better condition than the other? The answer is simply stewardship. For one there is a sense of ownership, therefore, upkeep is apparent. For the other, there is no pride of ownership, nor stewardship, and therefore, the condition is in need of restoration.

Think about how this applies to our own work in this world. As Christians we must understand our stewardship role as God's children. Jesus said:

"Blessed are the meek, for they shall inherit the earth." Matthew 5:5

How might we act differently knowing that where we live is going to be ours someday? It is our inheritance. Would we allow it to deteriorate? Wouldn't we try to keep up a proper appearance, fix that which is broken, restore what must be restored?

This is the work our Father has given us to do. Let our understanding be enlightened. Know what the hope of your calling is. Know "*what are the riches of the glory of His inheritance in the Saints*" (Ephesians 1:18). Be the restorers that God has called us to be.

There are many, even Christians, that have an escape mentality. This thinking has them being poor stewards, expecting to check out; they are leaving a mess for the generations to follow. May we not be like these. Begin by stewarding what you already have. Then God will give you ownership over more.

JULY 10

BATTLE FROM A SECURE FOUNDATION

The highest privilege and fundamental reality of the Christian's life is that we have been adopted into the family of God. Jesus gave His life so that we, who were born orphans, separated and at odds with the Father because of our sin, could become the adopted beloved sons and daughters of God.

"For we did not receive the spirit of bondage again to fear, but you received the Spirit of adoption by whom we cry out, 'Abba, Father.'" Romans 8:15-16

If we don't believe at the core of our being that we are "the beloved of God," then we are most susceptible to the devil's wiles. Our sense of value and worth is where our enemy will most likely launch his attack. We need to enter this battlefield with our identity secure. If we do not sense our worth as coming from God, we will seek it through the approval of others.

Jesus entered the wilderness (Luke 4:1-13) armed for battle: He clearly knew who He was to His Father, and the mission He was called to do. The devil kept addressing Jesus by saying, "*If You are the Son of God...*" This is the fundamental point. The battles we face need to be fought on a secure foundation of our identity in Christ. The Father had already spoken over His Son at His baptism:

"You are My beloved Son; in You I am well pleased." Luke 3:22

Jesus was rooted in this truth. We, too, must be rooted in the truth that we are the beloved adopted sons and daughters of God.

Thank you Lord for adopting us as Your beloved. Amen.

July 11

Pointing to "The Way"

Today I am doing a funeral service for a family that I honestly don't know. I have been asked by the funeral director to serve this family. While I do not know the deceased, I do know the One who is "The Way." For the man we are doing services for, his decision has been made, his fate sealed. For it is on this earth that we bow or stiffen our will for or against our Savior. But for those who will be attending, they still have an opportunity to respond.

Jesus told His disciples:

"Let not your heart be troubled; you believe in God, believe also in Me. In My Father's house are many mansions; if it were not so, I would have told you. I go to prepare a place for you. And if I go and prepare a place for you, I will come again and receive you to Myself; that where I am, there you may be also." John 14:1-3

Thomas still did not understand this saying and wondered just what was the way, for he didn't know how he would get to where Jesus was talking about. There are many others, also, who do not know the way. To make it real plain to Thomas, and all who would follow in the years ahead, Jesus told Thomas:

"I am the way, the truth, and the life. No one comes to the Father except through Me." John 14:6

This is the simple message that must be communicated. Jesus is the way, the truth and the life. No one comes to the Father except through Jesus. It is not religion, good works, or any great sacrifice on our parts that insure our salvation. It is only the great sacrifice already paid by Jesus that can insure our entrance into the kingdom.

Today is a day for decision. Today is a day that you and others can put their trust in the saving work of Jesus. May His word be proclaimed boldly, in the Spirit's power to those who might have ears to hear.

July 12

Why Has This People Slidden Back?

In reading the books of Joshua, Jeremiah and then Matthew this morning, there is a consistent theme of a people whom God has chosen; they refuse to hear His voice and obey Him. Their necks are stiff so they will not turn and repent. In speaking His words to the prophet Jeremiah God says:

"Behold this is what I commanded them saying, 'Obey My voice, and I will be your God, and you shall be My people. And walk in all the ways that I have commanded you, that it will be well with you.' Yet they did not obey or incline their ear, but followed the counsels and the dictates of their evil hearts, and went backward and not forward." Jeremiah 7:23-24

In addition to the fact that they are not advancing in God, they, in fact, are falling backwards in their character and destiny. They also trust in false teaching in order to go their own way. God answers the question for why they fall and will not rise and return:

"They hold fast to deceit, they refuse to return. I listened and heard, but they do not speak aright. No man repented of His wickedness, saying, 'What have I done?' Everyone turned to his own course." Jeremiah 8:5-6

Two important things must be seen in these passages: The first is that the Word of God must be preached fully, with all authority in order for people to encounter godly truth. The second is that once that Word is taught, we are accountable to obey that truth. Anything less will result in compromise and a falling back instead of an advancing forward.

If we are to be transformers of our culture, we must first show the way. Not teaching a Gospel of convenience, but teaching a pure Gospel that leaves its hearers with a decision to be made. We must also model that same Gospel through the actions of our own lives, giving living testimony to its ability to change lives.

JULY 13

THE PEOPLE HAD A MIND TO WORK.

I am late to put in my post for the day. Up early and out to prepare for Pastor's School. This is what Pastor Adelson calls doing construction work with me. He, and other young and older men and even a brave young woman, worked diligently today stripping wallpaper, cleaning, constructing, wall board hanging, compounding and even some trim work. It is an important part of discipline.

Nehemiah had a great work to do, repairing walls, rehanging doors, securing a city for God's glory. It took everyone working, joining together to see something visible being done. They were also experiencing something spiritual as well. Nehemiah comments about the progress and says:

"For the people had a mind to work." Nehemiah 4:6

Work is such an important aspect in which to be trained. Paul supplemented his missional expenses by being a tent maker. In exhorting the church, he instructed the Christians to be good workers, providers for their families, stating that if they did not work, they were acting like unbelievers.

So, Pastor's School had a summer session. Tomorrow, we will resume with another session. There is a lot one can learn in physical labor that gets us ready for real mission. In fact, what we were doing is part of that very mission. In case you are interested, you, too, can enroll in Pastor's School.

JULY 14

I HAVE SET BEFORE YOU AN OPEN DOOR...

I am reflecting on a passage in Revelations 3 that was preached at the 20th anniversary of our church. There was so much shared that day that is worth pondering and listening to in its entirety. What I am specifically thinking about this morning is that when Jesus is evaluating this Philadelphia church, he determines their future blessing based on their past faithfulness. Look what He says:

"I know your works. See, I have set before you an open door, and no one can shut it; for you have a little strength, have kept My word, and have not denied My name." Revelations 3:8

Have you given this some thought? That Jesus is watching over your works? That He knows what you are doing? He sees your great labor. He sees when you have to make decisions for the kingdom, even when others may not understand at the time. He understands when your labors have brought you to a point where your endurance is challenged. He sees the stewardship of using what resources with which He has entrusted you.

What is encouraging is that this church did not have the same abundant resources that other churches might have had, but what they lacked in strength, they made up for in faithfulness. Therefore, an open door is set before them. Can you imagine what that might mean? The door is set opened by Jesus. No one will be able to shut the door He has opened.

While this year has just as many challenges as past years for our ministry, I am encouraged by the fact that there is an open door. Whatever that might mean for the days ahead; it is an open door to the Kingdom of God. Only God knows His plans. For all of us, we need to continue to be faithful. For we want the door that He alone can open to remain opened for succeeding generations to follow.

July 15

Enter the Joy of Your Master!

Rewarding good stewardship is something God enjoys. But it isn't only God who enjoys this reward, so do those whom He determines as faithful, those who He promotes.

In reading the "Parable of the Talents" this morning, it is apparent that promotion in the kingdom comes from faithful stewardship. The quantity of our stewardship is not the important thing. It is the fact that we are faithful with whatever the allotment is. Some will have been given a greater deposit than others. However, the evaluation that the Master does is not based on what someone else has, but on what we have been given.

Being faithful then requires not only that we hold on to what we have been given, but that we use what we have been given to bring back increase to our Lord. If we do so, we are deemed as a "good and faithful servant" (Matthew 25:21). And the reward for this faithfulness is a greater stewardship along with joy.

"You have been faithful over a few things. I will make you ruler over many things. Enter the joy of your lord." Matthew 25:23

So we see that faithful stewardship brings promotion and joy: joy for our Master for the increase accomplished for the kingdom, and joy for the ability to trust us for even greater stewardship. This is a joy in which we also can enter. We can rejoice for being deemed faithful stewards, for being entrusted with greater things, and for celebrating with our Master. His joy now becomes our joy.

The choices we make today and tomorrow will have a bearing on the joy we can enter into today and forever. Be wise and diligent so that you might enter the joy of the Lord! He wants to share His joy with us.

JULY 16

IN THE CORNER OF A ROOF

We are in route to deliver my son's car to his new location in Florida. Not wanting to drive for 12 hours a day, my wife and I are doing about 6 hours of traveling a day. We are settled in a bed and breakfast for another day. We plan to visit the Site and Sound Theater today for their production "Joseph."

When we arrived yesterday, we were given keys to our room. Our room is on the third floor. No big deal you think. But this is not a hotel. There are no elevators. The ceiling heights are high, so the stairs are many. We did not pack for two days but for eleven. So, when the lady said room seven, on the third floor, I was thanking God that I can still walk and carry bags.

Our room is in the corner of the roof with slanted ceilings with dormers. I recall a scripture that says it is better to be in the corner of the roof, than to live with a contentious woman. I do not live with a contentious woman, but with someone who has been by my side for almost 36 years now. But in order to write this post, I needed to come down into the small lobby in order to be able to get my Bible program, read what I needed to for today, and now write, as I wait for the breakfast and my wife Bernice to appear.

We are glad to be able to spend some time alone together until we rejoin our family in Florida on Sunday. I am glad that wherever we go, the Lord is always close. His Spirit dwells with us. He is always near if we are willing to seek Him. So whether you are in a comfortable home, or in the corner of a roof, give Him praise. He alone is worthy. There is no other, or nothing that can compare.

Well my wife just arrived and so did the breakfast. Have a wonderful day. Give our Lord the praise He deserves.

JULY 17

ARE YOU STILL SLEEPING?

As I am reading Matthew's account of Jesus praying in a place called Gethsemane, I am reflecting on how the burden of intercession often falls heavier on the one who is carrying the weight of the impending trial or burden. While others might say they will pray, the burden for that prayer is often fleeting.

Jesus is about to face the greatest challenge of His earthly ministry and He asked His disciples to watch and pray with Him. Three extended times He prays and returns briefly to find His disciples sleeping. It provokes Him to ask:

"Could you not watch with Me one hour? Watch and pray, lest you enter into temptation. The spirit is indeed willing, but the flesh is weak." Matthew 26:41

That very night, Jesus is arrested but prepared for the ordeal that is part of His Father's plan. For the disciples, they lack the strength and fortitude needed at this time and scatter. They one day will come to the place of being prepared and empowered, then they will carry the same burden and be strengthened by prayer.

For us, we must ask, "Do we have the burden of the Lord's ministry?" When we do, we will pray. I saw a post of a mother yesterday that said she was hurting, but trying to put a smiley face forward. For me as a pastor, I began to pray for this woman.

People matter. If we say we will pray for someone, I hope it is more than a saying and is followed by deliberate action. Ask the Lord to draw you to Himself. May we be prepared spiritually to tackle whatever the Lord's plans are for our lives strengthened in the might of the Lord! May we also join in prayer for those who also need the Lord's strength and peace for their current situations.

JULY 18

CALLING FOR LABORERS FOR THE HARVEST

In the room we are staying is a Bible placed on a table. For many years the Gideons have served in getting Bibles into hotels and motels around the country. This Bible is also opened. I looked at what passage it was opened to, wondering if it was just a random turning or a strategic passage.

The passage clearly evident is Luke 10, when Jesus sent out the 70 and instructed them to go two by two into every city and place where He Himself would come. A key verse is in a summation that Jesus tells the 70:

"The harvest truly is great, but the laborers are few; therefore pray the Lord of the harvest to send out laborers into His harvest." Luke 10:2

Two things we see: (1) the harvest is great, and (2) more laborers are needed to reap the harvest. We live in a day where people think the harvest is lean. But is that the truth, or is it that we are not inclined to labor for the harvest?

It is clear to me that despite what we might see or think, the Word of God is the standard of what should motivate us to the truth. If Jesus says, "the harvest is plentiful," then I believe Him. Shouldn't you also?

What then must we do? Pray for the Lord to send out more laborers? Yes, please do. But do not sit by idle as we ask Him to do that of others. We must invest ourselves in the work of the Lord, being able laborers for Him. Where He sends you, He will also go.

Lord, give us a heart for Your harvest and a willingness to labor with you. Amen.

JULY 19

THE ENVIRONMENT OF THE CROSS

As I read the 27th chapter of Matthew's Gospel, I am struck with the tense, reviling nature of the crucifixion. I am not just talking about the physical torment that existed, but the great persecution offered towards Jesus as the Son of God. It came from the soldiers, people passing by, criminals, who themselves were condemned. Chief priests, scribes and elders also mocked Him. In all, those present mocked Jesus, spit on Him, shook their heads at Him, reviled Him and even challenged who He was. What a vile and challenging scene, yet Jesus never tried to defend Himself before them.

It reminds me of Jesus' word in the Sermon on the Mount. There He instructed His disciples about the difficulty of walking in righteousness, yet the necessity of keeping a proper focus on our blessedness if we are faithful.

"Blessed are those who are persecuted for righteousness' sake, for theirs is the kingdom of heaven. Blessed are you when they reviled and persecuted you, and say all kinds of evil against you falsely for My sake. Rejoice and be exceedingly glad, for great is your reward in heaven, for so they persecuted the prophets who were before you." Matthew 5:10-12

In the end, it was the testimony of Jesus life, death, and resurrection that verified that He was the Son of God. So too, in our lives, the testimony of His righteousness working through us will reveal who we really are. More importantly, through our lives, we will reveal to those around us, the reality of Jesus. Keep focused on the One who is the validator of your life. Then you will have the endurance to run the race and obtain your crown.

Lord, the only true validation we need in life comes from You. Today, we recommit our willingness to be identified with You. May our life point to our trust in You and bring glory to Your Name. Amen.

JULY 20

ALL AUTHORITY...IN HEAVEN AND EARTH

After Jesus' resurrection and before His ascension, He commissioned His disciples to go and make disciples of all the nations. They could do so because He had been given all authority and now was sending them out with this delegated authority.

When I consider the idea of authority, it is something that one uses with wisdom and discretion. Just because one has authority, it does not mean that they would wield their power in every circumstance. One must be wise and know when that power must be restrained.

For instance, when Jesus faced the cross, He could have called on the Father to send legions of angels to fight on His behalf, but He chose to submit to the Father's will instead. Jesus had the authority to complete the mission of His Father, but not the authority to operate in a way that would not honor His Father and His great plan.

If we are going to be the witnesses that Christ has called us to be, we must come to a better understanding of the power and authority we have in Him. Some people, when they are given authority, use it in wrong ways. I believe that some Christians do the same. Authority is not something we use for our own advantage. It is not something we just play with. It is something we must learn how to walk in with all discernment. If we can understand just who we are in Christ, we will have the confidence to whom we belong and use the authority we have been given for kingdom purposes.

Lord, help us understand authority as delegated from You. May we walk in rightful, lawful, delegated authority. May You be glorified as we walk in Kingdom power. Amen.

JULY 21

CONSIDER CHRIST, WHO HAS SPOKEN TO US!

The writer to the Hebrews begins his letter exhorting his fellow believers to go onto perfection; to not reverse their course of action because of any persecution, remembering that Christ is better than the Judaic system, Angels, Moses, the Aaronic priesthood, and better than the law. Pressing on in Christ produces tested faith, self-discipline, and a visible love seen in good works. Look at how he describes how God has spoken to us:

"In these last days [God has] spoken to us by His Son, whom He has appointed heir of all things, through whom also He made the worlds; who being the brightness of His glory and the expressed image of His person, and upholding all things by the word of His power, when He had by Himself purged our sins, sat down at the right hand of the Majesty on high, having become so much better than the angels, as He has by inheritance obtained a more excellent name than they." Hebrews 1:2-4

There is so much here to describe the worthiness of the Christ that we serve. Look at all these descriptions of our Lord. Our God has a face, and it is Jesus. Look at Him, the expressed image and brightened of God. The word of His power upholds all things. He has become a superior sacrifice, a once and for all sacrifice for our sins. He is not in the grave, but seated at the right hand of God. How excellent is His name!

Consider His majesty! Consider His humanity! Consider His superiority! Consider His power! Consider His great love! Let praise spring forth from your lips! Let joy fill your heart! Begin to express to God your great thankfulness! He is worthy to be praised!

JULY 22

HOW MUCH ARE WE PAYING ATTENTION?

As I continue my reading of the letter to the Hebrews, the writer transitions into the second chapter with a word "Therefore." This transition means that the first chapter, or the thought preceding consideration, must give light to what will come to follow. Having already spoken of the superiority of Jesus over the angels, he now exhorts those who believe to be careful. He wrote:

"Therefore we must give the earnest heed to the things we have heard, lest we drift away. For if the word spoken through angels proved steadfast, and every transgression and disobedience received a just reward, how shall we escape if we neglect so great a salvation, which at first began to be spoken by the Lord, and was confirmed to us by those who heard Him." Hebrews 2:1-3

Think about this for a moment. If what the angels spoke proved accurate and had abiding consequences, and Jesus is above the angels, how much more will His word stand firm? We have received the Word of God. His word is firm and able to lead us in His righteousness. However, if we neglect, or have little value for His word, we might drift away. The thing about drifting is that you don't really notice it until you are really off course.

Growing in our faith and in the knowledge of the Son of God will cause us to mature. Why do we need to be careful to mature? So "*that we should no longer be children tossed to and fro and carried about with every wind of doctrine, by the trickery of men, in the cunning craftiness of deceitful plotting*" (Ephesians 4:14). Growing in maturity and honoring the Word of God assures we don't drift.

May we be diligent to stay on the course given to us. Value the words of Jesus. His word will enable us to stand. Based on this standard, all will have to give an account.

JULY 23

ENTERING REST

So many people say they need rest, but have they ever entered true rest? There is evidently a difference between the two. In the fourth chapter of Hebrews, the author states that there is a promise of rest, but not everyone enters rest. Hardened hearts and disobedience keep us from experiencing true rest. Striving in our own works keeps us from this kind of rest.

Vacationing in a city given over to entertainment parks, I am amazed at the activity done under the guise of vacationing, and the apparent lack of real rest that so many are experiencing. Of course, you don't need to travel anywhere special to see this. It happens all around us, in our everyday life, at work, in our homes, etc. The rest promised by the Lord is not about how much sleep one gets, but how much of God's peace resides in our lives.

We are exhorted to "be diligent to enter that rest" ... "Seeing that we have a great High Priest who has passed through the heavens, Jesus the Son of God, let us hold fast our confession. For we do not have a High Priest who cannot sympathize with our weaknesses, but was in all points tempted as we are, yet without sin. Let us therefore come boldly to the throne of grace, that we may obtain mercy and find grace to help in time of need" (Hebrews 4:11, 14-16).

Whenever we are pressed with anything that takes our rest away, may we be reminded that the great sacrifice of our Lord and High Priest, Jesus, is the means that we have to come to the Lord and receive the rest we need. We do not need to strive or stay in a condition of unrest. May we come to Him by faith and receive what He has promised us.

JULY 24

REFRESHMENT IN A DRY AND THIRSTY LAND

As I sit praying and reading the Scriptures this morning, I can see the clouds thickening. It looks like it will be a rainy day for us to pack up and head to the airport and travel home. Thinking of what is natural has me searching for the supernatural as well. The earth is the Lord's and all its fullness, yet there are so many who do not see, nor experience this reality. They have a dryness of soul and spirit, badly in need of refreshment or hydration. I am reminded of a Psalm of David when he was in the wilderness of Judah. There he wrote:

"O God, You are my God; Early will I seek You; My soul thirsts for You; My flesh longs for You in a dry and thirsty land where there is no water. So I looked for You in the sanctuary, to see Your power and Your glory. Because Your lovingkindness is better than life, my lips shall praise You. Thus I will bless You while I live; I will lift up my hands in Your name. My soul shall be satisfied as with marrow and fatness, and my mouth shall praise You with joyful lips." Psalm 63:1-5

Thankfully, there is a sanctuary where the people of God can seek the Lord and His glory. He can be found. He desires to commune with us. No matter how dry the place we might find ourselves to be in, we can seek the Lord and He will be our refreshment. He will fill and sustain us. He will renew our strength. He will cause praise and worship to flow through us to Him and as a testimony to those all around us.

May we receive the refreshing of the Lord. May we allow His joy to flow through our lips today.

JULY 25

FLYING HOME - BUT THINGS ARE DIFFERENT

We are about two hours into our flight back home. The trip will only take a few hours. It took us several days driving down. It has been a real nice time to spend with our son's and daughter's families. But this was not just a normal vacation. One family will now stay relocated. I know that they are just hours away with a flight, or, can be seen on SKYPE or FACETIME. But something is different. We will live our lives around two different geographical areas. We will continue to grow diverse in some ways. Our grandchildren will have a new center around which they will learn to grow and call their home.

Yes, we will still be able to play an influential role in their lives, but just how much is the question? While I am excited for their new opportunities, I am also saddened in not having the frequency that we formerly enjoyed. In all my life, our extended family has lived close together. Yes, there were the brief times of service or college in which one temporarily went away, but the expectation was they were coming home.

I guess we now join so many other families who live in different centers. I don't know if the family is stronger this way, but we will trust that the Lord has His plan, and we will do our part to follow His leading. Intercession will be part of our duty, as it has been in times past. May the good Lord watch over all of us, and strengthen us for His journey.

July 26

Don't Worry About What Others Are Doing - Focus on the Lord

Reading Psalm 37 this evening is so instructive for all of us who want to live righteously for the Lord. There are times when we might be tempted to be envious of others who seemingly prosper, even though they do so with a lack of integrity.

There are so many exhortations for those of us who believe.

...Trust in the Lord, and do good;

...Dwell in the land, and feed on His faithfulness

...Commit your way to the Lord,

...Trust also in Him, and He will bring it to pass

...Rest in the Lord, and wait patiently for Him

The psalmist continues:

"The steps of a good man are ordered by the Lord, and He delights in his way. Though he fall, he shall not be utterly cast down; For the Lord upholds him with His hand. I have been young, and now am old; Yet I have not seen the righteous forsaken, Nor his descendants begging bread." Psalm 37:23-25

What a blessing it is to keep our lives in proper perspective. If we keep our eyes on the Lord, He will keep us, protect us, and prosper us in His time. If we fall, He will lift us up. If we delight ourselves in the Lord, He will give us the desires of our hearts.

So let us not focus on what is happening with others. Trust in the Lord, we will not be disappointed.

JULY 27

UNITY AND ONENESS - JESUS' PRAYER FOR US!

I don't know any family that doesn't want their children to get along or work together. What we long for is cooperation, maturity, and love to flow from our homes out to the community and beyond.

When Jesus prayed for His disciples, He also prayed for those who would follow Him and believe through the word that would be preached. His prayer was that we would be one that the world would believe that Jesus was sent by the Father. He also gave us the means for this to happen:

"And the glory which You have given Me I have given them, that they may be one just as We are one: I in them, and You in Me, that they may be made perfect in one, and that the world may know that You have sent Me, and have loved them, as You have loved Me." John 17:22-23

Two important things happen as we learn to grow in unity. (1) We mature into the people that God purposed. (2) Through this unity and maturity, we demonstrate a validation of the reality of Christ in our lives to the world to whom we seek to be a witness.

If this is a prime prayer request from Jesus to the Father, shouldn't it be a primary concern to us? What will it take for us to give this more consideration? How might we decrease so that Christ can increase among us? Until we get this right, our witness will be obscured, and honestly, our joy and peace will be minimized.

May we receive the enabling power of the Holy Spirit to walk together in the unity for which Jesus longed. He has already given us His glory. Let us now walk in it.

JULY 28

BY FAITH...

Yesterday was my first day back in the office after being away for a little over a week. That meant sifting through the mail and notes left in my in-box. I needed also to update our church and school budget. Like your homes and businesses, there are necessary things that we must forecast to do (upkeep, repairs, capital improvements), while we also seek to provide the necessary utilities, services, and to meet personnel needs. This is always a great balancing act. It seems like when it is just worked out, something changes that just makes it a bit more difficult. It's in times like this that we must remind ourselves of God's great faithfulness.

Reading the letter to the Hebrews this morning, the writer says:

"Now faith is the substance of things hoped for, the evidence of things not seen. For by it [FAITH] the elders obtained a good testimony." Hebrews 11:1-2

Thinking about this verse, I realize that if everything was always easy, we would not need faith. And faith by itself is not enough. What is required is that by faith we proceed towards the promises of God, seeing His unfolding provisions meet our most pressing needs. In doing so, we obtain a good testimony. It is a testimony that God has already purposed, but one we must walk out.

Because of the faithfulness of God, we can have faith to trust Him. This faith, then, must cause us to also be faithful to use the resources He provides for what He has purposed. It is in the balancing of these two tensions that we see the testimony of God made real, and rejoice in His provision.

If you are having a hard time seeing just how things will work out for you, ask God for His wisdom; be responsible in your actions, and then trust that He will be your provision. He is ever faithful.

JULY 29

SLOW AND STEADY OR DELUGE?

Yesterday we experienced a 1.2 inch rainfall in a 15 - 20 minute timespan. If any of you were traveling in our area, you surely experienced what happens when you get so much rainfall in a small amount of time.

While rain provides a needful resource, when it comes in that proportion, many of the benefits go away. There is not enough time for the rain to penetrate the ground, it simply overpowers and has to be shed into streams, culverts and drainage systems.

A steady light rain, on the other hand, penetrates the ground, provides what is needed for plant growth, greens up the lawns, and does not do any destruction to property and road systems.

We can learn something from this for our Christian walk. There are many who are like the quick storms. They make a great event, but it does little to penetrate the hearts of those who are near. Jesus said:

"Let your light so shine before men, that they may see your good works and glorify your Father in heaven." Matthew 5:16

I believe this exhortation is not just a quick outburst of light, but steady light seen and shown over long periods of time. Our works are steady and constant, providing a positive witness and cumulative resource which causes glory to God.

May our witness be like the steady light rain that brings refreshment to those who are near us. We are not called to bring storms, but refreshment to those who are near and far.

JULY 30

NONE OF THE THINGS MOVE ME...

I am encouraged with the focus and faith of the apostle Paul. Things did not always go as planned for him, but he used whatever opportunity he had to further the Gospel and fulfill the call of God on his life. In addressing the Ephesian Elders, he rehearsed some of their history together, and then spoke of what awaited him:

"I have kept back nothing that was helpful, but proclaimed it to you, and taught you publicly and from house to house, testifying to Jews, and also to Greeks, repentance toward God and faith toward our Lord Jesus Christ. And see, now I go bound in the spirit to Jerusalem, not knowing the things which will happen to me there, except that the Holy Spirit testifies in every city, saying that chains and tribulations await me. But none of these things move me; nor do I count my life dear to myself, so that I may finish my race with joy, and the ministry which I received from the Lord Jesus, to testify to the gospel of the grace of God." Acts 20:20-24

There is a real key to what Paul is saying. First of all, he knew to Whom he belonged. He was not focused on making an easy life for himself but carrying the responsibility and entrustment of the call given him. Secondly, he used all of the conflicts, setbacks, and difficult circumstances as a platform for proclaiming the Gospel to the watching world. It was ever unfolding through his personal story.

This is an incredible lesson. Our stories of faith create new life. Whatever pressure or difficulty we might be facing right now can become a testimony to our faith, and God's faithfulness that will bring new life to others. May we look on our situations with a new-found hope, recognizing that we have opportunity to tell His story through our own.

JULY 31

WARNING AND COMMENDATION

When the apostle Paul gave his concluding words to the Ephesian elders, he gave them strict warning and then commended them to God and the Word of His grace. He stated that he "*had not shunned to declare to [them] the whole counsel of God*" (Ephesians 20:27). He had held back nothing that was helpful for them. In other words, he spoke the truth of God's Word in its totality. He didn't pick and choose. He spoke the truth in love. He taught in a way that those who would hear could grow up in Christ. Become mature. Have what was necessary to be equipped as solid men and women, who could discern right from wrong. They could build their lives on godly principles and stand against the wiles of the devil.

Therefore, he now turns to the leaders who will carry out this work in the Ephesians community:

"Therefore take heed to yourselves and to all the flock, among which the Holy Spirit has made you overseers, to shepherd the church of God which He purchased with His own blood." Ephesians 20:28

In light of what these leaders were taught, they needed to carry out their responsibility with the greatest care. Understanding that their stewardship was given to them by the Holy Spirit, but the ownership was the Lord's. Given this understanding, Paul himself could release them knowing that it is the Lord who keeps us and builds the church.

So he commissions them with these words:

"*I commend you to God and to the word of His grace, which is able to build you up and give you an inheritance among those who are sanctified*" (Ephesians 20:32). It is before our Lord that we stand. It is His word that gives us the guidance we need. If we are ever before the Lord and trust in His word to guide our path, we will never be disappointed. This is what causes growth in the body, and at the same time, does not cause unnecessary cumbersome authority entanglements. May we learn from the models given us in God's Word.

AUGUST 1

THE SATISFACTION OF WORK

This summer has been especially busy. Every day needs to be thought through and used wisely. An old saying that I learned as a young person was, "don't put off till tomorrow, what you can do today". Saturdays, like other days, count also. I am just now getting to put down some thoughts. Though today has been filled to the hilt, there is a great satisfaction when I can look back, see things accomplished and check a few more things off the ever- expanding list.

The writer of Proverbs wrote:

"He who tills his land will have plenty of bread, but he who follows frivolity will have poverty enough!" Proverbs 28:19

We may or may not live in a farming community, but the idea can be understood in any of our occupations. If we are industrious with our time, we will have greater reward for our labor. Not only will it be a provision, it will also bring us great joy and satisfaction.

I wish I could tell you my list is almost accomplished, but that wouldn't be reality. There will always be more things that you and I will need to do. What is important is that we continue to make progress, use our time wisely, then reflect and enjoy the progress we have made.

Is there a project that you need to get started? There is no time like the present to begin. Sometimes beginning is the hardest part. May you be encouraged and enjoy new progress as you apply your time and effort wisely.

AUGUST 2

THE BLESSING OF A MOM

Today is my mom's birthday. My family and I are blessed to still have her. She is in good health and very active. There isn't a person that she meets or a family member that she doesn't give her full attention to. I have watched her serve others, thinking of their needs above her own. She has honored her own parents and many of our older relatives through the years. She still daily cares for her own mother who is ninety-nine years old. She loves on her children, grandchildren and greatgrandchildren, not to mention so many other family members.

Living in the house right next to hers, I have the privilege of seeing her often. Each morning as she reports for duty to care for my grandmother, we have a few moments of exchange to start off the day. Often in the evenings, I give, or get, a report of the happenings of the day, like who might have come over and what ministry things were done.

I can tell you that moms and dads do have a great influence on their children, especially by the example of their lives. The Bible calls us to honor our parents in the Lord and as children, we are admonished to obey our parents (see Ephesians 6:1-3). These foundational pillars must be kept in place if we are to thrive as a society. With the social programming attempting to dismantle the family and redefine it to its own choosing, there is so much at stake for the future generations.

For my family, we will continue to try and live according to the examples that have been passed on to us. Doing so is the best way we can honor our parents. Even if your dad or mom is no longer alive, you can show them honor through the way you live your life. This is how we build a heritage. This is how we are grounded in knowing who we are and what we as a family value.

Thanks mom for the great example that you have been to us. Happy Birthday! May the good Lord continue to bless you with good health and enable you to embrace all that your heart desires. We are so blessed to have you as our mom.

GOD'S PRIMARY PURPOSES FOR HIS EARTHLY FAMILY

Have you ever asked yourself this question? What are God's primary purposes for His earthly family? Let me just give you a few highlights this morning. The Father's highest goal for His children is that they inherit His heart.

In order to do so, believers must: learn to think as He thinks (Christian worldview); relate as He relates (*koinonia)*; live as He lives (strategic living); embrace His method of maturing us (ruler-ship training through obedience training and pressure); and see that exalting Christ is the door to His heart.

"I beseech you therefore, brethren, by the mercies of God, that you present your bodies a living sacrifice, holy, acceptable to God, which is your reasonable service. And do not be conformed to this world, but be transformed by the renewing of your mind, that you may prove what is that good and acceptable and perfect will of God." Romans 12:1-2 (see also Colossians 2:8-10; Philippians 2:5-8)

While these are the highlights, each one entails much detail. Starting with our thought process and developing an ability to think as our Father does affects every other area of our life (relating, living, maturing and exalting Christ). How we use what we know and learn is crucial to being able to solve problems in conjunction with others, some who will actually be opposing these views.

Growing in wisdom, discernment, character, and communication skills are also necessary to carry out our Father's heart. This all takes time, instruction, submission, training, and experience to fulfill His assignments and pass on a legacy where we can build generationally.

Father, give us Your heart to accomplish Your purpose. We understand this takes time. Mentor us according to Your ways. May we resemble You in all areas of our life, more and more, day-by-day. Amen

AUGUST 4

THE MISSING LICENSE...

This morning I was surprised to see my wallet and money spread out on top of a shelf. After working yesterday, I had failed to take my wallet out of my shorts and therefore, it got washed along with my shorts. I located a new wallet that I had been given and started to transfer the necessary credit cards, etc. In the midst of all this was a wild lightning storm. I received a text from someone, and after answering, went back to transferring the things to my new wallet. The only thing was, that now, my license was missing.

After looking all over for it, I decided to do what I always do: read my morning readings, pray and trust that the Lord will reveal what happened to the missing license. It is amazing how, when we put our trust in the Lord, He will do what seems like an insignificant thing (but very significant to me). The storm has now subsided substantially. I looked one more time in a place that I looked several times before, and there was my license.

The great thing is that the Lord can give you peace in the midst of the storm. Outside there was a great thunder and lightning storm. Inside was a storm of a different manner; I had lost my license. Both storms have now passed. When you find yourself in the midst of the storm, remember the Lord. He can calm any storm. He is our peace. Let Him be first; everything else will fall into place.

"Be anxious for nothing, but in everything by prayer and supplication, with thanksgiving, let your requests be made known to God; and the peace of God, which surpasses all understanding will guard your hearts and minds through Christ Jesus." Philippians 4:6-7

AUGUST 5

WHAT CAN BE FOUND IN THE FALLOW GROUND?

In reading the book of Proverbs, there is one verse that stuck with me this morning.

"Much food is in the fallow ground of the poor, and for lack of justice there is waste." Proverbs 13:23

When you think about this verse, it is evident that the ground that is spoken of is uncultivated. How can you expect a harvest, if you are unwilling to cultivate the ground? How many opportunities might exist for us, yet we are unwilling to put in the required effort, in the beneficial season, to be able to later reap a bountiful harvest? Note that the proverb says that much food is in this fallow ground. It is not just some small amount, but a rich abundant amount.

The second thing we see in this proverb is that because of injustice, some of what is able to be produced is not managed properly. It is wasted. So, in one case time and effort are not managed properly, and it leads to a lack of abundance. In the second case, material possession is not managed properly, and it leads to waste. This could be because one is not thinking about what others need, and doesn't fully appreciate the blessing one has received. It could also speak of the fact that seed for future sowing is not put aside, but consumed instead, making future harvest not possible.

For all of us, it speaks of our need to use time, work and material management in the wisest way. If we do so, not only will we have our needs met, but we will also be able to help meet the needs of others. There is much opportunity in the fallow ground.

This leads us to ask some important questions: What might be the fallow ground of our life that needs cultivating? What areas need better management? We must give some attention to this. If we do, we, and others, will reap the benefits.

AUGUST 6

AS THEY WERE ABLE TO HEAR...

Jesus often spoke in parables. Mark writes, "and with many such parables He spoke the word to them as they were able to hear it. But without a parable He did not speak to them. And when they were alone, He explained all things to His disciples" (Mark 433-34).

Jesus used life examples to depict kingdom truths. But if one was not in the kingdom, there would not be an understanding of this truth. One would need to press in and seek the explanation to further understand the implications of the truth presented by Jesus.

Jesus said to His disciples:

"To you it has been given to know the mystery of the kingdom of God; but to those who are outside, all things come in parables, so that 'Seeing they may see and not perceive, and hearing they may hear and not understand; lest they should turn, and their sins be forgiven them." Mark 4:11-12

Sometimes in the Christian culture we use the words believer and disciples rather loosely. If we applied what Jesus said as related to parables, shouldn't His disciples be those who want to press in to understand His Word, and then respond to that truth in application in their lives? For those outside, they don't bother. They never get past the initial story. Therefore, you can't expect that anything will change in their lives.

Jesus gave them more as they were able to hear what He first instructed (as they were able to hear). How about you and I? Are we pressing in to have the mysteries of the kingdom revealed to us? If so, more will be added to our understanding. If not, even what we have heard will be of little help.

Lord, speak to us and help us understand. We want to be Your disciples who desire to know Your truth and grow in that truth. Help us apply Your truth to our lives. Amen.

AUGUST 7

"DO NOT BE AFRAID, ONLY BELIEVE"

This is what Jesus spoke to a ruler of the synagogue. Someone had just come to the ruler to let him know that his twelve year old daughter had died. Therefore, he should no longer bother Jesus. But Jesus did not see in this situation a finality. He turned to this ruler and said:

"Do not be afraid, only believe." Mark 5:36

As you read the story, you will find that Jesus resurrects this young girl. He gives her back to her parents. He had taken her by the hand, and said to her:

"*Taltiha, cumi,*" *which is translated, "Little girl, I say to you, arise.*" Mark 5:41

This is one of three resurrections we see Jesus do in His ministry time. But, the lesson is not just about resurrection. It's about life itself.

When Jesus said, "do not be afraid, only believe," He was not saying mix fear and belief, but put aside fear and only believe. I wonder how many times we try to believe, but hold on to fear. In some way, isn't that being double-minded? James teaches us that a double-minded man cannot receive anything from God. How do we overcome this double-mindedness? Jesus tells us, "Only believe."

What are the situations in your life that you must put away? Is it fear and only believe? If I could only believe.... Fill in that sentence.

Is there someone close to you that seems dead to you? One that needs life restored, or given spiritual life for the first time? Only believe!

Are you struggling with a difficult situation that seems impossible? Only believe?

If we believe, Jesus will give us the instructions that we need to hear. Follow them and watch life come to your situations.

AUGUST 8

OLIVE PLANTS & CHILDREN'S CHILDREN

Today is my son's birthday. My wife and I can't believe that it has been thirty-five years since his birth. It makes us feel a bit older. He has grown up to be a fine young man, husband, and father. We are proud of who he is and the fact that he desires to please the Lord in what he does. He is surely precious to us, an olive plant that has been seated at our table. With his family growing, the table has become too small, but the blessing enlarged.

I am reminded of a Psalm of blessing this morning; one that I can surely affirm for my own self. One that I hope will also be a blessing to my children and to you.

"Blessed is every one who fears the Lord, who walks in His ways. When you eat the labor of your hands, you shall be happy, and it shall be well with you.

Your wife shall be a fruitful vine in the very heart of your house, your children like olive plants all around your table. Behold, thus shall the man be blessed who fears the Lord.

The Lord bless you out of Zion, and may you see the good of Jerusalem all the days of your life. Yes, may you see your children's children. Peace be upon Israel." Psalm 128:1-6

I have experienced this blessing and continue to be blessed. I pray you will also receive this blessing as you continue to fear the Lord and walk in His ways.

Happy Birthday Peter! You are much loved.

AUGUST 9

IT IS ALL GOOD!

I am considering what a week this has been. So much was accomplished and God's favor was evident in each and every day. Today, we had such a beautiful church service. The power and anointing of the Lord was present. We heard a challenging, heartfelt, even humorous testimony that directed us back to the importance of covenantal relationships and excitement about all that God has for us to participate in as we look to the future.

We had a wonderful church picnic which enabled us to continue to build our relationships with new and old friends. Even for one family with an emergency, others stayed with them and met the need with great service and love. As I watched the setting sun, I thought about the great peace of the Lord that He has for His people.

The psalmist wrote:

"I will both lie down in peace, and sleep; for You alone, O Lord, make me dwell in safety." Psalm 4:8

Isn't it good to lie down in peace? It doesn't mean that life is perfect, but we do not need to carry anxiety, anger, or unresolved conflict. With the Lord's help we can settle any issues, learn to forgive, keep short lists, and trust Him to lead us and keep us. Surely, with His help we can experience His peace. Sleep is a blessing for refreshment, not a means to escape.

May the peace of the Lord also settle, fill, and encompass you. May your sleep be fruitful and refreshing. For you dwell in safety. It is all good!

AUGUST 10

REMODELING VS. STARTING NEW

I spent the day taking things apart. It is often interesting to see just what one might find. One never knows what is hidden behind the surface. It is much different than when one starts building something from the beginning. In that case one can build orderly and predictably. In the former case, it takes much thought, undoing, redoing, and being creative enough to make it work out in the end.

As I think about this natural experience, I am also thinking about the importance in training our children in an orderly, biblical way. This is what we have been admonished to do in God's word. If we do not take the time to do this, we, and others, will have to work at undoing things in our children and young adults when they grow up.

Jesus gave us a clear description of how we need to build:

"Therefore whoever hears these sayings of Mine, and does them, I will liken him to a wise man who built his house on the rock: and the rain descended, the floods came, and the winds blew and beat on that house; and it did not fail, for it was founded on the rock. But everyone who hears these sayings of Mine, and does not do them, will be like a foolish man who built his house on the sand: and the rain descended, the floods came, and the winds blew and beat on that house; and it fell. And great was its fall." Matthew 7:24-27

There are many that bemoan in later years what they should have done in their younger years. Let it not be so with us. Let's build on a proper foundation, hearing and doing what Jesus has instructed us to do. Then, we will be wise builders. Then, we will see that what is built will endure.

AUGUST 11

THERE IS A RIVER...

Wherever we are, whatever we do, there is "a river whose streams shall make glad the city of God" (Psalm 46:4). This river is symbolic of the Holy Spirit. Jesus said that the Holy Spirit would abide in us and even spring forth from our innermost beings.

Jesus said to the woman at the well:

"Whoever drinks of this water will thirst again, but whoever drinks of the water that I shall give him will never thirst. But the water that I shall give him will become in him a fountain of water springing up into everlasting life." John 4:13-14

Jesus also spoke these words on the last day of the Feast of Tabernacles:

"If anyone thirsts, let him come to Me and drink. He who believes in Me, as the Scripture has said, out of his heart will flow rivers of living water." John 7:37-38

When Paul exhorted the Colossians, he stated:

"Let the word of Christ dwell in you richly in all wisdom, teaching and admonishing one another in psalms and hymns and spiritual songs, singing with grace in your hearts to the Lord." Colossians 3:16

It is amazing how in an ordinary situation, a song can bubble up and fill our spirit and mind. I am so thankful for this river. It is refreshing. It changes the landscape of dryness. It reminds me that I am not alone. This river is not just for me. It is meant to be shared. The presence of the Holy Spirit is empowering. He leads me into truth. He preserves my walk. He shapes my ways. He is ever faithful.

What can I say? The goodness of the Lord is beyond comparison. All I can do is praise Him. Thank you Lord for Your goodness and mercy. Thank you Lord for Your great favor.

August 12

WHERE IS YOUR PLACE?

In reading 1st Corinthians, Paul is instructing the church in relation to gifting, diversity and unity. He wrote:

"There are diversities of gifts, but the same Spirit. There are differences of ministries, but the same Lord. And there are diversities of activities, but it is the same God who works all in all. But the manifestation of the Spirit is given to each one for the profit of all." 1 Corinthians 12:4-7

Whatever gifting we might have is meant to be used for the betterment of others. Our gifting is not for ourselves, but for the building up of others. In other words, what kind of contribution can we make to others? How can we use our resources, reasonings, discernment, abilities, and spiritual gifting to make a difference to those we meet and with whom we covenant?

Paul continues to instruct us:

"But now God has set the members, each one of them, in the body just as He pleased." 1 Corinthians 12:18

Again, we see that in order to be fruitful and make a significant difference, we must stay in the place where God has set us. We are there for a reason. It is with divine direction. Our God is strategic. It is not a matter of chance. Until we understand this, we might not see the great wisdom of what God is doing.

So, let me ask you this question, "Are you in the place where God has set you?" If so, give what He has given you. If not, ask Him to direct you to your divine placement and begin to walk in your divine destiny.

AUGUST 13

GRADUATE OR PREMATURE HARVEST?

If we could settle one thing in our hearts, it would make such a difference in how we face life, build for the future, even endure suffering or hardships. God the Father has a destiny, purpose, and inheritance for Himself in Christ's people (*eklessia*)(see Ephesians 1:17-23).

Paul prayed that "the God of our Lord Jesus Christ, the Father of glory, may give you the spirit of wisdom and revelation in the knowledge of Him, the eyes of your understanding being enlightened: that you may know what is the hope of His calling, what are the riches of the glory of the inheritance in the saints, and what is the exceeding greatness of His power toward us who believe, according to the working of His mighty power which He worked in Christ when He raised Him from the dead and seated Him at His right hand in the heavenly places." Ephesians 1:17-20

At the end of earth's current history, Christ will return for His prepared bride and deliver her up to the Father for a gift and dwelling place (1 Corinthians 15:22-28; Rev. 21:3; Isa. 25:8-9). But before Christ can leave His throne to return (Psalm 110:3), the Father's purposes for the Church must first be accomplished.

One such purpose of the Father's heart is that the Church would learn to master stewardship skills ("wisdom" = skills; "instruction = discipline) on earth before we graduate to the work of the next age. We are to inherit the earth (Matt. 5:14); "occupy until He returns" (Luke 19:13); "rule in the midst of our enemies" (Psalm 110:1-3); display the light of God globally (Isa. 60:1-5), and scores of similar assignments.

To "graduate us" before we have achieved these goals would be to harvest a premature crop (Matt. 13:30). Ask yourself this important question: Has the Church fulfilled this expectation? If not, we must roll up our sleeves and get to work. Instead of putting the focus on ourselves (a man-centered gospel), let us refocus on Christ! It's time to grow up, take responsibility, in short, pick up our cross, endure hard work, and see the purposes of God unfold in the world right around us.

AUGUST 14

THE POWER OF YOUR LOVE

This is the song that keeps going on in my mind and spirit this morning. It is one of the songs we sing in worship, in fact, have so for many years off and on. Consider the introduction:

"Lord I come to You. Let my heart be changed, renewed. Flowing from Your grace that I found in You. Lord I've come to know the weaknesses I see in me will be stripped away by the power of Your love."

Another verse:

"Lord unveil my eyes. Let me see You face to face, the knowledge of Your love, as You live in me. Lord renew my mind, as Your will unfolds in my life, in living every day by the power of Your love."

The apostle Paul prayed for the Ephesian church that they would come to realize and experience Christ's love for themselves:

"For this reason I bow my knees to the father of our Lord Jesus Christ, from whom the whole family in heaven and earth is named, that He would grant you, according to the riches of His glory, to be strengthened with might through His Spirit in the inner man, that Christ may dwell in your hearts through faith; that you, being rooted and grounded in love, may be able to comprehend with all the saints what is the width and length and depth and height – to know the love of Christ which passes knowledge; that you may be filled with the fullness of God. Now to Him who is able to do exceedingly abundantly above all that we ask or think, according to the power that works in us, to Him be glory in the church by Christ Jesus to all generations, forever and ever, Amen" Ephesians 3:14-21

May the power of His love fill you, change you, renew you, and empower you for God's purpose and His glory, today and always.

AUGUST 15

FRAGRANT OIL

There is a story that has been recorded about a woman because of her worship. Breaking an alabaster flask of expensive spikenard, she poured it as an anointing over Jesus's head. Those around began to justify that she could have sold this expensive ointment and given the proceeds to the poor. But Jesus did not think so. In fact, He corrects their thinking and commends the woman for her act of worship, anointing His body prior to His impending death and burial. Let's take a look at the story:

"And being in Bethany at the house of Simon the leper, as He sat at the table, a woman came having an alabaster flask of very costly oil of spikenard. Then she broke the flask and poured it on His head. But there were some who were indignant among themselves, and said, "Why was this fragrant oil wasted? For it might have been sold for more than three hundred denarii and given to the poor." And they criticized her sharply. But Jesus said, "Let her alone. Why do you trouble her? She has done a good work for Me. For you have the poor with you always, and whenever you wish you may do them good; but Me you do not have always. She has done what she could. She has come beforehand to anoint My body for burial. Assuredly, I say to you, wherever this gospel is preached in the whole world, what this woman has done will also be told as a memorial to her." Mark 14:3-9

I wonder at what means we are willing to worship our Lord. Do we hold back, thinking some self-justifying thoughts? Do we hold in contempt those who are able to abandon themselves to worship? With what cost are we willing to bless the Lord? Are we even willing to give up our work on the Sabbath day to worship and gather together with the Assembly?

Let us consider our own forms of worship. Do we give Jesus the time and adoration He deserves? Everything we have comes from above. May we look to Him with thankful hearts and cultivate a heart of worship. He is deserving of our praise. He is worthy of our must heartfelt worship.

AUGUST 16

HOW GREAT IS THE LORD'S GRACE TOWARD US!

I am just meditating on the great grace of the Lord this morning. Oftentimes, I am overwhelmed that God would shower us with such great grace. Grace for salvation. Grace for enablement. Grace for favor with men. Grace for us to do above and beyond anything we thought was possible.

Paul writes to the Ephesians church:

"For by grace you have been saved through faith, and that not of yourselves; it is a gift of God, not of works, lest anyone should boast. For we are His workmanship, created in Christ Jesus for good works, which God prepared beforehand that we should walk in them." Ephesians 2:8-10

God has given us His grace for a purpose. When we realize this, we can begin to set our face toward Him and walk out His plan. When we do, what we experience is His great grace. How great is this grace that He has given us? Walking in this grace is a day-by-day experience. As we walk in obedience to the Lord's will for our lives, we come to understand the joy of being yoked with Him. He has designed us for what He purposed before our birth.

Coming to Him and surrendering to that design enables us to reach the mark of the upward call of God in our lives. May we all rejoice in Him today. Let His grace empower us for His work.

AUGUST 17

HE WHO CALLS YOU IS FAITHFUL...

I am reflecting on the faithfulness of God: faithful to get us through our day; faithful to have one of my friends be able to go back to work, after being out for more than a month; faithful to see us through different seasons; faithful to provide for our necessities; faithful to enlarge our ministry outreach; faithful to watch over our children and grandchildren; and faithful to work in us what is necessary so that our character reflects His own.

Paul wrote to the Thessalonians:

"Now may the God of peace Himself sanctify you completely; and may your whole spirit, soul, and body be preserved blameless at the coming of our Lord Jesus Christ. He who calls you is faithful, who also will do it." 1 Thessalonians 5:23-24

Did you catch that last part? God is not only faithful, He completes what He starts. If you are even a bit discouraged today, remind yourself about just how faithful God is. It will set your mind on a new course. You will begin to experience a new peace. Faithful is He!

Can we imagine that He who calls us is faithful. He will sanctify (set us apart) completely. He will preserve us body, soul and spirit to be blameless at His coming.

Thank you Lord, for Your great faithfulness. May we walk by faith trusting You to accomplish all that is necessary in our lives, families, work and ministry, until the Day of Christ Jesus. Amen!

AUGUST 18

CAN YOU EVEN IMAGINE?

When Paul wrote to the Corinthian church, he quoted from the book of Isaiah saying:

"Eye has not seen, nor ear heard, nor have entered into the heart of man the things which God has prepared for those who love Him." 1 Corinthians 2:9

He first was referring to those who missed the visitation of God, not realizing God's great plan. So much so, that they even crucified Christ.

Now he transitions to those who know the Lord:

"But God has revealed them to us through His Spirit. For the Spirit searches all things, yes the deep things of God." 1 Corinthians 2:10

While God has a great plan for us, it is possible for us to miss what He has planned. However, if we allow His Spirit to lead us and illuminate our ways, we will begin to see God's great plan develop in our lives. It is a plan that will exceed our expectations. We can't even imagine all He has planned for us.

As you give this some thought, it might be good to allow the Lord to begin to open up your imagination of His plan for you to a new, greater dimension. Perhaps you have limited what you think He could accomplish through you by trusting too much in your own ability, or you have not understood just how much God can do through you. Let this be a new day of revelation that God has great and greater things planned for your life. May today be the beginning of new doors of opportunity and new ways of expression of God's love and greatness through you.

AUGUST 19

LIVING WITH HOPE AND RESTING IN GRACE

Peter addresses the Christian of the dispersion. In reflecting on the great inheritance, they, and we, have been given, something we have received and angels desire to look into, he further admonishes us to a changed way of living:

"Therefore gird up the loins of your mind, be sober, and rest your hope fully upon the grace that is to be brought to you at the revelation of Jesus Christ; as obedient children, not conforming yourselves to the former lusts, as in your ignorance; but as He who called you is holy, you also be holy in all conduct." 1Peter 1:13-15

Note that we can set our hope on God's grace that is found in Jesus Christ. Having been given this great salvation, our lives should reflect outwardly what has been changed inwardly. Our conduct is expected to be transformed, as we allow the Lord to be our focus and hope. This transformation is a great witness to what the Lord is doing in our lives. It is the power of our testimony of the gospel. Without it, even if our testimony is true, our conduct will reduce the effectiveness of our witness.

The most important thing to realize is Who has called us. He is holy, and therefore, He calls us to be holy. We are to be like Father, like son (or daughter). If we keep our eyes on Him, we will become like Him.

As you pray today, ask the Lord to help you in this regard. Have Him search you and uproot anything that is contrary to His character. Let His power rest in you and rest fully in the hope and grace that He will reveal to you.

AUGUST 20

WE WILL REMEMBER THE NAME OF THE LORD...

Psalm 20 begins with a wonderful prayer for the Lord to answer, defend, send help, strengthen, and remember all our offerings. It continues to pray that our heart's desire be granted and we fulfill all our purposes. It turns to make a significant declaration of faith:

"Some trust in chariots, and some in horses; But we will remember the name of the Lord our God." Psalm 20:7

This is what gives strength to the beginning part of the prayer. We believe that God can do all that we have prayed because we have placed our trust in Him. Whenever, we have need, we can trust Him. Whatever we go through, we can trust in Him. He is the One we remember this morning. He is trustworthy.

Take some time before the Lord today. Ask Him for your specific needs; the needs of your family, the needs of your church community and the needs of your local community. Ask the Lord for the guidance that you need to make a difference in these areas. Trust that He will not only hear your prayer but also give you the answer to take specific steps. He is your strength.

CALLED TO BE A BLESSING

This morning I am concluding my Bible readings in 1 Peter. While he starts his exhortation with "finally", he isn't really finished with his letter, but concluding some previous thoughts. In summation he writes: "*Finally, all of you be of one mind, having compassion for one another, love as brothers, be tender hearted, be courteous; not returning evil for evil, or reviling for reviling, but on the contrary blessing, knowing that you were called to this, that you may inherit a blessing*" (1 Peter 3:8-9).

Just previous to this exhortation, Peter had been teaching about how we are to live before the world, work for our employers (in those days Master /slave relationship), and as husbands and wives. There is an expectation that we can be people of peace and blessing, knowing to whom we belong and serve. For God will bless His people.

Therefore, our actions are a result of a deep abiding peace that trusts in God's ability to make things right. So much so, that we do not have to always react to negative sayings and actions in like manner, but instead pronounce blessing to those who might be in opposition to us. It is so good not to have to keep a score card, or live life trying to get even. Instead, we love the Lord, trust Him, and as a result love and bless others.

May we use our day, and days, to be such a blessing to those we encounter. And even more particularly, may we be a blessing in our own homes, places of business, and to all we encounter.

"He who would love life and see good days, let him refrain his tongue from evil, and his lips from speaking deceit. Let him seek peace and pursue it. For the eyes of the Lord are on the righteous, and His ears are open to their prayers; but The face of the Lord is against those who do evil." 1 Peter 3:10-12

AUGUST 22

WORSHIP THAT GOD NOTICES

There are so many that try and get God's attention with many words, flashy actions, and loud noises. Others are trying to get His attention by what they do for Him. But what is it that really gets God's attention?

Isaiah writes:

"Heaven is My throne, and earth is My footstool. Where is the house that you will build for Me? And where is the place of My rest? For all those things My hand has made, and all those things exist," says the Lord. "But on this one will I look: on him who is poor and of a contrite spirit, and who tremble at My word." Isaiah 66:1-2

Everything that exists is already the Lord's. What can we in effect really give to Him? He does not seek to dwell in houses that we construct, even though it might be a proper thing to do. What He is looking for are humble people, who seek to honor Him by living according to His word.

This is true worship. We are to be His dwelling place. Can you imagine that? When we walk humbly, do justly and love mercy, God takes notice of us (see Micah 6:8). He puts His gaze on us. He abides in us. It doesn't get any better than that. There is nothing more valuable we could have.

Thank you Lord for setting Your eyes on us. Fill us afresh with Your mighty presence. You alone are worthy.

AUGUST 23

BIBLICAL SHEPHERDING

This morning's readings began in Psalm 23 and ended in 1 Peter 5. In the first reading David declares the Lord as his Shepherd; therefore, he has no want. In this last reading, Peter is exhorting the elders to shepherd as Christ would have us do.

"The elders who are among you I exhort, I who am a fellow elder and a witness of the sufferings of Christ, and also a partaker of the glory that will be revealed: Shepherd the flock of God which is among you, serving as overseers, not by compulsion but willingly, not for dishonest gain but eagerly; nor as being lords over those entrusted to you, but be examples to the flock; and when the Chief Shepherd appears, you will receive the crown of glory that does not fade away." 1 Peter 5:1-4

I have been blessed to serve with godly, humble men through the years, who love the Lord and have served Him and His people with all their strength. One such elder is celebrating his birthday today. Happy Birthday Pastor Adelson Nalini Junior! You have been a faithful servant, one who can be counted on by the people of the Lord. We are glad that you are serving with us. Your sacrifices have been many, but the Lord sees your faithfulness and will reward you with His glory.

May you and all of us who are called to shepherd God's people continue to trust Him, and allow Him to lead us in paths of righteousness for His name sake!

Perhaps take a moment and pray for your pastor and leaders today. Send them a note of encouragement for the responsibility that they carry. We can all be part of building up one another.

AUGUST 24

800TH DEVOTIONAL ENTRY

I was one of those who resisted using social media, thinking that for most people it was a distraction. But the more that I thought about this, I realized that this media could be used for positive influence and even edification if used properly.

In my own morning devotions, I began to write a small thought of the day in reflection to what I had read, or what impressed me during prayer. Keeping this in a digital notebook, I began to clip and paste this onto my Facebook page each day. It has now been more than two years that I have consistently done this, and it has built in me a habit that has enriched my own devotional time.

Today (August 24, 2015) marks the 800th entry into my notebook. I have not been concerned with just any happenings of the day, but just how in those happenings a truth can be exposed and held onto for hope and strength. Peter wrote:

"All flesh is grass, and all the glory of man as the flower of the grass. The grass withers, and its flower falls away, but the word of the Lord endures forever." 1 Peter 1:24-25

This has been my passion, sharing the Word of the Lord. It is His Word that is enduring. It is His Word that gives us strength in the seasons of our lives. I pray that if you have read some, or many, of these posts in the past few years or are reading this devotional book now, that you have been encouraged to deepen your trust in Jesus and His word. He will sustain you and strengthen you for the journey He has purposed for your life. He is worthy to be praised. Be most blessed.

AUGUST 25

FOR THIS REASON...

There was a great concern in the apostles of Jesus for truth to continue in each generation. Even when they were facing their own last days, they seemed to voice with greater conviction the need to have their own words, the words that they received and heard from Jesus, be received and remembered by those who would follow them. This was an inheritance that they would leave; one that would continue to bring strength, growth, and fruitfulness to those who would adhere to this truth.

The Apostle Peter wrote:

"For this reason I will not be negligent to remind you always of these things, though you know and are established in the present truth. Yes, I think it is right, as long as I am in this tent, to stir you up reminding you, knowing that shortly I must put off my tent, just as our Lord Jesus Christ showed me. Moreover I will be careful to ensure that you always have a reminder of these things after my decease." 2 Peter 1:12-15

In these verses Peter finishes by saying he will be careful to ensure that they would always have a reminder of what he is speaking after he is gone. We have been given such a gift in the writings of the apostles, which ensure that we have their thoughts and teachings continue with us to this day. As we continue in our own lives, what ways can we ensure that what we believe can be passed down and bring remembrance to those who follow us?

Our lives will be part of that testimony, but can we also practice putting our thoughts in writing? In doing so, we do not only communicate for the moment, but we also preserve for future generations truths that may help in their growth and fruitfulness. In our day we have so much more at our disposal to do something positive for future generations. Is it a concern for us like it was for founding apostles of our faith? I hope that I have given you something to consider, and the reason to do so.

AUGUST 26

LIVING FOR THE WILL OF GOD

There are many who think that Christianity is something that is easy, burden less and stress free. While we do walk in a wonderful victory, there is an identification with our Lord that we must also understand. When Peter wrote to those he was trying to instruct and encourage, he exhorted them to have a right mind about these things.

"Therefore, since Christ suffered for us in the flesh, arm yourselves also with the same mind, for he who has suffered in the flesh has ceased from sin, that he no longer should live the rest of his time in the flesh for the lusts of men, but for the will of God." 1 Peter 4:1-2

It was through Christ's sufferings that once and for all our sins were dealt with. We were brought near to God, death to our flesh was accomplished so that we might be made alive by the Spirit. We now live in sobering times. We are called to glorify God through our identity with Him. That means that others will reproach the name of the Lord, but the Spirit of glory and of God is upon us. Therefore, Peter gives us further instruction:

"Beloved, do not think it strange concerning the fiery trial which is to try you, as though some strange thing happens to you; but rejoice to the extent that you partake of Christ's sufferings, that when His glory is revealed, you may also be glad with exceeding joy." 1 Peter 4:12-13

I am glad that when I trusted in Christ, that trust was not partial. He is faithful to free us from sin, but He is also faithful to strengthen us in trials. The same Lord who calls us to Himself is present to clothe us with His mind and strengthen us with His Spirit. As we submit to His plan for our lives, He will shape us for His glory. The result will be a great joy in our hearts as we see His life being exemplified in us. There is nothing more rewarding than living for the will of God.

AUGUST 27

HIDDEN, SET AND LIFTED

Whenever we face certain obstacles and hindrances in our lives we need courage and proper perspective. We can find our strength in God, Who is able to show us the way, deliver us and give us the confidence we need to persevere. The psalmist expresses a great declaration of faith even in the midst of the reality of life. His focus and desire is in His Lord. Let's look at the expression of his heart:

"One thing I have desired of the Lord, that I will seek; that I may dwell in the house of the Lord all the days of my life, to behold the beauty of the Lord, and to inquire in His temple. For in the time of trouble He shall hide me in His pavilion; in the secret place of His tabernacle He shall hide me; He shall set me high upon a rock. And now my head shall be lifted up above my enemies all around me; therefore I will offer sacrifices of joy in His tabernacle; I will sing, yes, I will sing praises to the Lord." Psalm 27:4-6

Note that he is not just seeking the Lord in the day of trouble but is dwelling in the Lord daily as a lifelong pursuit. As a result of this kind of relationship, he has the faith to believe that God will help in times of trouble. He hides us in the secret place. He sets us high on a rock and lifts our head above our enemies. There we are established, unmoved, given a better perspective above our enemies. His care and protection encourage us to reorder our walk and strengthen our fight. Not only that, our spirit rejoices and praise becomes our testimony.

Knowing this is enough of a reason to get up and get going today. We do not need to be afraid. Lift up your head. Seek the Lord. He will hide you, set you, and lift you up.

AUGUST 28

WE HAVE A GREAT INHERITANCE!

This morning, I am looking at all the great exhortations and encouragements in Psalm 37. There are many comparisons between the righteous and the evildoers. We should not be envious or fret because of the existence of these evildoers. The Lord promises that "*the meek shall inherit the earth, and shall delight themselves in the abundance of peace*" (v. 11). "*The Lord upholds the righteous*" (v. 17). His "*steps are ordered by the Lord, and He delights in his way*" (v. 23).

So what are we called to do in light of these promises?

"Trust in the Lord, and do good; dwell in the land, and feed on His faithfulness, Delight yourself also in the Lord, and He shall give you the desires of your heart. Commit your way to the Lord, Trust also in Him, and He shall bring it to pass. He shall bring forth your righteousness as the light, and justice as the noonday. Rest in the Lord, and wait patiently for Him." Psalm 37:3-7

Repeatedly in these versus the psalmist reminds us that the wicked will be cut off and will be no more, but those who wait on the Lord, they shall inherit the earth. The righteous "*shall not be ashamed in the evil time, and in the days of famine they shall be satisfied*" (Psalm 37:19).

In light of all the negative things people put into our minds and hearts about the times we live in, isn't it a blessing to look at the reality of God's Word and find the promises that He has given? I, for one, have put my trust in Him and will continue to delight in the Lord, committing my way to His way and then simply resting and waiting patiently for Him. Will you join me?

AUGUST 29

BORN BEFORE HER TIME

Five years ago (August 29, 2010), my wife and I were praying in Woman and Infant's Hospital. My daughter had been admitted for almost two weeks. Her pregnancy had not come to full term, but for this child, it was complete. It was her time. Ready or not she was bursting forth into this world. She was ready to come and meet all of us almost three months premature. By God's grace she did. Only two pounds at birth, she continued to develop and get stronger and stronger, gaining the weight and functionality necessary to be able to be released by Thanksgiving.

She has continued to make us give thanks. Her personality, caring nature, and joyful countenance have given us so much joy these five years. Her love for music and dance comes naturally. She comes out with sayings that can astound us and make us give pause to wonder just how inspired her thoughts and words are. It is evident that God is at work, and in Him, we will trust.

This child, Mackenzie, our granddaughter, and all of her family and friends will celebrate her fifth birthday today. Five years ago, I was overwhelmed by the grace of God for giving her a healthy birth. Today, I am still overwhelmed by the grace of God for being our strength and the cohesiveness of our love for each other all these years.

Mackenzie, may the Lord keep His hand on your life to protect, guide, enrich, and instruct you in His ways and His plan for you. May He impart and train you in the gifts He has already designed for you to be a fruitful servant and powerful witness. May His joy ever be your strength and may you be a joy to the many you will encounter throughout your life. We love you. Happy Birthday from Memere and Pepere.

"Before I formed you in the womb I knew you; before you were born I sanctified you; I ordained you a prophet to the nations." Jeremiah 1:5

AUGUST 30

IF ONLY OUR EYES WERE OPENED

Paul prays a great prayer for the Ephesians. He realized that unless God gave this revelation, those Paul were leading would go about business as usual, but lack the hope and power needed to make a difference. Paul prayed:

"That the God of our Lord Jesus Christ, the Father of glory, may give to you the spirit of wisdom and revelation in the knowledge of Him, the eyes of your understanding being enlightened; that you may know the hope of His calling, what are the riches of the glory of His inheritance in the Saints, and what is the exceeding greatness of His power toward us who believe." Ephesians 1:18-19

This prayer is still so relevant for the church. So many do not realize who they are in Christ, nor do they realize the great inheritance that awaits them. Instead, they have been seduced to short-term, feel-good type of teachings that make them walk impotent and struggling to have any voice for those around to even take notice.

Can you imagine what could take place in a body of believers that began to believe just what God has done, and will do, in and through them? Knowing they have been empowered and seated in heavenly places, and that their inheritance is secure, they can lead from a position of security and confidence. Knowing that any difficulty or seeming set-back is momentary. For we are victors and will persevere and inherit the promises already secured for us.

Having this hope, which is greater than any fear, we embrace our calling and walk in the power already ascribed to us. Power, influence, and confidence all come from a strong sense of identity. We drift when we lose sight of why God left us on earth. Our goal is to participate in God's redemptive plan for the world. If we embrace purpose, we gain power. May He give us the spirit of wisdom and revelation in the knowledge of Him, so that we accomplish His great purpose for our generation.

AUGUST 31

FINDING TRUE REST

It's Monday again. Today's Monday is the last of the month of August. It seems like everyone is either just getting back from a vacation or trying to get one more in before the fall season approaches. Throughout the years I have heard some say, "I really need a vacation." Usually they say this because they are either exhausted or needing something that changes the routine of life. Oftentimes, what they then do on vacation makes them even more tired and not refreshed at all, needing a vacation following their vacation. Does this sound familiar to you?

What I have found that has helped me is the natural rhythms of life. In each day, I can set time aside for quiet contemplation, reading, prayer and reflection on lessons that the Bible and life teach me. Then, on a weekly basis is the day of rest (Sabbath) where I cease from my work and devote time to worship and the gathering of the saints. It is the reset button that provides the rest needed to continue on. It's no wonder that it has been given to us as an exhortation:

"And let us consider one another in order to stir up love and good works, not forsaking the assembling of ourselves together, as is the manner of some, but exhorting one another, and so much the more as you see the Day approaching." Hebrews 10:24-25

True rest can be found in the Lord and following His ways. It is wonderful when we do get the opportunities to have these special times of vacations. But, we don't need to get overly anxious if we don't always get that opportunity.

There is a rest for the people of God (see Hebrews 3 & 4). We can enter it by faith. Because of all our Lord has done for us, we can rest in Him. Try this out for yourself and see if you might find a greater refreshing for yourself.

SEPTEMBER 1

TIME TO SING - TIME TO WORK - TIME TO GROW

I was quickened to go to Isaiah's writing in chapter 54 this morning. He prophesied about God's perpetual covenant of peace to His people. He calls them to sing and break forth into singing because of what the Lord will do. I want to particularly look at verses 2 & 3. The instruction is as important for us today as it was for Israel when these words were written.

"Enlarge the place of your tent, and let them stretch out the curtains of your dwellings; Do not spare; Lengthen your cords, and strengthen your stakes. For you shall expand to the right and to the left. And your descendants will inherit nations." Isaiah 54:2-3

Can you get a vision of what God wants to do through us, even through successive generations? Look at the descriptive work that is involved:

- Enlarge the place of your tent;
- Stretch out the curtains of your dwellings;
- Lengthen your cords, strengthen your stakes.

We have to enlarge our territory, stretch out our influence and authority, build proper relationships and network, and finally drive down and teach the principles that are non-negotiable truths and hold on to them.

The promise is for generations to come. Can you envision your descendants inheriting nations? If you can, then you must build today for this to be possible for future generations. This is God's vision for us. Get it in your spirit. Declare it to each other. It is time to sing, to work, and to grow.

SEPTEMBER 2

SCHOOL BELLS ARE RINGING!

Over the past week I have seen many posts about children and adults that are returning to school for another year of challenge and growth. Our church school East Gate Christian Academy starts today. It is the first time that I can remember in the past 20 years that the start date had preceded Labor Day. However, because of the lateness of this holiday in September, it seems that many other schools have also got a jump ahead. With the winter we had last year and the Farmer's Almanac's prediction, we are more prudent to get going.

It is a blessing to begin our 21st year as a school. We are ever aware that God's favor and empowerment have kept us all these years. We look forward to engaging with the students and families of our students according to the basic principles of Christian Education. We hope that each will grow and be transformed in a safe environment. We pray for strength and health for our teachers and administrators as they dutifully perform their roles and responsibilities. We also pray for each parent and guardian that the Lord will bless you with every spiritual blessing and also provision for your family.

Welcome to this new school year. May the Lord be glorified in all that is done.

"Train up a child in the way he should go, and when he is old he will not depart from it." Proverbs 22:6

SEPTEMBER 3

EVERY TONGUE SHALL CONFESS...

What causes kings to speak of another kingdom? What makes people take notice of the living God? Reading a text from Daniel this morning reaffirms the faithfulness of God to His servants. We perhaps have all heard the story of Daniel and the lion's den through our Sunday School experiences. But have we considered what the outcome is when people who are faithful to God and are put to the test can accomplish in those who are conspiring, or might just be looking from the outside? God's deliverance of Daniel caused King Darius to send out this decree to all his people and beyond:

"To all people's, nations, and languages that dwell in all the earth: Peace be multiplied to you. I make a decree that in every dominion of my kingdom men must tremble and fear before the God of Daniel. For He is the living God, and steadfast forever; His kingdom is the one which shall not be destroyed, and His dominion shall endure to the end. He delivers and rescues, and He works signs and wonders in heaven and on earth, Who has delivered Daniel from the power of the lions." Daniel 6:25-27

Just give this some consideration the next time you go through a trial. Trusting God for the outcome will mean more than deliverance for you. It may mean the salvation for those who are watching. What they see demonstrated through you will say volumes about how you trust the Lord for yourself. Your testimony will verify your faith, one way or another.

SEPTEMBER 4

THE RIGHTEOUS SHALL FLOURISH LIKE A PALM TREE...

My wife loves palm trees. She can't get enough of their beauty. Unfortunately, we do not live in a climate where they flourish. However, when we have traveled in the southern states, or in Africa and Israel, they are in abundance. While we can't grow palm trees in our climate, my wife decorates with pictures, glassware, even clothes with palm trees to remind her of their beauty and climate.

The psalmist compares these trees to righteous people. Sometimes we might be tempted to think that righteous people don't flourish much in our climate either. However, that can be different. The psalmist declares:

"The righteous shall flourish like a palm tree. He shall grow like a cedar in Lebanon. Those who are planted in the house of the Lord shall flourish in the courts of our God. They shall bear fruit in old age; they shall be fresh and flourishing, to declare that the Lord is upright; He is my rock, and there is no unrighteousness in Him." Psalm 92:12-15

We need to have this vision: palm trees flourishing in the courts of the Lord; righteous people, who are planted and producing fruit. They are not just existing, but flourishing. May the Lord cause us to be planted, established, and flourishing in His courts, even in our old age.

SEPTEMBER 5

WHEN OVERWHELMED YOU CAN FIND ASSURANCE AND PROTECTION

This past evening my sleep was tentative. Getting up a few times gave me opportunity to pray for individuals that are in need of God's intervention in their lives. One woman just lost her mother, another is still struggling with the grief of losing a loved one. There are those who are battling sicknesses and diseases. Others who need direction, and still others who are recovering from past surgeries. Some badly need deliverance from controlling substances and habits, and others who just want to continue to grow in their love and service to the Lord.

The psalmist prays a prayer that gives us hope and can serve as a model in our own prayer times. He cries out:

"Hear my cry, O God; Attend to my prayer. From the end of the earth, I will cry to You. When my heart is overwhelmed; Lead me to the rock that is higher than I. For You have been a shelter for me, a strong tower from the enemy. I will abide in Your tabernacle forever; I will trust in the shelter of Your wings." Psalm 61:1-4

Today, if you are overwhelmed by your own burden, or if you are carrying someone else's burden, you can turn to the Lord and find relief. He can be trusted to hear your prayer and act accordingly. He will give you the secure footage you need. He will provide you with a safe place where you are protected. Trusting Him will give you great peace and comfort.

May your burdens be lightened as you find that secret place under the Lord's shadow. Be most blessed.

SEPTEMBER 6

JUST A COUPLE OF QUESTIONS TO PONDER!

God has called us for an important work in our generation. In order to be able to fulfill this calling, it is important for us to deal with a couple of questions:

1. What is the task (or tasks) that we have to still complete to fulfill our calling and purpose in our generation?

2. What giants need to be slain in order for us to progress and insure that another generation does not need to fight this battle over again?

If we can answer these questions, we will have great direction and foresight and know what warfare must be engaged. We can walk in victory! If we leave these things undone, we will walk in general weakness. The choice is ours. What will we choose?

For the Apostle Paul, he chose to move forward:

"Not that I have already attained, or am already perfected; but I press on, that I may lay hold of that which Christ Jesus has also laid hold of me. Brethren, I do not count myself to have apprehended; but one thing I do, forgetting those things which are behind and reaching forward those things which are ahead, I press toward the goal for the prize of the upward call of God in Christ Jesus." Philippians 3:12-14

May we press on, ever reaching to grasp what Jesus has already grasped for us.

WORK IS SOMETHING THAT IS HONORABLE AND GLORIOUS

Today in America many of us are celebrating Labor Day. We are thankful for the ability to be able to work and ironically rejoice in this fact by taking a day off work to celebrate it. For me, work is an expression of who I am and allows for a creative outworking of the abilities that God has given me. Beyond the fact that in our work our families are provided for, we also are able to do things that allow others to be blessed as well.

The psalmist expresses this thinking about God's work:

"The works of the Lord are great. Studied by all who have pleasure in them. His work is honorable and glorious, and His righteousness endures forever. He has made His wonderful works to be remembered; the Lord is gracious and full of compassion. He has given food to those who fear Him; He will ever be mindful of His covenant. He declared to His people the power of His works, in giving them the heritage of the nations." Psalm 111:2-6

If we can view our work in light of God's work, we might not look at work in the same light. Instead of thinking of the toil of it, may we begin to understand our work as a heritage that we are building to be remembered and a blessing to those whom we serve.

May we also see in our work an opportunity to be creative as our Lord is. We have the great ability to steward what has been given to us and bring about increase. May we follow our Father's work ethic and produce works of righteousness that will endure testing and reap eternal rewards.

SEPTEMBER 8

EVERY NEW SEASON

With the start of school, the season begins to change. Some of us might be excited about this and others not ready for a new season. In life we all go through seasons. In New England, where I live, we experience the variety of four seasons. Each has their own beauty and challenge.

It is comforting to know that God created the seasons. We must discern what God wants to do through our experience in these seasons or in the coming seasons that He has for us.

Here is a thought that we can ponder: what is this season of my life? What does God want to do in me, and through me, because of the experiences I will encounter? How might He be purposing to change me through this season? How might I be able to know Him in a more intimate way through the experience of this season?

Here is a reminder for us, no matter what kind of season we might be experiencing:

"And we know that all things work together for good to those who love God, to those who are called according to His purpose." Romans 8:28

Let's trust the Lord to shape us for His glory in the seasons of our life. Even in our present season, may His grace be sufficient and His love abounding.

"To everything there is a season, a time for every purpose under heaven." Ecclesiastes 3:1

Yes, God has a purpose for us in this season. May we bless Him, learn contentment, and find rest in each season of our lives.

SEPTEMBER 9

CLEANSING POTS TO CELEBRATION POTS!

Of all the miracles that Jesus could have performed, it is interesting the first one that He did perform, changing water to wine (see John 2:1-11). John records it as the first sign of seven that he writes about, although he says that, "*Jesus did many other signs in the presence of His disciples, which are not written in this book; but these are written that you may believe that Jesus is the Christ, the Son of God, and that believing you may have life in His name*" (John 20:30-31).

Here is the key to signs - they point to who Jesus is! He is the Bread of Life, the Living Water. He is our healer, deliverer, sustainer of life. He is above nature and can change circumstances. This first sign shows us something about His life. While we come to Jesus through faith and receiving His forgiveness for our sins, He calls us to walk in freedom and enjoy life.

What a contrast this was to the religious leaders of His day, and might I say the same is true today. Their yoke was, and is, hard, but Jesus's yoke is easy and His burden is light (see Matthew 28:30).

Jesus took the water in ceremonial cleansing pots and turned it into wine. When we receive His cleansing, it is time for rejoicing. This first miracle tells us something of why Jesus came: to exchange mourning into joy. It's time to get up and dance. Let us rejoice in Him!

"Come to Me, all you who labor and are heavy laden, and I will give you rest. Take My yoke upon you and learn from Me, for I am gentle and lowly in heart, and you will find rest for your souls. For My yoke is easy and my burden is light." Matthew 11:28-30

SEPTEMBER 10

THANKFUL FOR THE IN-BETWEENS!

We have had such nice weather for a long stretch. Today, I was to begin a project that I was looking forward to tackling. On top of that, today was the day that I could get some help to mix cement which needed to get accomplished. But the forecast was rain. The morning confirmed the forecast. But there seemed to be a possibility that while the showers would come, there might be some let up in-between the showers.

Here is where the great contemplations take place. Work in-between, or don't work?

"The lazy man says, 'There is a lion in the road! A fierce lion is in the streets!" Proverbs 26:13

For me the lion in the street was the rain. However, by God's grace and some determined help, what needed to get done, did get done. The so-called lion did not stop us. The day was not wasted. Progress was continued.

Sometimes when I talk to people they say that they lack the time to get something done. Could it be that they do not take advantage of the in-between times of life? We are to be good stewards of our time. I believe that includes those in-between times.

Thank you Lord for all the moments that You give us. Tonight, as I reflect, I am satisfied with the windows of opportunity You allowed.

SEPTEMBER 11

THIS DATE HAS SIGNIFICANCE FOR ME.

While many will remember the grave happenings of September 11, 2001 and rightfully so, I have memories of September 11 that precede that date. They go back to September 11, 1977. That is the day that I met the woman that was destined to be my wife. I know you will need to use a calculator, but let me do the math for you, that was 38 years ago. In a couple of weeks (September 29, 2015) we will celebrate our 36th wedding anniversary.

As I look back on that day, I can only give thanks to an Almighty God, who orders the path of His saints. The Bible says:

"He who finds a wife finds a good thing, and obtains favor from the Lord." Proverbs 18:22

I can testify that this scripture is true. Not only did I find her, I believe that the Lord prepared her just for me. She is the Lord's favor given to share and be a suitable companion to me for life.

How can I express my gratefulness to the Lord, except to simply say: "Thank you Lord for Your great favor. You are the One who deserves all glory and praise."

If you are married, perhaps you could take a moment and pray for your spouse. Give God thanks for His gift to you. Ask Him to bless your spouse and help you show appreciation to your spouse.

If you are not married, pray for couples that you know that the Lord would strengthen their marriage, help them to appreciate each other and commit their marriages to the Lord's care and help.

SEPTEMBER 12

STRENGTHEN ONE ANOTHER

The past few days, I have been building a ramp for a gentleman in our church. He has been such an encouragement and strength to so many over the years. He is a great example of an older man who is "*sober, reverent, temperate, sound in faith, in love [and] in patience*" (Titus 2:2). He has quietly been gracious to many who have been in need. He always wears a smile. Even in his own health struggles, he has minimized them in his testimony and shown such perseverance in the midst of trials.

Seeing him look out his door and interact or smile while working there has been such a joy for me. To know that he will be helped, and that this project will be useful to him and his family, makes the work more special.

Paul instructed Titus saying:

"This is a faithful saying, and these things I want you to affirm constantly, that those who have believed in God should be careful to maintain good works. These things are good and profitable to men." Titus 3:8

Like this older gentleman, we, too, are called to do good works for others. It is profitable to those we serve. It is also profitable to those who witness our serving. May the Lord cause us to abound in love and good works.

THOUGHTS TO PONDER FROM TODAY'S MESSAGE

While the man with a withered hand was healed (Luke 6:6-11), the others were filled with rage. What is it about moving in God that gets some people unglued?

"So the scribes and Pharisees watched [Jesus] closely, whether He would heal on the Sabbath, that they might find an accusation against Him. But He knew their thoughts, and said to the man who had the withered hand, 'Arise and stand here.' And he arose and stood. Then Jesus said to them, 'I will ask you one thing: Is it lawful on the Sabbath to do good or to do evil, to save life or to destroy?' And when He had looked around at them all, He said to the man, 'stretch our your hand.' And he did so, and his hand was restored as whole as the other. But they were filled with rage, and discussed with one another what they might do to Jesus." Luke 6:7-11

Can you believe that this is the response to God working in a synagogue - the very place that God's presence should be? Why would those who walked and talked with this man not rejoice in his new-found freedom?

There seems to be two different things at work here:

1. The first is that God is calling us to step forward, stretch forth, and be restored.

2. The second thing that is noticeable is the power of the religious crowd to intimidate the others from doing the same.

Will we trust God fully and be willing to stand out to make a difference? Or, will we shrink back and settle into the religious conformity of impotency and regret? The choice is ours!

SEPTEMBER 14

RESPONDING TO THE LORD'S CALL TO STRETCH FORTH

God wants to express His authority through you and I. He is able to restore and redeem us from failure and fatigue to fruitfulness. We need to make a genuine decision to move out of the limitations of our lives.

The world around us might be saying, "Pull back, hide, give up and retreat." But God is telling us, "Step forward in the midst of your situation." It is time to rise up and move forward. Begin to reach for what the Lord directs you towards.

"Then the Lord said to Joshua, 'stretch out the spear that is in your hand toward Ai, for I will give it into your hand." Joshua 8:18

"[Moses] lift up your rod, and stretch out your hand over the sea and divide it. And the children of Israel shall go on dry ground through the midst of the sea." Exodus 14:16

"Stretch out your hand." Luke 6:10

The Apostle Paul said: "Not that I have already attained, or am already perfected, but I press on, that I may lay hold of that for which Christ Jesus has also laid hold of me." Philippians 3:12

Keep stretching. Make it a lifelong pursuit and habit. Trust God and see what a difference you can make with His power in your life.

Have the very best Monday!

SEPTEMBER 15

PRAYING FOR HIS FAVOR!

Today, I hope to be able to finish a project that I have been working on. However, I am well aware that I need the favor of God to do so. Therefore, I pray for His favor in all that must be accomplished, the circumstances that may be faced, and the things that are beyond my control.

We all go through seasons in our lives, even seasons of discipline. Yet, the psalmist puts our life in perspective when he declares:

"For His anger is but for a moment, His favor is for life; Weeping may endure for a night, but joy comes in the morning." Psalm 30:5

This is something that we must hold on to. His favor is for life. Everything else is small in comparison to His favor. Another word that could be used is the word "grace." His grace for us is His unmerited favor. The Apostle Paul made this clear when writing to the Ephesians:

"For by grace you have been saved through faith, and that not of yourselves: it is the gift of God, not of works, lest anyone should boast. For we are His workmanship created in Christ Jesus for good works, which God prepared beforehand that we should walk in them." Ephesians 2:8-10

Let that sink in for a while. He has favor for you and I. His grace has also been poured out in our lives. He has destined us for specific works. May we walk and experience God's grace and favor today and everyday as we do the works He has prepared us for.

SEPTEMBER 16

"WHO THEN IS THAT FAITHFUL AND WISE STEWARD...

Whom his master will make ruler over his household, to give them their portion of food in due season?" Luke 12:42

This is a question that Jesus asks, but He is going to follow it up with an answer. Peter had just asked Jesus a question in relation to the previous story describing faithful servants. Peter's question was:

"Lord, do You speak this parable only to us, or to all people?" Luke 12:41

Jesus follows up His own question with this answer:

"Blessed is that servant whom his master will find so doing when he comes. Truly, I say to you that he will make him ruler over all that he has." Luke 12:43-44

In the first parable, Jesus taught about servants being watchful, waiting, and ready to serve their master. It didn't matter what time of day or night, they were ready to serve. In the second parable, He again states that even if there is a delay in the coming of the master, the servant is always working, waiting, and watchful. Because of the servants responsibility, the master will have a certain expectation of him. Even if he comes unexpectantly

Are we behaving like wise and faithful servants? Have we been watchful and productive, ever serving and building up with the resources entrusted into our care? We have been given a great privilege of being servants of the Lord. May we be found faithful with the responsibilities assigned to us. Our promotion is dependent on faithfulness.

SEPTEMBER 17

AMBASSADORS FOR CHRIST

Last night in our Bible study we were discussing the need for integrity in being faithful witnesses for Christ. Those around us are watching to see if what we say matches up with what we do. Paul told the Corinthians:

"We are ambassadors for Christ, as though God were pleading through us; we implore you on Christ's behalf, be reconciled to God." 2 Corinthians 5:20

But in order to understand what it means to be an ambassador, or what will authenticate that role, we have to go back a few verses.

Christ has done something to enable us. We also must do something to testify of Him. Paul wrote:

"For the love of Christ compels us, because we judge thus: that if One died for all, then all died, and He died for all, that those who live should no longer live for themselves, but for Him who died for them and rose again." 2 Corinthians 5:14-15

It is through what Christ has done for us, that we are empowered to testify of Him. Our allegiance is to Him. Our strength comes from Him. The transformation in our lives is because of Him. May we allow His Word to shape us as we adhere to His principles. Then, and only then, will we walk in integrity and be powerful witnesses in our communities.

SEPTEMBER 18

ANOTHER SPECIAL DATE

Today marks my wife Bernice's birthday. I have been so privileged to share so many years with this woman. Her quiet spirit and dutiful service are among some of her greatest qualities. Her love for her family and friends is seen in her expressions of care and encouragement that she continues to bring. She is not one to seek any fanfare, or to bring attention to herself. But her very presence brings strength and blessings to all who are near.

She has been such a blessing to our children, grandchildren, extended family, and many who have had the privilege of being taught by her. She has always been ready to walk with me in whatever the Lord has called us to do together.

I could not have fashioned a more suitable wife and companion if I had tried to make up some lists long ago. My mom says that Bernice's birthday follows mine by nine months and four days, because after I was born, the Lord gave thought and fashioned a woman just for me. I think she is right. He did bless me with someone whom He fashioned. So on this birthday, I first must thank the Lord for such a great gift to me personally and to so many others.

"She watches over the ways of her household, and does not eat the bread of idleness. Her children rise up and call her blessed; her husband also, and he praises her: 'Many daughters have done well, but you excel them all.' Charm is deceitful and beauty is passing, but a woman who fears the Lord, she shall be praised." Proverbs 31:27-30

Bernice, may you have a very special day. Happy Birthday! May the Lord continue to give you great health, strength and favor for His great purpose in your life!

SEPTEMBER 19

ON BUILDING WALLS AND PEOPLE

Tomorrow, I am planning on beginning a new series in our church. Twenty years ago, we visited this topic and it was so relevant to where we were as a new church. I believe that it is just as relevant as we remind our founding generation and teach our second generation of leaders to build for a third generation and beyond.

When you think of building walls and people there is a similarity: one you build with mortar and stone (material things); the other with intangible things (spiritual and motivational). Those doing the building seek permanence, protection and performance. How you go about building and the materials you use will largely determine the durability of what you are building.

A reference in the Old Testament book of Deuteronomy comes to mind and applies here:

"When you build a new house, you must place a guard-rail (wall) around your roof. Do not allow a dangerous situation to remain in your house, since someone can fall from an unenclosed roof and you bring the guilt of bloodshed on your house." Deuteronomy 22:8

In mid-eastern countries the roof was a place of retirement, relaxation, and communion - much like our patios of today. At times it served as a parlor, sometimes as a study, and at other times a place of entertaining visitors. If there was no protecting wall around this favored place of meeting, it could turn into a place of danger instead of a place of friendship. The man of the house - the leader - was commanded to make sure that wall of safety was adequate and secure.

To build spiritually, you need leadership, building principles, and a willingness or determined focus to see it accomplished. I hope you will be a part of this great work. We need to build walls and people. You can make a difference in closing in the gaps, building the walls, and seeing a people restored. Can I count on you to participate?

SEPTEMBER 20

EXCERPT FROM TODAY'S MESSAGE AT MASTER BUILDER MINISTRIES "ON BUILDING WALLS AND PEOPLE"

Leadership entails an ability to bring out the best in people in whatever work or ministry they may be involved in - an ability that seems to be an attitude more than a skill learned."

"To be a person who 'sees the big picture' is not a leader unless that person has a corresponding ability to move the followers to accept, achieve, and accomplish that vision."

One Christmas morning after our children had opened their gifts, I was moved to retreat into my room and pray. That proved to be a special time for me. I grabbed my notebook and wrote down what I had sensed the Lord speak to my Spirit. Part of the message was that He had called me, like Nehemiah, to a work that He had purposed. I had been a builder and was accustomed to working with certain materials, but the Lord was now calling me to build with people. That time of prayer began to shape what He would do in my life in the coming months prior to launching out in faith and beginning Master Builder Ministries in 1995.

When you think of building walls and people there is a similarity: one you build with mortar and stone – material things; the other – intangible things – spiritual and motivational. Those doing the building seek permanence, protection, and performance. How you go about building and the materials you use will largely determine the durability of what you are building. To build correctly requires physical oversight and a coordination of materials and people. To build spiritually, you need leadership, leadership principles, and a willingness or determined focus to see it accomplished.

Perhaps God is calling you to lead. By His grace you can!

SEPTEMBER 21

WHEN LOST IS FOUND...

This morning my readings included Luke 15. Here, Jesus tells three parables. The main idea in each is the joy that accompanies repentance, the turning from being lost to being found in God; once going our own way, now trusting in Him. Accompanying this transformation there is joy, joy for those who were praying, searching, waiting, hoping and believing.

"I say to you that likewise there will be more joy in heaven over one sinner who repents than over ninety-nine just persons who need no repentance." Luke 15:7

"And when she has found it [a lost coin], she calls her neighbors and friends together, saying, 'Rejoice with me, for I have found the piece which I lost!' Likewise, I say to you, there is joy in the presence of the angels of God over one sinner who repents." Luke 15:9-10

"It is right that we should make merry and be glad, for your brother was dead and is alive again, and was lost and is found." Luke 15:32

Jesus tells us that it is only right to celebrate and be glad, for the former condition was dead and lost, but the present condition is alive and found. As a pastor it has brought me so much joy to see people who were going down a wrong path in life be enlightened, equipped, and encouraged to turn their life around because of what Jesus has done for them. To see thoughts change and responsibility emerge, softness of heart and humility demonstrated, and a willingness to follow the path outlined in God's Word, brings such joy to those who walk along the side of them.

I am not saying that life will necessarily be easy. Commitment, persistence, and a willingness to see things through are necessary. But by God's grace He can and will make all things new. Hope becomes the anchor for our souls, and God's love gives us the assurance to be secure as we persevere. If you have headed down the wrong path in life, know that if you turn around (repent) and seek God's forgiveness, He will rejoice in your coming home to Him. And He won't be the only one rejoicing, so will we!

SEPTEMBER 22

WHAT DOES JESUS MEAN WHEN HE SAYS "MY CHURCH"?

Today, I am pondering Christ's love for the church. Jesus' church-centeredness came out clearly when He spoke this word:

"'But who do you say that I am?' Simon Peter answered and said, 'You are the Christ, the Son of the living God.' Jesus answered and said to him, 'Blessed are you, Simon Bar-Jonah, for flesh and blood has not revealed this to you, but My Father who is in heaven. And I also say to you that you are Peter, and on this rock I will build My church, and the gates of Hades shall not prevail against it.'" Matthew 16:15-18

He states that He, in person, will build a church that is His, and it will triumph over all forms and powers of death.

When we in the West speak of "our church," we are normally referring either to the building or the denomination that we are associated with. We call these entities "ours" because we have chosen to link up with them. "Ours" signifies identification, not possession.

When Jesus spoke of "My church," possession was central to His message. What He had in view was a community unified by a shared allegiance to Himself that would have a common acknowledgement of His claim upon them and His Lordship over them. Included would be a common bond of love, loyalty, and devotion to Him.

The question for us is whose church are we a part of, His or ours? How we answer that question will make a significant difference in how we seek to go about being a part of the building of the church. Just something to give some thought to. One way is limiting; the other way is freeing and opens up a greater appreciation to the Kingdom of God and all of God's people in various cultures. Our vision is expanded; our hearts enlarged.

SEPTEMBER 23

EVENING MUSING

It has been a busy, but productive day. The Kingdom of God is alive and well. The Lord is moving in His people. Despite our cultural decay, there are a remnant people who are standing fast, holding on to the truth of God's Word, and willing to make an impact for His kingdom through sincere lives of integrity.

In the several meetings that I had the privilege to be a part of, I can see an honest stirring to shake things up, get involved, solidify testimony and stand to make a difference. There is also a coming together of people with like-mindedness to work together in a more corporate way.

I for one am encouraged. We must continue to walk by faith and not by sight. God is bigger than any obstacle we might encounter. He brings down Jericho walls and strengthens the faint hearted. May we take courage tonight knowing He is faithful and able to do what is necessary and beyond our expectations. Be healed, strengthened and encouraged. Don't be afraid of your next step. You will not walk alone. You belong to Him. We can take comfort and direction in the words of the Apostle Paul:

"Rejoice in the Lord always. Again I say, rejoice! Let your gentleness be known to all men. The Lord is at hand. Be anxious for nothing, but in everything by prayer and supplication, with thanksgiving, let your request be made known to God; and the peace of God, which surpasses all understanding, will guard your hearts and minds through Christ Jesus." Philippians 4:4-7

May the peace of the Lord be with you as you exercise your thoughts toward Jesus and bring any cares that you might have to Him through prayer.

SEPTEMBER 24

CONTENT NOT SELF-SUFFICIENCY

Independence and inter-dependence are two different things. In one case we strive for independence, where there is no need for anyone else. In the second, we realize that we are in need of community, for we were fashioned for this, though at times we might need to go it alone. The Apostle Paul tried to communicate this idea through his own ministry experience as he penned some of his closing words to the Philippians.

"But I rejoice in the Lord greatly that now at last your care for me has flourished again; though you surely did care, but you lacked opportunity. Not that I speak in regard to need, for I have learned in whatever state I am, to be content: I know how to be abased, and I know how to abound. Everywhere and in all things I have learned both to be full and to be hungry, both to abound and to suffer need. I can do all things through Christ who strengthens me. Nevertheless you have done well that you shared in my distress." Philippians 4:10-14

Paul learned that in whatever state he was in, he could be content. This included the times when he had to walk alone. This might not have been because no one cared, but they could have either lacked the knowledge of what he was going through or lacked the opportunity to be able to help. While this could have developed in Paul an independent spirit, instead he exhibited a great graciousness to include the help of others.

This balance of what he is communicating is between having unrealistic expectations of others to meet our deepest needs on one hand, and the knowledge that real help comes from the Lord alone on the other hand. The lesson we must learn is both a dependence on the Lord and interdependence on those whom He will use to help us.

SEPTEMBER 25

A SIGN OF OUR TIMES...

I have been pondering some thoughts that I have been waiting to share. While we live in challenging times, we also must be wise in whose counsel we listen to, and the leadership we follow. The Scriptures give some light as to what we might experience in times of correction or judgment. It is important that we do not fall prey to what is happening around us. In fact, we must be even more careful and determined to develop those who can lead with integrity and skill.

In the time of Judah and Jerusalem's judgment, the prophet Isaiah described what was happening and the condition of that time. He wrote:

"For behold, the Lord, the Lord of hosts, takes away from Jerusalem and from Judah the stock and the store, the whole supply of bread and the whole supply of water; the mighty man and the man of war, the judge and the prophet, and the diviner and the elder; the captain of fifty and the honorable man, the counselor and the skillful artisan, and the expert enchanter. I will give children to be their princes, and babes shall rule over them. The people will be oppressed, everyone by another and every one by his neighbor; the child will be insolent toward the elder, and the base toward the honorable" (Isaiah 3:1-5).

Not only do we see in this time of judgement an economic press, we also see a leadership that is young, inexperienced, even arrogant. There is no consideration of the wisdom of the wise, nor is their counsel sought. The strength of the nation declined militarily, economically, and in the development of goods and services. In the end, not only was there want, but oppression, not freedom.

In light of this, may we consider who we are applauding and raising up to lead in our communities and nations? Do we seek those who can give us some immediate gratification to our pet peeve, or do we look for those who, with careful consideration, will be honest and build for the long haul, drawing on experience, wisdom and godly character? In the end we will get the leadership we deserve. By God's grace, I hope it will not be so.

SEPTEMBER 26

HANDS-ON VS. NEW TECHNOLOGY

Today I spent a good part of the day cleaning and organizing my garage and tools. After a busy season of projects, it was necessary to get some things sorted out, arranged in a proper order and to get rid of what was unnecessary. Having things in order feels good and enables greater production for the future.

I also updated my iPad and phone with the latest updates. I wish I could say I enjoyed the ordering of this as much. Somehow, each time there is an update, something doesn't work like it did before. There is always a need for me to get some help to get it working properly.

These two things have me thinking. While I am dependent on the technology of our day, I much prefer being able to do things hands-on. There I can see what needs to be done and take the necessary steps to see it come to fruition. I wonder if this new generation that spends so much time on the tools of technology will have the insight to be able to do what is necessary with their imagination and coordination of their own hands to be artisans in their generation? What will the builders of the next generation look like?

There sure is a need to mentor the next generation, not only in technological knowledge, but also hands on experiential, concrete learning experiences. When Jesus called His disciples, He bid them to come follow Him, be with Him. He sent them in front of Him, and then eventually, He gave them their own commission. May we learn to follow His model.

"After these things the Lord appointed seventy others also, and sent them two by two before His face into every city and place where He himself was about to go." Luke 10:1

"But you shall receive power when the Holy Spirit has come upon you; and you shall be witnesses to Me in Jerusalem, and in all Judea, and Samaria, and to the end of the earth." Acts 1:8

SEPTEMBER 27

ON THIS ROCK I WILL BUILD MY CHURCH

In Matthew 16, Jesus states that He in person, will build a church that is His, and it will triumph over all the forms and powers of death. Jesus' thought clearly was that He Himself would form a community bonded together by a common grasp of the reality that Simon Peter had just confessed.

Jesus was the appointed and anointed Christ, the Son of God both officially and personally, the Maker and Master of all things, the Lord of life, the Determiner of all destinies, and the Savior of His servants. When Jesus thought of the church, He was thinking of the process by which the truth about Himself was received and responded to. Increasingly those who respond are conformed to share in what the church does, come under the leadership of the Lord and depend on His power.

"For we are God's fellow workers; you are God's field; you are God's building. . . . For no other foundation can anyone lay than that which is laid, which is Jesus Christ. . . . Do you not know that you are the temple of God and that the Spirit of God dwells in you? If anyone defiles the temple of God, God will destroy him. For the temple of God is holy, which temple you are." I Corinthians 3:9, 11, 16, 17

The question for us is do we understand the church as Jesus does? Is our heart changing to the place where repentance, faith, and obedience are becoming more and more the pattern of our life? Are we exhibiting humility, purity, love, and zeal for God? Are we fulfilling Jesus' call to worship, work, and witness in His name?

None of this happens in isolation. None of this can happen if we hold on to individualism. Only as we esteem what Christ esteems and allow Him to form us in community can we be fitted for the destiny He desires and be transformed through the power of His Spirit. Let's not just go to church - let us be the church that Christ is building!

SEPTEMBER 28

PRAY THAT YOU MAY NOT ENTER INTO TEMPTATION...

This Jesus says twice to His disciples.

"Pray that you may not enter into temptation." Luke 22:40

"Why do you sleep? Rise and pray, lest you enter into temptation." Luke 22:46

It is the two slices of bread surrounding Jesus's own prayer in the Garden. His prayer was wrestling with the call of God to be our sacrifice. Through earnest prayer, He was able to say:

"Father, if it is Your will, take this cup away from Me; nevertheless not My will, but Yours, be done." Luke 22:42

We might look at His admonition that prayer is important so that we can evert sin in our lives. I do believe that this is part of the truth that we must understand, that the Holy Spirit strengthens us in our times of temptation. But, notice that this admonition is surrounded in the context of Jesus doing the Father's will. Could it be that Jesus is exhorting His disciples, and us as well, that prayer is necessary for us to be able to discern and have the strength to do the Father's will?

We might think that we are generally not committing sins, but have we considered that we might not have the fervent desire to do all that God has called us to do? This prayer that Jesus calls us to is to get out of our own comfortable redefinition of what it means to be a Christian and pray seeking just what God's definition for us really is.

Are we willing to pray this kind of prayer today? Can you imagine what might happen if we all do?

SEPTEMBER 29

THE JOY OF 36 YEARS

Across from my chair are four pictures hung up on our living room wall. There is a picture of Bernice and I on our wedding day (36 years ago today, September 29, 1979), my son and his wife's wedding picture, my daughter and her husband's wedding picture and a family picture with all of us including our four grandchildren (and one on the way). What a reminder of the joy that we have experienced and remains with us, since Bernice and I were joined together in marriage.

I have been blessed with such a perfect partner all these years. The fruit of our union is all around our table. It is as the Psalmist describes:

"Blessed is every one who fears the Lord, who walks in His ways. When you eat the labor of your hands, you shall be happy, and it shall be well with you. Your wife shall be like a fruitful vine in the very heart of your house. Your children like olive plants all around your table. Behold, thus shall the man be blessed who fears the Lord." Psalm 128:

The grace that God has bestowed on us is beyond measure. His faithfulness to lead and guide us through the years is unsurpassed. His peace is beyond any comprehension. I am thankful for His providence in my family's life.

While Bernice and I will celebrate these 36 years of marriage, may we both pause and give God thanks for all that He is to us, the third chord that keeps us bound together strongly.

Happy Anniversary Bernice! Looking forward to the rest of my life with you.

SEPTEMBER 30

IT ALL BOILS DOWN TO THIS...

This morning, I am thinking about two different themes: one which I will probably be preaching about on Sunday, the other I will briefly share today. When we think about our lives as Christians, we sometimes think we must do complicated things. While that might be so in some instances, it is not generally the theme that we are taught in the Bible. Our culture has us thinking that we need to be going here, there, and everywhere. We must keep our kids busy, and find we ourselves bringing them from one event to another. At the end of the day everyone is frazzled, but are they enriched?

In the concluding verses of Ecclesiastes, the writer tries to sum up the gist of all he has been writing about. He has warned of the vanity of a lot of things we seem to put greater value on. While he is a knowledgeable and wise man, his words seem too simple. I don't know why we shutter at simple. Life is not as complicated as we make it to be sometimes. Here is what he penned:

"Let us hear the conclusion of the whole matter: Fear God and keep His commandments, for this is man's all. For God will bring every work into judgment, including every secret thing, whether good or evil." Ecclesiastes 12:13-14

When we order our lives around the principles of God's word, there is so much blessing for us. It is not all that complicated. We must however, seek to know just what these principles are and then set sail in that direction. These principles and commands are not straight jackets in our lives. Instead, they are more like life boats. They keep us safe, and give us a future and hope.

Today, why don't we just keep things simple. Enjoy our lives, the way God intended for them to be enjoyed.

October 1

Eyes and Understanding Must Be Opened

In two consecutive accounts that I read this morning, there was a need for Jesus to open the eyes and understanding of His disciples. It happened on the road to Emmaus, when, "*beginning at Moses and all the Prophets, [Jesus] expounded to them in all the Scriptures the things concerning Himself*" (Luke 24:27). It also happened in the Upper Room when Jesus appeared to His disciples and reminded them:

"'These are the words which I spoke to you while I was still with you, that all things must be fulfilled which were written in the Law of Moses and the Prophets and the Psalms concerning Me.' And He opened their understanding, that they might understand the Scriptures." Luke 24:44-45

Paul also prayed for the Ephesian church that they would receive "*the spirit of wisdom and revelation of the knowledge of Him, the eyes of your understanding being enlightened; that you might know...*" (Eph. 1:17-18). Paul continued to pray that his disciples would get a real picture of the church and their placement in it as being central to God's work in the world. How they would understand that would make a significant difference in whether they could walk out that high calling.

In all these instances it was the disciples who needed to have their eyes opened, their understanding opened or enlightened. It suggests to me that there are many who might go through the motions of some religious faith, at the same time walk with a blindness and lack of understanding to the power and position to which Christ has called them. Unless their eyes and understanding are opened, they cannot rise up to that call.

Prayer and expounding of the scriptures are necessary for this revelation to become real. Only through the work of the Holy Spirit can this revelation be understood. May we pray, expound and study the scriptures and ask the Lord to open our eyes and understanding, revealing His sovereign purpose in our lives and the lives of those we seek to lead.

OCTOBER 2

WHY DON'T WE ASK QUESTIONS?

Last night I had the privilege of sitting with a group of people who are part of a grassroots swelling in our community. We listened to someone who was part of the Department of Education for many years talk about an initiative that we hope to be a part of. Without going into the detail of this right now, one of the issues that she brought up is so important. It has to do with local self-government. The ability for people to be participants in the governmental process.

One interesting question that she presented, I have thought of many times. She has often reflected in her own dealings with things that centralized governments are pushing down the pike: Why more people do not ask questions? In other words, why don't we seem to care? We are talking about our sons and daughters. We are talking about our future as a community and a nation. Why don't we care? Making a difference begins with showing some concern. We have to overcome the sin of indifference! Otherwise we will increasingly be brought under oppression by those who have an agenda. Nehemiah showed his concern for the welfare of his countrymen and then developed a plan to make a difference in their lives.:

"It came to pass in the month of Chislev, in the twentieth year, as I was in Shushan the citadel, that Hanani one of my brethren came with men from Judah; and I asked them concerning the Jews who had escaped, who had survived the captivity, and concerning Jerusalem." Nehemiah 1:1-2

Do you think it is time that you and I have an agenda? Of course, that requires us to think, strategize and then act. If we take some responsibility for where we presently are, then together (not isolated) we can rise up and build the broken down walls of our communities. It is time we ask the proper questions, raise up the dissenting views when needed, and care about what is going around us. We can make a difference in our generation!

OCTOBER 3

PROFESSING TO BE WISE THEY BECAME FOOLS...

As we look at the evil of our day, we can't help to consider why the behavior we see is so corrupt on every level. Not only are the things that should be common sense being distorted, but the things that are true are exchanged for what are lies. This is happening at such a rate that you almost cannot trust any credible source to supply you with any truth about a particular matter.

In reading Romans 1 this morning, the issue is clear: because people have not accepted the truth about their own creation (which requires them to acknowledge their Creator), then an exchange is needed. Worship, allegiance, truth, right thinking, proper behavior - all are exchanged to follow after the futility of a foolish, darkened heart.

"For since the creation of the world His {God's] invisible attributes are clearly seen, being understood by the things that are made, even His eternal power and Godhead, so that they are without excuse, became, although they knew God, they did not glorify Him as God, nor were thankful, but became futile in their thoughts, and their foolish hearts were darkened." Romans 1:20-21

Unless hearts are changed, heads will continue to lead in foolishness. Unless hearts are changed, wrong conclusions will be made. Unless hearts are changed, there is a continued slide in character and demonstrations that are not only vile but also approved by others. Only true repentance can bring about the change that is needed in our communities. That won't happen if truth continues to be suppressed. Someone needs to care enough to tell the truth. And truth can only be found in the One who is truth!

May we search for the truth of God's Word and align our lives accordingly trusting in the grace of our Savior to enable us to be transformed by His power.

OCTOBER 4

REESTABLISHING THE STRENGTH OF LIFE

Today, in our church, we continued a message in our Nehemiah Series. In particular we considered how we can follow Nehemiah's example to rebuild areas in our lives that have deteriorated. In an individual's life, the rebuilding of the walls would be a picture of re-establishing the strength of life.

Many have had their defenses crumble away. This leads to a state of feeling hopeless and helpless. By God's grace re-building can take place. The principles that must be applied are the same for any life, local church, community, or nation. Re-building can take place. You do not need to feel helpless or hopeless. You can gain strength, power and purpose.

Tune in tomorrow to our link for this message. Learn the five principles (STEPS) that are basic to any reconstruction:

1. Concern about the ruins;
2. Confession for how you have forsaken God;
3. Committing yourself to God's project;
4. Courage to take the proper steps;
5. Caution – don't jump into things. First make a honest assessment of the facts.

I believe that if we apply these principles consistently in our lives, we will not only gain strength in our own lives, but we will be poised to be rebuilders of our communities as well.

OCTOBER 5

WHY THE DISCONNECT?

I know that in our day that students are taught that they cannot know the meaning of what a writer intended. They have been taught deconstruction of the very words and meanings that have been written. We see this being applied today even in interpreting the Constitution of the United States and many other documents. But what about in the churches? Have we also taken the texts of the Bible and claimed they cannot be understood? Or are we free to change the author's intention to come under the preference of our own interpretation?

I wonder why some people have heard things taught for so long, yet feel like it should not apply to them. Instead of the Ten Commandments they have turned it into the Ten Suggestions. No wonder the watching world sees this as being hypocritical. In fact, you don't have to go that far; your children, spouse, co-workers can also see the disconnect. This is why Paul exhorted his disciple Timothy so strongly:

"Take heed to yourself and to the doctrine. Continue in them, for in doing this you will save both yourself and those who hear you." 1 Timothy 4:16

"Hold fast the pattern of sound words which you have heard from me, in faith and love which are in Christ Jesus." 2 Timothy 1:13

"All Scripture is given by instruction of God, and is profitable for doctrine, for reproof, for correction, for instruction in righteousness, that the man of God may be complete, thoroughly equipped for every good work." 2 Timothy 3:16-17

Unless we live with integrity, how could we have the respect of others? Maybe that is why Paul included so many times in his letters, "*walk worthy of the gospel*." Perhaps if we did so, others might want to ask us the reason for our hope.

I hope this is something worth pondering.

OCTOBER 6

ENTITLEMENT THINKING WITHOUT GRATITUDE!

One of the basic ideas that must be learned in economics is that everything has a price that must be paid. In other words, nothing is free. If you receive something free, it is because someone else absorbed the price. This is true of promotions. It is true of life.

Recently my wife read on one of the utility bills that we received that the rate had gone up to absorb those whose bills were delinquent. So the people who pay their bill promptly have to pay more for those who do not pay at all. It's not just utility companies, food, clothing and material goods have costs factored in for the items taken by thieves.

All over our communities, we have people feeling entitled to receive things free, even though it is costing someone else for their feelings of entitlement. I wonder if they understand exactly that their ability to receive something is at the expense of someone else paying the price? I wonder if they realized it fully that they would be more thankful or have some gratitude for what they have received.

Even when it comes to our salvation, we understand that we paid no price to receive it. We simply needed to have faith in Jesus. But again, what came freely to us was at a great cost. Jesus gave His very life and paid fully for our own sins. Do we realize this fully? If we did, wouldn't we be more thankful? Knowing this, wouldn't we want to give back to the One who made us free with thanksgiving in our hearts?

"For the wages of sin is death, but the gift of God is eternal life in Christ Jesus our Lord." Romans 6:23

"For you were bought at a price: therefore glorify God in your body and in your spirit, which are God's." 1 Corinthians 6:20

Gratitude and humility go a long way in defeating the thinking of entitlement in our lives.

OCTOBER 7

THOUGHTS OF A FRIEND GROWN QUIET

During the past few days I have been praying for an old friend that is preparing for glory. In our younger years, we were part of the same church family and enjoyed life there with our children having fun times. I can remember one camping trip in particular. Over the course of years, we lost track of each other, but through Facebook were able to reconnect many years later.

I can tell you that even though this friend has gone through so much medically, you would never know through her posts, comments and likes and relationships. She has always shown such positive, cheerful, hopeful, caring concern for others throughout her own ordeal. I am sure that those close to her would have their own stories to tell and could surely tell of the difficulties, endurance and courage in which she had lived her life.

For me, she has modeled what a Christian, full of faith, can be. I am not talking about perfection, but maturity. I can still picture her great smile and laugh. Today her voice has gone quiet. We may never see her posts, or be encouraged with her words. But one thing for sure, we can remember her life. I, for one, have been enriched to have known her. As I continue to pray for her and her family and friends, I am reminded of how important our testimony is. Our lives are short in comparison to eternity. Yet, how we live our lives can alter the eternity for so many. Be blessed my friend.

"Behold, I tell you a mystery: We shall not all sleep, but we shall all be changed – in a moment, in the twinkling of an eye, at the last trumpet. For the trumpet will sound, and the dead will be raised incorruptible, and we shall be changed. For this corruptible must put on incorruption, and this mortal must put on immortality; so when this corruptible has put on immortality, then shall be brought to pass the saying that is written: 'Death is swallowed up in victory.'" 1 Corinthians 15:51-55

OCTOBER 8

IS "HARD WORK" IN OUR VOCABULARY ANYMORE?

Am I the only one noticing a gradual change in our culture that needs to be of grave concern to all of us? It used to be that hard work was thought of as a virtue and a discipline of responsible people. Even those who might not have had a chance at higher education, prided themselves in their ability to work hard with their hands.

In reviewing Paul's letter to Timothy, we can't help seeing words like, "*be strong*," "*endure hardship*," "*engage in warfare*," "*be diligent*." He uses examples of farmers, soldiers and athletes to give pictures of those who are diligent in their disciplines.

When Paul wrote to the Thessalonians, he exhorted them to:

"Aspire to lead a quiet life, to mind your own business, and to work with your hands, as we commanded you, that you may walk properly toward those who are outside, and that you may lack nothing." 1 Thess. 4:11-12

He even went a bit further in his second letter to them:

"For even when we were with you, we commanded you this: If anyone will not work, neither shall he eat. For we hear that there are some who walk among you in a disorderly manner, not working at all, but are busybodies. Now those who are such we command and exhort through our Lord Jesus Christ that they work in quietness and eat their own bread." 2 Thess. 3:10-12

I believe that having a good work ethic begins early in the raising of our children. We must model this ourselves, and then also help them in this discipline. If we do not do this for our children, who then will do it for them? I know parenting is "hard work", but someone needs to take this responsibility.

OCTOBER 9

NOT ONLY THAT...

Last night and this morning I have been quiet in contemplation. The news of a friend passing into glory is always filled with a mix of sadness for the loss for their family and friends and the joy that faith gives us for someone entering their eternal rest. Life is so precious and these are times when people reflect on what is important and how life can be lived to the fullest.

In reading Romans 5, I am reflective of how Paul is encouraging the Romans of faith triumphing in trouble. It seems that he cannot just make one statement about this, but twice following, adds other thoughts to expand the understanding of his readers to all that we have in Christ.

"Therefore, having been justified by faith, we have peace with God through our Lord Jesus Christ, through whom also we have access by faith into this grace in which we stand, and rejoice in hope of the glory of God." Romans 5:1-2

.... And not only that, but we also glory in tribulations, knowing that tribulation produces perseverance; and perseverance, character; and character, hope." Romans 5:3

... And not only that, but we also rejoice in God through our Lord Jesus Christ, through whom we have received the reconciliation." Romans 5:11

There is so much more in what he said. It would be good to go and read all the fullness of what Paul wrote. For me this morning, it is about what we have in Christ. If we sat around and had a conversation about it, I believe we could all add, "and not only that" telling our own experience.

If that has not been your experience, may I suggest that there is hope in times of trouble? The great Author and Finisher of our lives, promises to be with us always. That includes in life and death; in good times and in times of trouble. All we need to do is put our trust in Him. Peace can flow like a river in our lives. Not only that...

OCTOBER 10

CHILDREN LIKE OLIVE PLANTS...

Our house is full again this weekend. It is a joy to be reunited again. What a blessing to see our children and grandchildren gathered for a special time together. I am reminded of the expression of the psalmist who in reflecting on the blessedness of the Lord wrote:

"Your wife shall be like a fruitful vine in the very heart of your house, your children like olive plants all around your table." Psalm 128:3

There are numerous ways in which olive plants and its fruit were used in the Scriptures: olives and olive oil were used for food (Deut. 24:20), illumination (Lev. 24:2), consecration of religious workers (Exod. 3:22-33), cosmetic purposes (Ruth 3:3), medicinal and hygienic functions (Luke 10:34), religious ceremonies (Gen. 28:28), and even as a commodity of exchange (1 Kings 5:11; Luke 16:6). In addition, the olive tree and its fruit are symbols of joy, prosperity, and peace (see Isaiah 61:3; Psalm 45:7).

What does this suggest about our children? They are highly valuable in the eyes of God and in the wellbeing of our communities. Therefore, we should have high expectations for them, keeping with their personal giftings and stage development. We must bring them up in the instruction and discipline of the Lord (Eph. 6:4). We must provide an environment that is conducive to the development of godly character and conduct.

Well, for today, there are extra chairs needed to be put around our table, but each one that is seated is precious. Each one has great potential in God's design. Surely, the Lord has blessed us. I will need to resume my writing later – right now, apple picking awaits us.

OCTOBER 11

HOW DO YOU DEFINE SUCCESS?

One popular modern definition of success might be that "Success is the freedom to live your life the way you want to." Others might say that "freedom is getting what you want." Still others would say that "freedom is doing what you want, when you want to." But what does the Bible have to say about success? I believe the lesson taught is that "success is to live your life the way God wants you to."

The widespread belief in our time that success and happiness are tied to self-seeking pursuits must be challenged. Our strategies for self-fulfillment will not work unless they are tied to the pursuit of God's will. The idea that "the will of God" and "the good life" are one and the same is not always evident. The good life, in our culture, is tied to wealth, leisure, recreation, and material possessions. The will of God, throughout the Bible, is tied to love, mercy, justice, caring for the poor – all requiring giving and sacrifice.

Micah the prophet of the Lord answered the people of his generation with what the Lord was requiring of them. It was not in their great sacrifices, it had to do with their response to His love:

"He has shown you, O man, what is good; and what does the Lord require of you but to do justly, to love mercy, and to walk humbly with your God?" Micah 6:8

Jesus does promise us an abundant life, but He also insists that "*it is more blessed to give than to receive*" (Acts 20:35). Using this criteria we can ask ourselves an important question, "Are we living a successful life?" Depending on the answer we give, we may need to adjust our way. May we see success according to the way the Lord defines it and not the world around us.

OCTOBER 12

WHEN TIME RUNS OUT YOU HAVE TO HAVE S'MORE!

We have had a wonderful, fun-filled time with our family this weekend. It was nice to have the north and south parts of our families reunited. The time seemed to go by too fast. But we will look forward to new adventures and reunions soon in the future.

The sun has gone down, but the energy of the grandchildren has not waned. I don't know if it is the same with the adults. We have not had much quiet time. I was tempted to write late yesterday but chose to go to bed instead. I am presently writing while the fire is simmering. The marshmallows have been cooked and eaten. The mosquitoes are now taking over.

I just want to give God thanks for His grace and goodness in our lives. It is His grace that enables us to live, grow and fulfill His plan. It will be His grace that will enable each member to find His strength and peace for their lives as they continue to see it unfold in each and every facet. It is because of God's faithfulness that we can rest in our trust in Him for the future. All is good.

Allowing God's mercy and truth to lead us helps us to find His favor as well as the favor of others. Trusting in His ways is crucial to having our paths rightly directed. His ways and thoughts are higher and perfect. For our lives, we endeavor to continue to acknowledge the Lord, His wisdom, His way. We accept His leading. We are at peace.

"Let not mercy and truth forsake you; bind them around your neck, write them on the tablet of your heart, and so find favor and high esteem in the sight of God and man. Trust in the Lord with all your heart, and lean not on your own understanding; in all your ways acknowledge Him, and He shall direct your paths." Proverbs 3:3-6

OCTOBER 13

A LESS ANIMATED SUPPER!

Tonight, the supper table had a lot of empty chairs. My wife Bernice and I were able to carry a complete conversation, but it was not quite the same. For the past weekend, we have been blessed to have five generations sharing a meal together. Right about now, our southern group should be landing and heading back to their home.

In life we must take the opportunities that present themselves, or create opportunities. Each person is precious and we never know how life will change. Recently, we lost a friend. In looking back at a writing that I did a couple of years ago about the theme of eulogizing, I commented that we should use each present opportunity to share how precious someone is to us and not to wait till they have passed. This friend commented that day that she was thinking the same. Little did we know that she would now be the one gone.

Let us enjoy each day that we have to make a difference; to love and be loved. Time passes quickly. We don't want to miss any precious moments. Each day is a gift. Let's not waste time on the trivial, when the important is right before our eyes.

"See then that you walk circumspectly [carefully], not as fools but as wise, redeeming the time, because the days are evil. Therefore, do not be unwise, but understand what the will of the Lord is." Ephesians 5:15-17

"Walk in wisdom toward those who are outside, redeeming the time. Let your speech always be with grace, seasoned with salt, that you nay know how you ought to answer each one." Colossians 4:5-6

OCTOBER 14

NOT YOUR AVERAGE BIBLE STUDY

Who says that church can't be exciting? This evening following our opening prayer the fire alarm went off. We use the expression that we want to be on fire for God, but I don't think we expected this kind of interruption. Anyway, while the fire department did what they needed to do, our group moved outside and continued in prayer. When things were all cleared, they moved back in for praise and worship and then continued in three different breakout groups.

We had new people join us this evening. I assured them that this (having fire alarms go off) isn't a regular occurrence; however, they enjoyed the interaction in our small group Bible study and said they were so glad of the experience that they were coming back Sunday morning.

Our study focused on the vision Paul painted for a mature global church. There was great input from everyone. I am thankful for the vision that God is continuing to enlarge in the heart of His people. Looking forward to all the Lord is going to do in our community and beyond.

"And [Christ] Himself gave some to be apostles, some prophets, some evangelists, and some pastors and teachers, for the equipping of the saints for the work of ministry, for the edifying of the body of Christ, till we all come to the unity of the faith and of the knowledge of the Son of God, to a perfect man, to the measure of the stature of the fullness of Christ; that we should no longer be children, tossed to and fro and carried about with every wind of doctrine, by the trickery of men, in the cunning craftiness of deceitful plotting, but, speaking the truth in love, may grow up in all things into Him who is the Head – Christ – from whom the whole body, joined and knit together by what every joint supplies, according to the effective working by which every part does its share, causes growth of the body for the edifying of itself in love." Ephesians 4:11-16

OCTOBER 15

EVERY PART DOES ITS SHARE...

The mystery of the body of Christ is so profound, yet simple. It is as simple as learning to grow up, knowing what is to be shared in common with each other according to the principles that Christ has laid out for us; and working together, each one doing his or her part in His purpose which will cause further growth in love (see Ephesians 4:11-16).

I think that sometimes we only think of this as how our church service or family should function. But the potential is so much greater than an organized service. Paul is referring to how we are all to play our part in the progress of the gospel and be witnesses to the watching world.

As we mature in our faith and understand our own need to be a contributing member of His body, we can look at the issues of our own day and be those who make a difference for all people. Getting out of the four walls and living the incarnation of Christ in the midst of our own communities.

This requires that we respect the value of the Kingdom of God and His global church . . . *"endeavoring to keep the unity of the Spirit in the bond of peace"* (Ephesians 4:3). To each one of us grace is given according to the measure of Christ's gift. We are all called to mature and help in the maturing process of building others up. When we do our share, growth happens and love is built up.

Today, give some thought as to how you can be God's instrument of love right where you are. Go ahead; do your part. You can make a significant difference.

OCTOBER 16

IT'S NOT EASY TO EXPRESS WHAT WE ARE FEELING

Do you ever have times where you just can't express what is going on inside of you? You might have some deep thought, or are considering a solution to a problem, or just some strategic plan that you must be able to communicate. Probably, the best word that I can associate with this is the word groaning.

Paul wrote to the Romans communicating this idea. The whole of "*creation groans and labors with birth pangs together until now (speaking of the revealing of the Sons of God). Not only that, but we also who have the firstfruits of the Spirit, even we ourselves, groan within ourselves, eagerly waiting for the adoption, the redemption of our body.*" Romans 8:22-23

What Paul is saying is that even though we have a hope in the Lord, we are still waiting for the full revelation of this hope to be revealed. Therefore, we must wait with perseverance. In a like manner, he instructs us that "*the Spirit also helps in our weakness. For we do not know what we should pray for as we ought, but the Spirit Himself makes intercession for us with groanings which cannot be uttered. Now He who searches the hearts knows what the mind of the Spirit is, because He makes intercession for the saints according to the will of God.*" Romans 8:26-27

Here is where I can find comfort. Even when I don't know how to pray, the Spirit of God does know. He is at work in me, as He is also at work in you. The wisdom that I seek, He has. In my limitations, He is not limited. All I need to do is trust in His intercession for me. As I do, I will understand His will more fully. Even if I have no words, my groaning is sufficient for the moment, and He will lead me to greater hope.

If you are in the same kind of place tonight, trust the Lord. Let the Holy Spirit help you in your weakness, for He knows how to intercede for you. And the situation you might be facing, or have experienced will come to greater clarity as you understand God's good purpose in your life (see Romans 8:28).

OCTOBER 17

NETWORKING: IS IT IMPORTANT?

We have been studying the book of Nehemiah the past several weeks as a church. One thing that is clear is that Nehemiah built a network, which was foundational upon which the rest of his ministry in Jerusalem would be based. Nehemiah was not the only biblical networker we find in the Bible: among the finest were Moses and Paul. Through God's providence, each was prepared and used their preparation well.

"Then I said to them, 'you see the distress that we are in, how Jerusalem lies waste, and its gates are burned with fire. Com and let us build the wall of Jerusalem, that we may no longer be a reproach.' And I told them of the hand of my God which had been good upon me, and also of the king's words that he has spoken to me. So they said, 'Let us rise up and build." Then they set their hands to this good work." Nehemiah 2:17-18

This idea of networking should have us thinking in a couple of ways: First, how has God shaped our individual lives to enhance our ability to network with others? Second, how can we network effectively through our lives and into our communities?

What networking can do for us individually and as churches is to prepare us to take the next risky step that can transform our ministry and our relationship with our community and city. It is through this networking where we can gain credibility, properly assess needs, and encourage others to join us to rise up and build the solutions.

May God give us wisdom and clarity to discern how He has prepared us for this time and season of our lives. May we then act on this revelation and involve ourselves in His work.

OCTOBER 18

REFLECTIONS ON KNOWING CHRIST

My wife and I had a beautiful day in the Lord today. We enjoyed meeting new people and the faithful alike as we worshipped, prayed and shared the Word of God in our church service. It is always amazing how the Holy Spirit is able to move us to His direction if we are willing and open. We also had a beautiful dinner and fellowship this afternoon with wonderful friends. Our conversation was edifying and thought provoking. What I am thinking on now is some of the discussion that we had in Our First Principles Class following our morning service focused on "Laying Hold of Christ."

The Scripture that we examined is Philippians 3:1-21. When Christ's call and cause are first and when we live according to the pattern set down and modeled by Paul for community life, we are truly beginning to lay hold of Christ and are really getting to know Him. Unless we follow Him and are involved in His discipleship in of our lives, in community, we will never come to fully know Him. It is in laying hold of God's call and pursuing that call that we experience Christ and lay hold of Him. We do so sharing in both His suffering and resurrection.

I believe the church needs to recapture the priority of community in Christian discipleship. The church which rediscovers something of the God-given quality of such a sharing community will speak with great relevance, credibility, and spiritual power to the world today. It is a visible manifestation of Christ's body on earth! Can you imagine what kind of impact we can have if we lay hold of Christ, individually and corporately?

"Therefore let us, as many as are mature, have this mind; and if in anything you think otherwise, God will reveal even this to you. Nevertheless, to the degree that we have already attained, let us walk by the same rule, let us be of the same mind. Brethren, join in following my example and note those who so walk, as you have us as a pattern." Philippians 3:15-17

OCTOBER 19

PRESSING ON!

In sports and other areas of life, there seems to be a peaking of performance and then a decline. The interesting thing about the Christian life is it is not the same. If we have peaked and find ourselves in decline, we haven't correctly apprehended the truth that we find in the Scriptures. Paul, the apostle, wrote to the Philippians about this very such matter.

Paul desired above all else to know Christ. To know the power of His resurrection and the fellowship of His suffering as he looked forward to the future resurrection promised by God. In reflecting on his own life he says:

"Not that I have already attained, or am already perfected; but I press on, that I may lay hold of that for which Christ Jesus has also laid hold of me. Brethren, I do not count myself to have apprehended; but one thing I do, forgetting those things which are behind and reaching forward to those things which are ahead, I press toward the goal for the prize of the upward call of God in Christ Jesus." Philippians 3:12-14

You see, to know Christ we must follow Him, work with Him, identify with Him and be discipled by Him. As we answer His call in our lives, we recognize that He has made an eternal investment in us. Our desire should be to know Him and continue to grow in our knowledge and intimacy with Him. We can't rest in past accomplishments or get stuck in past failures.

Today is a new day. May we grow from our past experiences and press into new experiences as we trust Him to continue to reveal Himself more fully in our lives.

OCTOBER 20

EVERYONE WANTS PEACE!

Everyone wants peace, or do we? How can one live in peace? Is peace just something that we feel, or does it require something from us to know peace? Paul tells the Philippians:

"Be anxious for nothing, but in everything by prayer and supplication, with thanksgiving, let your request be made known to God; and the peace of God, which surpasses all understanding, will guard your hearts and minds through Christ Jesus." Philippians 4:6-7

Paul first begins with the idea of putting our dependence on the Lord. By bringing our needs before Him we can trust in His provision and timing in our lives. This trust will keep us centered in His peace.

Secondly, he continues to instruct on what our mind should be fixed on in verse 8. If we continue to focus on the negative, we will not experience God's peace. We need to train ourselves to look at what is good and worthy of our reflection.

The third area he deals with is how we must walk. This is very important. People who lack peace often don't walk in the manner that will bring them peace, but instead will steal their peace even more. Paul exhorts the Philippians:

"The things which you learned and received and heard and saw in me, these do, and the God of peace will be with you." Philippians 4:9

God has a plan and purpose for our lives. Walking in His way is coming to know Him. This knowledge of God leads us to a greater intimacy and trust. This trust helps to frame us into right thinking. Right thinking leads us into right walking. What does all this produce? Peace beyond expectation.

OCTOBER 21

BEARING WITH THE WEAKNESSES OF THE WEAK

I was challenged this morning reading Romans 15. Paul admonishes the Roman Christians saying:

"We who are strong ought to bear with the scruples (weaknesses) of the weak, and not please ourselves. Let each of us please his neighbor for his good, leading to edification." Romans 15:1-2

I don't know about you, but often I get frustrated with how some people live and try to take advantage of other people's kindness and generosity. They seem to live in a perpetual state of immaturity and do not follow the counsel given, nor ever put themselves out of the way to help others. They are always on the receiving end, never the one giving. But are these who the apostle is talking about? Those who continue in sin? Surely not.

He is speaking about those who might have a weak conscious, who possibly because of some legalism in their lives, do not seem to be able to walk in the fullness of liberty and therefore can have stumbling blocks put before them if we do not exercise our liberty properly. For their sake, Paul is requiring from the strong to consider their weakness and try to build them up with patience, preferring them even if you have the liberty to do as your conscience dictates.

Therefore, he is not condoning sinful actions. These must be confronted. He is talking about walking out the maturing process. We must have patience and seek the good of our neighbor in order to build up. In other words, use your strength to lift up others and not tear them down. May God's grace be with you as you apply this word.

OCTOBER 22

DIRTY BIRD CATERING SERVICE

There is a provision for the people of God who move in obedience to the Lord's commands. Elijah had just proclaimed that it would not rain to King Ahab until he proclaimed that it would. This drought would cause famine in all of Israel, to show the king that God rules over the affairs of men, and for him to repent of his evil ways. The judgment, however, also affects those who live in the region. But for those who trust in God there is an appointed place of blessing.

The Lord instructed Elijah saying:

"Get away from here and turn eastward and hide by the Brook Cherith, which flows into the Jordon. And it will be that you shall drink from the brook, and I have commanded the Ravens to feed you there." 1 Kings 17:3-4

Elijah obeyed the word of the Lord and when he got to the place where he was assigned to go, "*the Ravens brought him bread and meat in the morning, and bread and meat in the evening; and he drank from the brook*" (1 Kings 17:6).

I am sure that Elijah never thought that his provision would come in this season of his life from a dirty bird catering service. We don't know where the bread or meat came from, but they were presented to Elijah routinely morning and evening. I like to think that the Ravens took it from Ahab's table. In any case, we learn from this story (and the story that follows - see 1 Kings 17:8-16), that God has a provision for His people. The important thing is that we go to the place of our appointment. "There" is where your provision will be.

Are you where the Lord has appointed you? Only "there" will you have the provision that He has provided for this season of your life.

OCTOBER 23

FRIENDS IN THE WORK OF THE GOSPEL

As I am reading the concluding chapter of Romans, I am pondering the final greetings that Paul sends to his friends now residing in Rome. While he is looking forward to coming to be with them in the future, his letter is sent to support the basis of the gospel and in what these precious saints should persevere, as he encourages them to stand and contend for that same faith.

As I look at these greetings, I count at least 27 different individuals that he names (in this chapter alone - not counting those with him at present), along with several house churches. In some way, they have all been instrumental in the networking and spreading of the gospel. Many have worked as part of his team; some have sacrificed greatly to see the gospel advance and even put themselves out there in support and defense of Paul.

One thing that is apparent in this letter is the appreciation and love that Paul has for the people with whom he has worked and shared his life. We might want to focus on all that Paul did to advance the gospel in his generation, but we must not miss how much he networked with others to see this accomplished. It was a team effort.

As I look back on my own life today, I am thankful for the many that I can call out by name who, throughout the years, have given of themselves in the service of God, and in great humility, have been of great support and encouragement to me personally. I just want you to know how much you are appreciated. I greet you today.

May *"the grace of our Lord Jesus Christ be with you all. Amen."* Romans 16:24

OCTOBER 24

CONSIDER YOUR WAYS!

In reading the first chapter of Haggai this morning, I am reminded of how easy it is for people to get preoccupied in their own lives, and then give excuses as to why they are not available for others. In this case, the house of the Lord was left unfinished, but the people said that it was not the time to build because the Lord had evidently not given them the resources to do so.

Haggai confronts them with their poor excuse. He addressed why their self-focus was not getting them to experience satisfaction. He asked them to consider their ways. Here are his direct words:

"You have sown much, and bring in little; You eat, but do not have enough; You drink, but you are not filled with drink; You clothe yourselves, but no one is warm; And he who earns wages, earn wages to put into a bag with holes." Haggai 1:6

What the Lord was asking of His people was to do the things that He would take satisfaction in - building His house. Because they instead had focused only on themselves, their productivity and supply had dwindled. In fact, the blessing on their lives had been withheld. What was needed was for them to obey the Lord's voice as He stirred them up with the prophet's message.

Are you in need of stirring up today? Has your focus been on your own comfort and wants? Have you neglected how you can be a builder in the house of God? The church is not just a place we can take or leave. It is the pillar and foundation of the truth. It is the wisdom of God displayed to the watching world. It is where we have opportunity to encourage each other in how we should walk. It is a family of families where we know we belong. It is where the very presence of God encourages us to be builders and re-builders of our communities.

If you have had a different focus, would you consider your ways? Return to the Lord's house. You will not only find rest, you will also find purpose.

OCTOBER 25

THANKFUL END OF DAY REFLECTION

One of the great things about the Lord's Day is that it helps to reset us each week. We can take the time to worship, learn, encourage each other, and just do something that is not the usual thing we do every other day.

As I think about today, I am thankful for the gathering of the saints to worship and share in a communion service as we continued to look at how we all can have a significant part in the building up of the wall in our church and community. We also had a great discussion in a small group setting following the service. This afternoon my wife and I were able to have wonderful fellowship with several families as we also watched a victorious Patriots game. Just spending time with these friends was precious.

We are now resting at home; thankful for our family, friends, fellowship, and faith. Surely, this is a gift from God. There is wisdom in God's ways. We have been reset; ready for the challenges of a new week, but not until we can give the Lord thanks for all His bounty in our lives which includes you.

"I thank my God upon ever remembrance of you, always in every prayer of mind making request for you all with joy, for your fellowship in the gospel from the first day until now, being confident of this very thing, that He who has begun a good work in you will complete it until the day of Jesus Christ." Philippians 1:3-6

OCTOBER 26

A CRY FOR GODLY LEADERSHIP

We are only days away from another community election. As I survey the field of those from whom we can choose, I am also struggling with the absence of real leaders who can unite and get our community to work together and solve some of our most pressing needs. Instead, we see factions and many of the individuals who have their own personal causes and goals to advance. What would real leadership look like? The church is called to be a city on the hill, an example of proper leadership and administration which those in civil government are able to get ideas and convictions from. However, oftentimes the church is also a reflection of what we see played out in our civil sphere.

For those in the church, I believe that leaders are charged with the responsibility of mobilizing and empowering people to do God's work. This does not mean that leaders should not get their hands dirty; instead, they should lead by example. People from all ages and all walks of life are to be inspired to join in the work of transformation. God works through people. It is the responsibility of leaders to help people accomplish their work, by helping each one to know where they can serve and find their piece of building the walls of our community.

The church of Christ needs the participation of each member. We spend so much of our lives on projects destroyed "*by moth and rust*" (Matt. 6:19; see also 1 Corinthians 3). What a fulfilling contrast to see our efforts contribute to God's great work on earth. Our lives find ultimate meaning in knowing that we have labored - as parents, as church workers, as doers of justice, as communicators of God's truth and love - for what will last.

"If anyone's work which he has built on it endures, he will receive a reward." 1 Corinthians 3:14

As you survey the condition of our communities, do you see the condition that we are in? If we are going to do something about it, we need to come together and take responsibility and put our best efforts to becoming solutions to the problems. This won't happen unless we all unite and participate together.

OCTOBER 27

WHO IS WISE?

Who is wise? Perhaps to answer that question we must first ponder, "What is the fruit of wisdom?" First, we know that wisdom is not the same as knowledge. There are many who are knowledgeable but not wise. Then, there are different kinds of wisdom, earthly and heavenly. One has its focus on self and controlled by self-seeking and envy which produces confusion and every evil thing. But there is a wisdom that is from above that "*is pure, then peaceable, gentle, willing to yield, full of mercy and good fruits, without partially and without hypocrisy*" (James 3:17).

James wrote:

"Who is wise and understanding among you? Let him show by good conduct that his works are done in the meekness of wisdom." James 3:13

There are many who profess to be wise, but do not follow their own counsel. They know what is right, but do not walk in that way. James links wisdom with doing. Jesus also linked the two, when He said that a wise man hears and does (see Matthew 7:24). If we hear and do not build our lives around this truth, Jesus calls us foolish because what we build will ultimately be tested by the storms of life and not endure.

One of the greatest obstacles we have in sharing our faith is the discrepancy between what we profess and what we actually do. If there is a great difference, we deserve others calling us hypocrites.

Let us pray and ask God for the wisdom we need, but also let us trust in the abiding help of the Holy Spirit to do what He instructs us to do. If we live our lives in this way, we will see the fruit of God's wisdom. If we do not, anything goes, and the picture is not pretty.

OCTOBER 28

OVERCOMING ADVERSITY & SYSTEMS

I am amazed with the parallel political pressures and ridicule pressed on the Jews who were working at reformation in Nehemiah's day and ours. The establishment was benefitting by exploiting the Jew's cheap labor. The political and economic establishments of Palestine were the ones who resisted the action of the people of Jerusalem as they sought to improve their conditions. They were the primary systems shaping the lives of all the people around Jerusalem.

The Sanballats and Tobiahs of today take the form of bureaucrats who see any version of Christianity that challenges the status quo as subversive, unnecessary, unwise, and destructive rather than constructive in its thrust.

They value routine above revival - snuffing out spiritual life. Sanballat & Tobiah were "*deeply disturbed that a man had come to seek the well-being of the children of Israel*" (Neh. 2:10). Many people are not concerned about others, only about how things will affect them. What they tried to do was affect the morale of the group working together. One of the oldest weapons of the enemy is an open attack with a barrage of words. May I say that ridicule needs no factual ammunition.

I have never seen such outright lying as we see in our day. People in high offices continue to hold back the truth and nothing happens to them because the establishment does not want you to know the truth and protects its own. Debates are not about facts and persuasion. They are filled with non-truths or misspoken words (to be politically correct). All of this is so that you and I stay under the thumb of oppression while they paint for us a deceptive picture that actually says we are free (based on their own ideology).

We must be well founded in what we believe (based on truth) so that these lies do not undermine our own determination to do right. It is high time we wake up. May we not be deterred by this subversive plot, but continue to work to enable true freedom for those who are part of our communities.

OCTOBER 29

GOSPEL OF SELF

I was disturbed yesterday by a conversation that I had. Not only were the roots of someone's thinking wrong, it was sending a contrary message to the people he was boasting to about his plans. Actually, a stumbling block to others as they try and make sense of the Christian faith, which gives rise to the following thoughts.

There is another gospel being preached today that does not find its roots in the biblical texts. It is a gospel of self. In this gospel, you are told you can have anything and be anything because God wants to give you whatever you desire. What many fail to understand is that what they desire often is personal pleasure, lusting for what they do not have; and coveting what they cannot attain.

You, yourself, may even pray for these things and not receive, "*because you ask amiss, that you may spend it on your pleasures*" (James 4:3). In other words, you cloak your selfish desires in religious posturing. Outwardly you may look religious, but inwardly you are filled with self-seeking.

James goes on to say:

"Do you not know that friendship with the world is enmity with God? Whoever therefore wants to be a friend of the world makes himself an enemy of God"...."God resists the proud, but gives grace to the humble." James 4: 4, 6

The gospel of self puts us against the true gospel. The gospel of self is just that, it is self-seeking and self-fulfilling. It is motivated by self and focused on this present world. The true gospel tells us to crucify self and become a servant, like our Master. In the true gospel we use our time and resources for His great purpose. Therefore James tells us to "*submit to God. Resist the devil and he will flee from you. Draw near to God and He will draw near to you*" (James 4:8). It is only as we humble ourselves in the sight of God that we can expect Him to lift us up (see James 4:10).

OCTOBER 30

RENEWING STRENGTH

I am in the middle of covering a study hall in our school today and don't know if I will be able to get this devotional thought completed. However, as I read Isaiah's words this morning, I am encouraged by them. As we get older, there are times where we think we do not have the energy of those who are younger. Yet, we can fool ourselves into thinking that we are not as important or able to bring to the battle what is needed for victory.

Isaiah begins by saying:

"The Creator of the ends of the earth, neither faints nor is weary. His understanding is unsearchable. He gives power to the weak, and to those who have no might He increases strength. Even youths shall faint and be weary, and young men shall utterly fall, but those who wait on the Lord shall renew their strength; they shall mount up with wings like eagles, they shall run and not be weary, they shall walk and not faint." Isaiah 40:28-31

What I read in this text is strengthening. God is the One who gives us power. He can do so even if we feel weak. He not only gives us His strength, but can increase that strength in us.

Even when others are falling and fainting, we do not need to do so. The issue is trust, dependence, and a willingness to walk in the power of His might and not our own. Others will not make the journey because they are trusting in the strength of their own selves. Only those who trust and wait on the Lord are ever being strengthened.

May the Lord strengthen you today so that you may continue to walk with Him. Let the Lord's Spirit fill you and renew you in His purpose.

OCTOBER 31

TRANSFORMATION OR CONFORMATION

Today was a good day to get through so many things that needed to get done around the house. Bernice and I are now able to pause and focus our attention on other things as we prepare our minds and hearts for ministry tomorrow. As I sit to write today's thought, I am reflecting on Paul's exhortation to the Romans. While it is probably a familiar passage for most Christians, it is often not given much thought. We have been so affected by our culture that we often don't even see the consequence of it.

Paul strongly admonishes the Romans saying:

"I beseech you therefore, brethren, by the mercies of God, that you present your bodies a living sacrifice, holy, acceptable to God, which is your reasonable service. And do not be conformed to this world, but be transformed by the renewing of your mind, that you may prove what is that good and acceptable and perfect will of God." Romans 12:-12

Lately, I have been so disappointed in how so many who know what these verses say are living their lives in conformity to the world instead of trusting in God for transformation. Something needs to change. Attention to the word must become a priority. There needs to be a heart and mind change, but this doesn't happen until we present ourselves as living sacrifices to Lord.

Tonight, many have chosen to glorify much that is not godly. But if you think that I am hopping on Halloween, this is only one display. How about immorality that is condoned in homes? Addictions that are not addressed? Marriages that won't seek after help because individuals are too stubborn to care about the other? I think you might be getting the point.

Until we bow before One Greater than us, we will never know what real freedom and transformation is. As we assess our situation tonight, would we consider the cross, instead of ourselves. Only there can we find forgiveness and the grace needed to live changed lives.

NOVEMBER 1

GRANT US BOLDNESS!

The early church leaders witnessed the crucifixion of Jesus, had been beaten and threatened themselves, and now just being released from this harassing treatment of religious leaders, they pray that God would give them boldness to continue to speak the message that only they could speak.

"'Now, Lord, look on their threats, and grant to Your servants that with all boldness they may speak Your word, by stretching out Your hand to heal, and that signs and wonders may be done through the name of Your holy Servant Jesus.' And when they had prayed, the place where they were assembled together was shaken; and they were all filled with the Holy Spirit, and they spoke the word of God with boldness." Acts 4:29-31

The disciples were called to be the witnesses of Jesus. Surely, it required courage, boldness, an informed mind, and a trust in the One who had called them. They were not immune to fear, or the knowledge that just as Jesus was persecuted, they would be also. Yet, they turned their attention to the One who called them. They knew that it would be in His strength that they could go forward. It was not their power that would deliver them, but the power of the Living God who resided in them.

What can we learn from their example? As they were able to answer the call of God on their lives, so can we. It is time for us to stand up and be bold! We have to answer an important question, "When was the last time that we stood up for anything that required boldness?" Or, "When have we prayed a prayer that shook things up?" It is time for us to wake up, stand up, and be witnesses for the One who has confessed us to the Father. Let us not just believe; let us behave as we are called to do!

NOVEMBER 2

HOW DOES WORK AND PRAYER RELATE?

In reflecting on Nehemiah's leadership there are two strong elements in his example: a life of prayer and a life of hard work. How are these two qualities related? You could say that our praying determines the quality of our working, just as our working reflects the quality of praying. We can see this clearly in Nehemiah's story.

William Temple said:

"We think our real work is our activity, to which prayer is an adjunct, our prayer is our real work, and our activity is the index of how we have done it".

J. I. Packer on reflection on this statement wrote:

"Prayer . . . that centers on the hallowing of God's name and doing His will - has, among its other effects, a reflex effect. It purifies the heart; it purges our attitudes and motives; melts down all the self-centeredness, self-sufficiency, and self-reliance that as fallen creatures we bring to it and programs us to work humbly, in a God-honoring, God-fearing, God-defendant way."

You see, real prayer (not superficial prayer), places our hearts and motivations in view (God already knows them) for God to inspect and mold for His glory. It is out of presenting ourselves as this kind of living sacrifice that He then proves what His will is for our lives. Then, our work becomes a reflection of our inward state. That is why James could write:

"Show me your faith without your works, and I will show you my faith by my works." James 2:18

May our real work of prayer motivate and shape our external work and activities to reveal God's glory.

NOVEMBER 3

THE POWER OF CHOICE!

Today is Election Day in the city of Fall River. Those of us who are citizens and live in this city have a responsibility to choose able servants who will lead this city. Like any other city, we have enormous challenges as well as opportunities. It is important that we all use our best judgment and participate in making our city successful.

It is instructive that when the early church was facing difficulties, or you could say growing pains, the apostles sought to bring about a solution. What they said to the people was:

"Seek out from among you seven men of good reputation, full of the Holy Spirit and wisdom, whom we may appoint over this business." Acts 6:3

What they did was give some criteria from which to be able to evaluate who to choose, but the choice was theirs. Poor choices would bring poor leadership. Good choices would secure wise leadership.

If there is ever a day when we need wise leadership it is today. May we seek out those who have good reputations, a fear of God more than man and are wise for the task. Only then can we secure that we will be properly represented. If we do nothing, we must live with the consequence of not exercising our voice.

Let us pray for our leaders and also pray for the wisdom to select leaders in the future. Our diligence is needed. Get informed the best that you can. Ask the Lord for discernment. Remember, character is weightier than promises.

NOVEMBER 4

THE CALL TO BE!

This morning, in our community the votes have been tabulated and the people have exercised their voice in our democratic system of government. We now must live with the choices made and seek to unite in a way that is constructive and not destructive. All who have been elected in office will need our prayers and cooperation. Included in this should be our involvement and example.

Jesus instructed His disciples (and by inference all of us who are His disciples today):

"You are the salt of the earth ... you are the light of the world...a city that is set on a hill cannot be hidden." Matthew 5:13-14

In each of these descriptions was the alternative idea of what it would be like if we didn't take our place. The salt would be no good, the light would be hidden, the city would not be seen. In other words, we have a tremendous responsibility to be people who demonstrate what a healthy city looks like. How laws are to be followed. How families love each other. How work is to be done. How character is to be developed and demonstrated. How interactions with people are to bring out the best in others.

This means that heart and head issues need to be dealt with. What will follow are actions that demonstrate right thinking and being. We do have a part to play, and it hasn't ended because we have voted. We must all ask the question how we can be part of the solution and not just part of the problem.

Let us follow the concluding thought that Jesus spoke:

"Let your light so shine before men, that they may see your good works, and glorify your Father in heaven." Matthew 5:16

It is time for us to rise up and be builders in our homes, churches, and communities!

NOVEMBER 5

NEED REVELATION AND HARD WORK TO MAINTAIN UNITY

I am considering a pivotal section in the letter to the Ephesians this morning. For the first three chapters, Paul tells the Ephesian church all God has done for them. He is praying they get this revelation of the importance of the church in God's plan for their lives. If they can see what this great inheritance is, and God's plan for the world, they can strategically participate in making that revelation known through their very lives. He now is going to make a transition to all that must be embraced to see that this revelation becomes a reality.

"I, therefore, the prisoner of the Lord, beseech you to walk worthy of your calling with which you were called, with all lowliness and gentleness, with longsuffering, bearing with one another in love, endeavoring to keep the unity of the Spirit in the bond of peace." Ephesians 4:1-3

Here begins the hard work on our part. In order to walk worthy of our calling, there is an attitude and aptitude that must be acquired. We must be humble, patient with those called to work with us, and we must also learn the principles of what a redeemed life looks like. Not only learning but doing.

Becoming one-minded requires that we accept training and dialogue with others to come to the place of one-mindedness. This is not just something that is automatic. It takes a maturing process. Becoming one-minded is becoming Christ-minded. It is not just that we agree on doctrine, but how that doctrine is worked out in our life-choices and actions. This takes great effort to do in our families and churches, but even more so among several churches.

What Christ Jesus wants revealed is His wisdom (see Ephesians 3:10). This is part of Christ's eternal purpose. You and I are privileged to be a part of this. Knowing what Christ has already done for us, may we accept the second half of the letter to the Ephesians as clear instruction to how we can walk worthy of our calling. Don't be faint-hearted. You can do it. The same power that raised Jesus from the dead resides in you.

NOVEMBER 6

WHAT IF WE ONLY HEAR AND UNDERSTAND PART OF THE MESSAGE?

This morning I am reading a familiar passage. Jesus encounters a Samaritan woman at a well. His conversation leads Him to compare the water she is drawing from the well with eternal life, and the indwelling Spirit. What she hears is a possible way for her to have an easier life. Look at the words spoken:

Jesus answered and said to her:

"Whoever drinks of this water will thirst again, but whoever drinks of the water that I shall give him will never thirst. But the water that I shall give him will become in him a fountain of water springing up into everlasting life." The woman said to Him, "Sir, give me his water, that I may not thirst, nor come here to draw." John 4:13-15

If this woman simply said, "Give me this water so that I may not thirst", she would have been hearing and understanding the comparison that Jesus was using for what she needed to have eternal life and a sustained life. Because she added that she would no longer need to come and draw water makes one question if she saw this water as something more than spiritual; therefore, she would no longer need to labor for life's necessities.

Thankfully, Jesus continued in His dialogue with this woman so that she could come to a full understanding and by faith believe. The question we must ponder is, "Have we explained fully the gospel so that those making a commitment have a proper understanding for their faith?" If we don't properly teach, others might believe another gospel, one that promises life to be easy. If so, will those that are not fully discipled endure or develop the fruit of walking in the kingdom?

Lord, help us to communicate the truth of your Gospel!

NOVEMBER 7

ON EAGLES' WINGS

This morning I attended a funeral where a song was sung about rising on eagles' wings. This afternoon, one of the scriptures chosen for a wedding ceremony that I will be performing is from Isaiah 40 which says:

"But those who wait on the Lord shall renew their strength; they shall mount up with wings like eagles, they shall run and not be weary, they shall walk and not faint." Isaiah 40:31

Isn't it curious that this symbol of eagle's wings is something that both the grieving and hopeful are both looking to? In one case, it points to the acknowledgement of God's promise in the resurrection, in the other the promise to strengthen us for our walk here on the earth. But there is another scripture that might help us to tie these two together. It is found in Exodus 19. Here the Lord speaks to the children of Israel saying:

"You have seen what I did to the Egyptians, and how I bore you on eagles' wings and brought you to myself." Exodus 19:4

What we see in this verse is how the grace of God is what brings us close. It is not anything we do, but all about what He did. When we were still sinners, Christ died for us. He is the one who bore us on His wings. He is the One who will sustain us in this life. He is the One who will carry us home.

There is nothing mysterious about this. It is His grace that enables our faith. When we get a revelation of so great a love He has shown us, we can't help but love and serve Him now and forever.

Lift us on Your wings today, Lord! Thank you for your great grace in our lives.

NOVEMBER 8

WHERE IS MY HONOR? WHERE IS MY REVERENCE?

This afternoon, I began reading the Book of Malachi as part of my regular daily readings. Malachi the prophet was probing the situation of his own day where there were deep problems of hypocrisy, infidelity, mixed marriages, divorce, false worship, and arrogance. So sinful had the nation become that the words of God spoken to the people no longer had any impact.

It is interesting that this book becomes the last of the Old Testament where the voice of God remains silent for over four hundred years. If Israel would no longer listen, then the word of God remained silent.

One of the indictments is found where the prophet writes two of God's questions:

"A son honors his father, and a servant his master. If then I am your Father, where is My honor? And if I am a Master, where is My reverence?" Malachi 1:6

As I consider these questions, I have to ask the same in our own generation. Where is the honor? Where is the reverence? Where is the fear of God? If we will not follow the words already spoken, should God speak more? If we have no fear, can we possibly find wisdom?

Until we learn to honor and show reverence, we will not demonstrate to our generation these qualities. Maybe in this thought is the answer to our own generation. If we demonstrate the right example, perhaps others will follow our lead. If not, it is anything goes, and we will suffer the fruit of our own hypocrisy.

Lord, teach us to honor you properly with our words and actions. Help us rightly demonstrate this quality to our own friends, family, and associates. May you be glorified through our lives. Amen.

NOVEMBER 9

HONORING PARENTS WHEN ROLES ARE REVERSED

When parents grow weak and the child grows strong, and the child becomes the parents' caregiver when the parents' economic value is small and the child's is great (Lev. 27:7), the child remains a child called to honor his or her parents.

Today, more than any other time, our culture is concerned with its happiness over its responsibilities. Biblically, we are called to embrace our responsibilities. Our parents are to continue to be esteemed in our lives. Though the power of our parents might wane and their active authority diminishes, they should never lose their dignity as caregivers and teachers.

"Children, obey your parents in the Lord, for this is right. 'Honor your father and mother,' which is the first commandment with promise: 'that it may be well with you and you may live long on the earth.'" Ephesians 6:1-3

"But if any widow has children or grandchildren, let them first learn to show piety at home and to repay their parents; for this is good and acceptable before God. . . . But if anyone does not provide for his own, and especially for those of his household, he has denied the faith and is worse than an unbeliever." 1 Timothy 5:4, 8

What we distill from the command to "honor your father and mother" is a moral commitment to filial respect and long-term loyalty. This includes material care and support. A hug or a kiss on the cheek is very pleasant, but nothing suits honor better than carrying out the legacy of what your parents have instilled in you. God is honored as we honor our parents and grandparents.

Consider the practical ways in which you can show honor to those who have been in authority over you. May we learn new expressions of honor as we value those who have given much in times past to strengthen us.

YOU SEEK ME - WHY?

Have you ever noticed how some people gather around those in power? These same people can't be found when that same person is no longer in the position to better them. What might seem to be a great following is really just people looking for their own needs, without any real concern with what sacrifice they might need to make for others.

People had followed Jesus after one of His miraculous feelings. In this case, over five thousand had been fed. But Jesus probes why they are following Him. Because the reason they follow makes a huge difference. He said:

"Most assuredly I say to you, you seek Me, not because you saw the signs, but because you ate of the loaves and were filled." John 6:26

In other words, "you profited by being associated with Me." It wasn't an association to see what they could do for Jesus, or because they had a great love for Him. No, it was an association where they thought, "if He can give us bread, what else can He do for us." It saddens me to think of the times we have all experienced these kinds of relationships.

But Jesus now tells them how this relationship can change, "*Do not labor for food which perishes, but for food which endures to everlasting life, which the Son of Man will give you, because God the Father has set His seal on Him"* (John 6:27). Jesus had to continue to explain this concept. Many of the people just could not understand. They said it was a hard saying. I have come to understand that because of the filters and preconceived thoughts we have, it can make us deaf and dumb to any real understanding of what the Lord is leading us to. Instead of changing their minds, many of His disciples went back and walked with Jesus no more (see John 6:66).

The whole chapter was focused on believing. Who are those that believe? How is that belief expressed? How about us today? Do we believe? Or, are we just in association for the benefits? What happens if the bread line dries up, then what?

NOVEMBER 11

DECLARE YOUR STRENGTH AGAIN LORD!

As I ponder the great sacrifice of our veterans, I am also wondering how our present generation understands the cost of freedom and the importance of working to preserve it? The psalmist writes:

"O God, You have taught me from my youth; and to this day I declare Your wondrous works. Now also when I am old and grey headed, O God, do not forsake me, until I declare Your strength to this generation, Your power to everyone who is to come." Psalm 71:17-18

We have had the enormous privilege of living in a secure country. We know that the example of so many to give of themselves for a greater cause has been etched in our minds. We must never stop telling the stories and taking the time to remind each other of this on-going demonstration of courage and sacrifice. If we fail to, this generation will not know what the costs were, nor will they have the courage themselves to protect what has been fought for. It seems that in these days, the greater enemy is not across the shores, but those within our own borders who no longer take pride in what it means to be an American.

May God give us the strength to declare the truth to this generation. Reminding them also of the fact that "*unless the Lord guards the city, the watchmen stays awake in vain*" (Psalm 127:1).

Thank you to all who have served, and also are presently serving. Your sacrifice is appreciated and is noticed.

NOVEMBER 12

THURSDAY NIGHTS!

My various responsibilities have me reading and studying on different levels. The problem with that is trying to reduce some of this thinking to some unifying thought. For now, I will leave that for another day.

Thursday evenings are a special time when my daughter and grand-daughter have dinner with my wife and I. Included around our table are my mom and grandmother. Five generations together - something that I know is a real blessing. Somehow the complications of life are easily reduced to simply loving family.

We are able to talk about our respective days, enjoy each other's company. Have a competition with my grand-daughter as to who can get to my chair first, and tonight some Lego building.

Life can seem complicated at times, but it is good to enjoy the simple things, For in the large scheme of things, loving God and loving family and friends are the things that are fulfilling and most important. So simple is good. Tomorrow is soon enough to try and solve all the other problems of the world.

"The Preacher sought to find acceptable words: and what was written was upright-words of truth. The words of the wise are like goads, and the words of scholars are like well-driven nails, given by one Shepherd. And further, my son, be admonished by these. Of making many books there is no end, and much study is wearisome to the flesh. Let us hear the conclusion of the matter: Fear God and keep His commandments, for this is man's all. For God will bring every work into judgment, including every secret thing, whether good or evil." Ecclesiastes 12:10-14

NOVEMBER 13

OVERCOME EVIL WITH GOOD

Tonight (November 13, 2015), we have learned of such great atrocities in Paris, France. We recognize that the world we live in has changed so much. Fear has a way of gripping each of our hearts, and it seeks to paralyze us in what we seek to do. I know that we feel so small and insignificant in times like these, but is that the truth?

If we are honest with each other we would admit that recoiling, retreating, and relinquishing our ground are always pressing in on our own thinking and being. But, if that is what we do, we succumb to the enemy's plot. What are we to do? How can we make a difference? Paul told the Roman Christians:

"Do not be overcome by evil, but overcome evil with good." Romans 12:21

This was spoken to a people who had to face great atrocities themselves.

So with grieving hearts we pray for France, as we also pray for so many parts of the world, including our own neighborhoods. But may we not just retreat, we must stand our ground, fight the good fight of faith, take our places in our communities as the light we were meant to shine. If we all do this, we can overcome evil and shine the light of Christ's love to those around us.

IS IT WHERE THE BLOOD IS SPILLED THAT MAKES A DIFFERENCE?

Like many of you, I am saddened by the events that took place in Paris. Surely, we should pray for those and others being affected by terrorism. What is troubling me though is why other events do not move us as much. For an extended time, Ukraine has gone through great battles, many people have died, others have had their land confiscated, and the West has been silent. There has been great genocide in African countries that go unreported. I could go on and on, but that is only part of the problem.

You see, if we want to be real, there is blood being shed on our own land. That blood is shed in clinics all over our nation. The blood is shed on the most innocent and undefended. I am talking about babies. While we make room for others to come to our nation, we legally allow the extermination of others. We do not use gas, but drugs, knives, and any other instruments that efficiently snuff out life.

How can we point the finger at other nations and peoples when we the people have such a barbaric existence? I know that many would argue with me using personal rights as their defense. But whose personal rights are they talking about? In any case - the blood is spilled. I can't even count the number of the carnage to date. I wonder if this blood spilled cries out, or is it important to anyone anymore? If we are really about life - maybe we have to do some inspection of our own. Then there would be a proper focus for our prayers.

"Then the Lord said to Cain, 'Where is Abel your brother?' He said, 'I do not know. Am I my brother's keeper?' And He [the Lord] said, 'What have you done? The voice of your brother's blood cries out to Me from the ground.'" Genesis 4:9-10

"Deliver me from the guilt of bloodshed, O God, the God of my salvation. And my tongue shall sing aloud of Your righteousness." Psalm 51:14

NOVEMBER 15

GIVE US HELP FROM OUR TROUBLE!

In reading Psalm 108, the last two verses catch my attention. There was a song we used to sing many years ago that had these verses imbedded in the chorus. The condition of our times can overwhelm us. If we are not resolute and keep our eyes and trust on God, we can easily be distracted and even defeated. But that is not our focus. Therefore, we sing praises to the Lord among the nations, knowing that His great mercy is above the heavens and His truth reaches to the clouds.

What we must understand is that we need His intervention. Our own human wisdom or strength will only get us so far. We must be inspired, empowered, and informed by the Lord's wisdom and strength. Therefore the psalmist says:

"Give us help from trouble, for the help of man is useless. Through God we will do valiantly, for it is He who shall tread down our enemies." Psalm 108:12-13

For the times in which we live, may we be encouraged to trust in the One who makes us valiant. Only with His help can we overcome trouble. Only with His lead, can we see the enemy defeated. It is time we stop trusting in what is useless and start putting our trust where it belongs. Only then can we expect to see victory come to pass.

NOVEMBER 16

NOW THAT IS A REAL PRAYER!

This morning, one of the scripture readings that I have read and pondered is Psalm 109. If you would take the time to read this psalm, you will notice the reality and difficulty that David must have been experiencing. He is not mincing words here. He is surely not being politically correct. For a guy that is after the heart of God, you could even say he has a rough edge.

I bet many people reading this psalm might be quick to judge and say "where is your mercy David?" "You call yourself a God-fearing man, why such strong speech and condemnation?" "Shouldn't you just take it on the chin, and turn the other way?"

I am so glad that the Bible shows us real men and women, not some plastic sanitized versions. It teaches us real life situations, difficulties, enemies, struggles, pressures, and yes, even false accusers. I am glad that God is big enough to listen to our honest rant. Knowing the circumstances we are already in, He helps us sort out the frustrations, the way we see things, and empowers us to move ahead in a righteous albeit real way.

When David gets everything off his chest in prayer, he then declares:

"I will greatly praise the Lord with my mouth; Yes, I will praise Him among the multitude. For He shall stand at the right hand of the poor, to save him from those who condemn him." Psalm 109:30-31

Go ahead, pray a real prayer to the Lord! He wouldn't want you to come to Him any other way. It could be the beginning of a real breakthrough in your relationship with your Heavenly Father.

NOVEMBER 17

IF WE COULD APPRECIATE THE PARTS - WE COULD ACCOMPLISH EVEN MORE

This morning I had the privilege of touring with the director of the Veteran's Association in the city of Fall River. Our children and families from East Gate Christian Academy had collected canned goods and food items to be able to donate to the veterans. There ended up being more than they could fit in one truck, so we filled mine and I went down with these men to unload.

The director was kind enough to show me around and explain what they do, how different people and businesses have helped and the volunteers that give their time to help veterans and their families in our community. I am thankful for organizations like this one in the city that give of their time to be of help to those who are in need. I can only imagine how many of these kinds of groups, individuals, businesses and non-profit organizations including churches and schools are giving of themselves in the service of helping others. Can you just imagine if we could in some coordinated way use our time, talent and treasure to the maximum?

While I hope we can move more towards this ideal in the future, we can take the time now to celebrate and support those who are doing their part. If we could only appreciate this, and each other, think of the possibilities that could be?

"Continue earnestly in prayer, being vigilant in it with thanksgiving; meanwhile praying also for us, that God would open to us a door for the word, to speak the mystery of Christ, for which I am also in chains, that I may make it manifest, as I ought to speak. Walk in wisdom toward those who are outside, redeeming the time. Let your speech always be with grace, seasoned with salt, that you may know how you ought to answer each one." Colossians 4:2-6

NOVEMBER 18

ASK OF ME, AND I WILL GIVE YOU...

In times of trouble and turmoil, we have a tendency to recoil, retreat, and retire. When we search out the pages of the Bible, there were plenty of opportunities for such retreat. Pressures have been felt in every generation. Wars and rumors of wars continue to this day. If fear led us, we would not go. But in all of this, is there also an opportunity? It all comes down to who we see as above all. If it is self, or government, or kings and rulers, we have a right to be afraid. But if we understand that there is a King set and seated in the heavens, our perspective must change.

I am reminded of Psalm 2 this morning. You read at the beginning about the nations rage and the people plotting vain things, kings of the earth setting themselves and taking counsel together for power and destruction. But then there is a second scene, the one from above, where He who sits in the heavens has the final say. He is the One with ultimate authority. He speaks of His anointed Christ:

"Ask of Me, and I will give You the nation's for Your inheritance, and the ends of the earth for Your possession." Psalm 2:8

When Jesus commissioned His disciples, He sent them and us out with delegated power. He proclaimed that all power and authority had been invested in Him; therefore, He now was sending us (See Matthew 28:18-20). If we can only get a glimpse of what this means, we might just rise up and begin to build the Kingdom as He has already commissioned us to do.

We have a King who is seated. What we now need to experience is an enemy put under His feet. The only way to do that is to be hid in Him and work together as His body. If He is our head, we will lack no authority or direction to do what He has called us to do.

Today is not a day of retreat or to be polarized with fear. It is a day to rise up and do what He has commissioned us to do.

NOVEMBER 19

CHOSEN BY GOD

Why did God choose us? Not because we did anything great that impressed Him. It wasn't the size of our faith or the depth of our intellect. It certainly wasn't because we first chose Him. It was entirely by grace. Grace prompted by love.

The Lord chooses us for reasons only He can answer. He is sovereign, and He can give grace to whomever He pleases. He sets His love upon us because, out of the goodness and grace of His own heart, He declares, "I want you to be Mine."

Isn't that humbling? Jesus said to His disciples:

"You did not choose Me but I chose you, and appointed you that you would go and bear fruit, and that your fruit would remain, so that whatever you ask of the Father in My name He may give to you." John 15:15

In other words, we didn't hunt Him down; He hunted us down. We did not initiate this encounter; He initiated the call. We didn't work half of our lives to find Him; He gave His life so that we might be found. Being chosen by God says a lot more about Him than it does about us!

Nevertheless, think of the value of being owned by God. What incredible worth that He has bestowed on us. What incredible dignity we have been given! We are *"a people for God's own possession"* (1 Peter 2:9).

As those belonging to Him, we are called to bear fruit, fruit that endures. This can only happen if we trust that the same Lord who chooses us, sends us out in His name. He will empower us to accomplish whatever He desires. He remains available to answer our call in prayer for the task at hand. Chosen by God for a purpose, what a privilege!

NOVEMBER 20

SUFFERING WITHOUT SEPARATION

When I consider the contemplations of Paul as he wrote to the Romans, I can also consider the reality of our own lives in ministry. Some people, maybe even you, have had the notion that life with Christ is an easy one. Everything will fall into place without much difficulties, for after all, doesn't Christ give us His grace? What we often fail to see is that we are being groomed to steward His kingdom. We cannot possibly take on this responsibility without ever increasing training and development. Here is where it gets interesting.

Paul says, "*For I consider that the suffering of this present time are not worthy to be compared with the glory which shall be revealed in us*" (Romans 8:18). Why would Paul talk about suffering? Is it because some of us might experience tribulation, distress, persecution, famine, nakedness, peril, or even the sword? (see Romans 8:35)).

Two thoughts here: First, are the things we go through just to hammer us down, or shape us up? In other words, the challenges in our lives, if faced up to, can develop us into better stewards so that we can take on greater responsibilities for the Lord. He who is faithful in the little will be faithful in the much.

The second thought is, where is Christ in relation to these difficulties, pressures, principalities, and powers? He is right there with us. Paul writes, *"Yet in all these things we are more than conquerors through Him who loved us. For I am persuaded that neither death nor life, nor angels nor principalities nor powers, not things to present nor things to come, nor height nor depth, nor any other created thing, shall be able to separate us from the love of God which is in Christ Jesus our Lord"* (Romans 8:37-39).

If you can give some thought to this, I know you can be encouraged. Instead of the pressure you are feeling right now getting you to despair, recognize the love of God that is near and is inseparable. Ask Him by His grace to give you the wisdom, endurance and the strategic ability to continue the race with success. The glory is only going to get greater.

NOVEMBER 21

MULTIPLY OUR SEED!

It is only natural to be concerned with having enough to meet our needs and the needs of our family; but when we begin to look beyond ourselves and out to others, there is something important being done in our lives, while blessing others. Of course, this will require discipline and faithfulness on our part.

Paul wrote to the Corinthians:

"God is able to make all grace abound toward you, that you, always having all sufficiency in all things, may have an abundance for every good work. As it is written: 'He has dispersed abroad, He has given to the poor; His righteousness endures forever.' Now may He who supplies seed to the sower, and bread for food, supply and multiply the seed you have sown and increase the fruits of your righteousness" (2 Cor. 9:8-10).

It is important that we do not mix up these two things. Bread is meant for eating and seed for sowing. God provides us with both. If we use our seed for our own consumption, where will the return on our planting take place? If we have sowed ample seed, we must trust and pray that God will multiply that seed sown. Finding the delicate balance is important.

The Lord knows we need provision for our homes. He also calls us to trust Him as we sow into His field. The simple reality is no seed sown reaps no future harvest. If we sow much seed, we have the potential for a great harvest.

As we pray, may we ask the Lord to multiply our seed! As we put aside some of the harvest for future sowing, may the Lord increase the fruit of our hands. It's not one or the other, but both together: seed for the sower and bread for food. May we never take what was meant for sowing and mistake it as our food.

NOVEMBER 22

PREPARATION AND PROVING MUST PRECEDE LEADERSHIP

It seems that we are facing a growing crisis of leadership in our culture as well as in the church. Many leaders have been elected into prominent national offices with little experience or training for the important responsibilities that they hold. Then we wonder why there is such a lack of integrity and ability for them to properly make the difficult choices that are needed for our well-being as a people.

From a Biblical perspective (which is instructive for civil and ecclesiastical office) a leader does not become one overnight. Nor do they become one simply because of popular vote. They must be tested first.

"But let these also first be tested; then let them serve as deacons, being found blameless." 1 Timothy 3:10

"Do not lay hands on anyone hastily, nor share in other people's sins; keep yourself pure." 1 Timothy 5:22

Leaders must first undergo the preparations of God, which both breaks and strengthens them. Moreover, the more a person wants to be used by God as a leader, the more they must submit to the deeper dealings of God in their life.

This goes against our culture, which wants instant success. We want to start at "the top," but that is not the way of God. In the Kingdom of God, the way up is down (humility). We are called to serve those who we lead. If we ignore God's way in leadership development, we do so at our own risk! Emerging leaders must be given time to learn, to be proven, to learn discipline and to be broken, in order for character to be formed. Moreover, emerging leaders must also learn that faithfulness in a little is required before they will receive responsibility for much (see Luke 16:10).

How does this apply to our own lives? Is the Lord trying to shape something in us in order for us to take on the next greater responsibility? Should we be careful to whom we extend authority, by our own vote, whether or not they have the sufficient character for the office?

NOVEMBER 23

ARE WE PROPERLY DRESSED?

It is important that we discern where we are and who we are so we can present ourselves in a proper way. It used to be if someone was traveling that they dressed up for the occasion; same with church, business, social events. If one was dressed improperly, one might attract attention, but not in a good way.

Paul uses this terminology in different ways. For instance, in battle one must dress with proper armor (see Ephesians 6). But in Colossians, he speaks of another kind of dress. He speaks of how one must put on the proper attire of one who is elect and holy before God. What might this attire look like? Paul gives us insight:

"Therefore, as the elect of God, holy and beloved, put on tender mercies, kindness, humility, meekness, long suffering; bearing with one another, and forgiving one another, if anyone has a complaint against another; even as Christ forgave you, so you also must do. But above all these things, put on love, which is the bond of perfection." Colossians 3:12-24

Beyond this, we must have our hearts ruled by the peace of God, and let the Word of God dwell in us richly (see Colossians 3:15-15). Of course, we must understand the calling for which we have been called and be thankful.

Can you imagine what would happen if our wardrobe was changed to these items? While we think of putting on something as external, in reality what we put on is mostly internal. But the revelation of what is put on internally is experienced externally. Those around us will see how we are dressed.

Instead of starting another fashion trend like putting on ugly sweaters, let's put on Christ. This will be a welcomed sight for sore eyes. Maybe it will catch on and we will help shape a better, spiritual fashion trend.

NOVEMBER 24

A POWERFUL PRAYER MEETING

In my office, directly facing me is a picture of the first prayer in Congress. I know that many Americans today, including many Christians, have fallen into believing that Christians should not be involved in civil government and that faith should be some sort of compartmentalization. They think that faith should be kept in one arena and real life in another.

God was so important to the Founding Fathers of our nation, that when they met in Congress for the first time, in September of 1774, they opened with prayer. This prayer was not the kind of prayer we have perhaps witnessed that is routine, ordinary, or sanitized. According to the writings of those who were there, that time of prayer in Congress was momentous as well as extended. In fact, John Adams explained that Congress not only prayed but that they also studied four chapters of the Bible.

That Bible study had such a profound effect upon the delegates, that John Adams wrote to his wife Abigail these words: "I never saw a greater effect upon an audience. It seemed as if Heaven had ordained that Psalm to be read on the morning . . . I must beg you to read that Psalm . . . Read this letter to your friends. Read it to your father." (Her father was the Rev. William Smith, the pastor of their local church).

There is no doubt that America has been a successful nation with stable, successive government because of the foundation on which it was built. This is the same foundation we must return to in our day.

As we prepare for our Thanksgiving celebrations, may we be ever so thankful for the founding of our nation. First, with the faith of the pilgrims that became the bedrock or stepping stone of the later establishment of a Christ fearing nation. Secondly, may we pray for a reawakening that will cause us to kneel once again, in our homes, our churches and yes, even in Congress so that we might once again put our trust firmly on the One who has all providence and is deserving of our utmost allegiance.

NOVEMBER 25

THE SWORD OR THE CUP?

Reading the account of Jesus' arrest in Gethsemane this morning, I came to the point of where Peter cuts off the ear of the high priest's servant. Jesus had just told those who came for Him who He was and for them to let go of the others. Peter quickly draws his sword and does damage. I suspect he wants to defend Jesus. One might look at this and say that Peter is a man of courage, willing to stand up for his Master.

But Jesus does not encourage him in his action. In fact, he rebukes Peter:

"Put your sword into the sheath. Shall I not drink the cup which My Father has given Me?" John 18:11

Here is the real issue: flesh vs. Spirit. Do we respond in the flesh or according to the Spirit? There are times when the sword is the appropriate instrument to use. This is not the time. God has a plan and it involves Jesus submitting to that plan. Jesus understood this. Peter did not.

Do we ever have times when we must surrender to the plan of God, and we draw our swords and fight against this plan? We might even think we are doing the righteous thing, but we haven't discerned properly. Perhaps when confronted with a fearful situation it tends to elicit a sword type reaction from us. However, because of Jesus discernment of the Father's will, He had the courage and foresight to drink the cup instead.

May we, too, be this discerning. It takes more courage to walk this road.

NOVEMBER 26

HAPPY THANKSGIVING

We have so much to be thankful for; the love of God, love of family and friends. May each of you, who are so dear to us, reflect on God's great blessings.

- Take some time today and give Him thanks.
- Take some time and appreciate those who are dear to you.

Bernice and I want to extend to you God's richest blessing on you and your families.

"Enter into His gates with thanksgiving, and into His courts with praise. Be thankful to Him, and bless His name. For the Lord is good; His mercy is everlasting, and His truth endures to all generations." Psalm 100:4-5

"Oh come, let us sing to the Lord! Let us shout joyfully to the Rock of our salvation. Let us come before His presence with thanksgiving; let us shout joyfully to Him with praises." Psalm 95:1-2

"Thanks be to God for His indescribable gift!" 2 Corinthians 9:15

"Be anxious for nothing, but in everything by prayer and supplication, with thanksgiving, let your request be made known to God; and the peace of God, which surpasses all understanding, will guard your hearts and minds through Christ Jesus." Philippians 4:6-7

NOVEMBER 27

HAVE WE TURNED THE PAGE ON THANKFULNESS?

This morning, I turned to the Drudge Report for some news and six of the top stories on the list were incidents of fighting associated with Black Friday. I just read the titles of the articles and couldn't believe, or wish I couldn't believe, that this is my country.

Let me give you some of the headlines: "Kentucky Mall Brawl Kick Off Violence" ..."Brutal Fights Across America" ..."Woman Steals Veggie Steamer from Child, Wrestles Mother"... "Santa Stampede". The sad thing is that these were not the only articles about how people are behaving across America today. It really makes one question why this kind of behavior? James gives us insight:

"Where do wars and fights come from among you? Do they come from your desires for pleasure that war in your members? You lust and do not have. You covet and cannot obtain. You fight and war. You do not have because you do not ask. You ask and do not receive, because you ask amiss, that you may spend it on your pleasure." James 4:1-3

The reality is that we cannot find peace in things. Stuff never satisfies. The latest gadget will be broken soon and outdated. There are some things that are of more value than stuff. Can you imagine if you could wrap up kindness with a bow; love through your unselfish service; joy in seeing someone else get a hand up; satisfaction, because of a life well lived; contentment, because of a heart of gratitude for all of God's care and time that you were willing to share with a friend in need?

All of these expressions of love are more worthy than any material possession we may obtain. They are of the substance that make for enduring qualities. They are the sentiments that hold us in difficult times. We can never really appreciate life if we continue to try and grab and claw at ways to obtain an advantage for ourselves. It is only when we see things from a different perspective (a God-like perspective) where we turn and instead of lusting (which focus on self) we love (which has its focus on others). Only then will we really walk in true thankfulness.

NOVEMBER 28

CATCHING UP ON SOME READING

In my continued studies the past few years, I have come across many quotations or ideas presented by a missionary. His name is Roland Allen. The book that I just finished is part of a classic reprint series. Written in 1912, the book "*Missionary Methods St. Paul's or Ours, a Study of the Church in the Four Provinces*" is one I would highly recommend to anyone serious in mission work, church planting and administration. I could even go as far as to say that some of these principles would hold true in developing our families into maturity.

We often build with methods we have become accustomed to in our own generation without giving serious consideration to the principles we are using. Sometimes those principles we seek to implement do more harm than good, often creating cultures of dependence. We see these principles at work in the world around us also.

If we rediscover the principles we find in the founding of the first churches, we can have greater success and develop communities that will thrive, be self-sustained and self-propagating. The Christian faith, when properly received, should lead us to freedom and responsibility. One in which we can be empowered to deal with the uniqueness of our own community situations, develop leadership within that community, and be a light-bearer of the gospel in our culture. Only when we are discipled to take personal responsibility and participate in bringing solutions to our own culture will we begin to grow into full maturity.

What is one area of responsibility that you need to focus on? Without excuse or blame-shifting, how might you embrace that responsibility? What specific steps could you take beginning today?

May God's grace and enablement strengthen you to take the proper action.

NOVEMBER 29

ARE YOU THIRSTY?

The lyrics of an older song that I love to sing is taken from Psalm 42 which reads, "As the deer pants for the water brooks, so pants my soul for You, O God." Deep in all of us is what Augustine described as a "God-shaped vacuum." One that only God can fill. It rejects all substitutes. Oh, we might try to substitute this need with many material or relational things, but nothing finite will last or quench the thirst. Whether we know it or not, what we are longing for is to know and experience the presence of God in our lives.

The water brooks are springs which flow continually from subterranean rivers. Jesus promises us that those who come to Him and drink will have streams flowing from their hearts.

"On the last day, the great day of the feast, Jesus stood and cried out, saying, 'If anyone thirsts, let him come to Me and drink. He who believes in Me, as the Scripture has said, out of his heart will flow rivers of living water." John 7:37-38

It is the same kind of water that Jesus offered the woman at the well:

"If you knew the gift of God, and who it is who says to you, 'Give Me a drink,' you would have asked Him, and He would have given you living water. ... Whoever drinks of the water that I shall give him will never thirst. But the water that I shall give him will become in him a fountain of water springing up into everlasting life." John 4:10, 14

The living water God promises us will satisfy us like the streams of water satisfy the deer. Jesus promises: *"Blessed are those who hunger and thirst for righteousness, for they shall be filled"* (Matthew 5:6). Here is the invitation, *"Everyone who thirsts, come to the waters"* (Isaiah 55:1).

NOVEMBER 30

I WAS GLAD...

I have been quoting from the beginning of Psalm 122 for several days now. When Jesus came to Jerusalem on what we now reflect on Palm Sunday, there were shouts of praise. The Pharisees did not like the fact that people were praising Jesus. They wanted it stopped. They told Jesus so. But Jesus affirming the rightness of the praise told these religious leaders that if these would not praise Him, even the rocks would cry out.

Sometimes, in our day, it seems that people are more like the Pharisees than those praising. There is something in us that wants to quiet the joyful expressions of thanksgiving; the joy that is centered on the One who is faithful; the joy that comes because of trust and intimacy; a joy that transcends any circumstance or storm.

Instead of joy being expressed among the people of God there is sadness. Why? Is it unfulfilled expectation? Misplaced expectation? Is it legalism? Have people exchanged some ritual from the real; religion instead of relationship; self-absorption instead of life-giving?

The psalmist says:

"I was GLAD [my own emphasis] when they said to me, 'Let us go into the house of the Lord.'" Psalm 122:1

What if we reoriented ourselves in this way. Instead of some grudging duty, we were so filled with love and anticipation that we couldn't wait to be present in the Lord's house; so much so that we made this a priority in our lives? What if we guarded this time from any other preoccupation or distraction? If we did, do you think we might be glad again.

If we were glad to go to the Lord's house, might not others also be glad when we invite them? Of course they would. We have no problem promoting the things that we enjoy. Let us ask God to renew gladness as a fruit of our lives. It is high time we begin to rejoice in a new and fresh way.

DECEMBER 1

WHERE SHOULD OUR AFFECTIONS BE CENTERED?

Reading John's Epistle this morning an important question must be settled. John writes, "*Do not love the world or the things of the world. If anyone loves the world, the love of the Father is not in him. For all that is in the world - the lust of the flesh, the lust of the eyes, and the pride of life - is not of the Father but is of the world. And the world is passing away, and the lust of it; but he who does the will of God abides forever*" (1 John 2:15-17).

While this exhortation seems to be clear, it can also raise some questions. The same writer also wrote, "*For God so loved the world that He gave His only begotten Son that whosoever believes in Him should not perish but have everlasting life*" (John 3:16). Is there a difference between God's love for the world and the kind of love for the world that John does not want us to have? Another scripture might help us reconcile what is meant.

"And you He made alive, who were dead in trespasses and sins, in which you once walked according to the course of this world, according to the prince and power of the air, the spirit that now works in the sons of disobedience, among whom also we once conducted ourselves in the lusts of our flesh, fulfilling the desires of the flesh and of the mind, and were by nature children of wrath, just as the others. But God, who is rich in mercy, because of His great love with which He loved us, even when we were dead in trespasses, made us alive together with Christ (by grace you have been saved), and raised us up together in the heavenly places in Christ Jesus, that in the ages to come He might show the exceeding riches of His grace in His kindness toward us in Christ Jesus." Ephesians 2:1-7

Our old allegiance was to the world and the things of the world. But God's mercy and grace raised us out and up from that existence, He changed our eternal state. We must place our trust in Him and His Love for us, not in any temporal material thing or other worldly power. Only then will the love of the Father be in us. Only then will we be able to also love others around us and desire to call them to this same walk of grace.

DECEMBER 2

AT HOME WITH GOD

God wants to be our dwelling place. He has no interest in being a weekend getaway or a Sunday summer cottage. We cannot consider using God as a vacation cabin in the woods, nor as an eventual retirement home in a far off place. God wants you and I under His roof now and always. He wants to be our mailing address, our point of reference; He wants to be our home.

Jesus declared to His disciples:

"If anyone loves Me, he will keep My word; and My Father will love him, and We will come to him and make our home with Him." John 14:23

For many, the idea that God wants to be our home is a new thought. We think of God as a deity to discuss, not a place to dwell. We think of God as a mysterious miracle worker, not a house to live in. We think of God as a creator to call on, not a home to reside in. But our Father wants to be the one in whom "*we live and move and have our being*" (Acts 17:28).

Jesus promised this kind of relationship when He encouraged His disciples:

"Let not your heart be troubled; you believe in God, believe also in Me. In My Father's house are many mansions; if it were not so, I would have told you. I go to prepare a place for you. And if I go and prepare a place for you, I will come again and receive you to Myself; that where I am, there you may be also." John 14:1-2

It does not get any better than this: "Christ in us the hope of glory!" This is what I want: my home is His home!

DECEMBER 3

THE OLD HAS TO GO FOR US TO EXPERIENCE THE NEW!

Jesus declares Himself to be the Alpha and the Omega, the Beginning and the End. As the Omega, there are things that must be finished in us, so that we can have new beginnings. Jesus, as the Omega of our lives, can bring an end to deep wounds, broken hearts, mistakes, negativity, and unforgiveness. These things have to be let go.

What hinders our life of possibility? The framework of old assumptions we carry with us; framing our future with old assumptions that evolve from older beliefs and conditions of the past; allowing ourselves to shrink and live in a rut of "sameness," with no change; not breaking out and doing new things because it is illogical, too out of normal (by our own definition); not willing to make a shift in our thinking, our seeing things, our perceptions that lead to new things; not breaking the old frames of our mind that define and confine what we see possible.

Paul tells us that when we came to Christ:

"Old things have passed away, behold the new has come." 2 Corinthians 5:17

The new is the world of possibility. Lift off the world of limitations. Today is a new day! What was old has disappeared, now everything has become new. The new is a dynamic relationship with Jesus. It involves a New Covenant, new heart, new creation and a new life. In Christ is the new!

This is what caused Paul to write:

"I have been crucified with Christ; it is no longer I who live, but Christ lives in me; and the life which I now live in the flesh I live by faith in the Son of God, who loved me and gave Himself for me." Galatians 2:20

You, too, can experience this newness of life. Jesus can help you put an end to some things and enable you to start new. He won't only help you jumpstart a new life, He will see that you cross the finish line!

DECEMBER 4

IF WE REALLY DO CARE ABOUT THE POOR...

We are not limited to one kind of expression but many:

Surely, we should care about the homeless and hungry and work to provide some place warm and provide food to eat. This is very much needed, and I hope that you all consider how you can meet this need. But is this the end of our expression? Do we feel like we have done all that is necessary?

May I suggest some additional ideas: creating opportunities for someone to be educated with skills that would enable them to supply for themselves. This includes job and skill training; teaching on stewardship and responsibility; coaching and counseling to encourage change and overcome poor habits or thinking; literacy skills and mentoring.

In addition, we should be encouraging people in creating new businesses, providing needed services to those in our communities. We should support legislation that enables this while opposing legislation that creates a greater obstacle on independence. In doing so, we should oppose candidates for public office who do enslave the poor with dependency programs and support those who want to cut the red tape and release people to their greater potential.

In short, we practice the gospel and offer it to those whom we encounter. The gospel is "Good News" and, when received, sets us on a course for blessing, renewed thinking, and community advocacy. It is in fact real freedom. So do not let the first go undone, but may we also embrace a full picture of what it means to help the poor.

"Then Jesus said to those Jews who believed Him, 'If you abide in My word, you are My disciples indeed. And you shall know the truth, and the truth shall make you free." John 8:31-32

"The thief does not come except to steal, to kill, and to destroy. I have come that they may have life; and that they may have it more abundantly." John 10:10

DECEMBER 5

SOMETHING WORTH MEDITATING ON TODAY!

Whoever believes that Jesus is the Christ is born of God, and everyone who loves Him who begot also loves him who is begotten of Him. By this we know that we love the children of God, when we love God and keep His commandments. For this is the love of God, that we keep His commandments. And His commandments are not burdensome. For whatever is born of God overcomes the world. And this is the victory that has overcome the world - our faith. Who is he who overcomes the world, but he who believes that Jesus is the Son of God?" 1 John 5:1-5

God is light. Therefore, to engage in fellowship with Him we must walk in light and not in darkness.

God is love. Since we are His children, we must walk in love. Our love must be practical; it is more than words; it is actions.

God is life. Those who fellowship with Him must possess His quality of life. Spiritual birth occurs through faith in Jesus Christ.

Believing is more than a thought process; it is a changed life orientation that through intimacy, dependence and willing obedience, one receives the power of God's grace to produce fruit. Faith, therefore, results in action. Not an action of drudgery, but joyful agreement.

God's ways are a delight, His people are our people. His victory is secure and we walk in His promise.

May the joy and fruit of our lives be evidence of Whom we are in union with. May His light, love and life be seen through our lives as we stay in communion with Him.

JESUS IS MIGHTY GOD

Knowing Jesus as "Mighty God" will change the way you live, think, see, and act. God is valiant, powerful, strong, prevailing, unmatched, and champion. He uses His power to fulfill His purpose. His will is never frustrated. Nothing is too difficult for Him to accomplish.

Jesus is bigger than you think and greater than you can comprehend. Nothing is beyond His ability.

Knowing Jesus as "Mighty God" will change your life!

- God can do without effort and by volition whatever He wills.
- Nothing is too difficult to accomplish.
- Nothing is beyond His capability.
- There is no limitation with God.
- God's will is never frustrated.
- What He chooses to do; He accomplishes. He has the ability to do it.
- God uses His power purposefully.
- He has unlimited power within Himself.
- God uses that power to fulfill His purpose in us and in the world.

Knowing Jesus as "Mighty God' changes everything:

- Our prayers are not limited.
- Our faith is ever increasing.
- Our obedience is quick.
- Our miracle supply is visible.
- Our troubles do not discourage us.
- Our battles will end in victory.
- Our mountains will be moved.
- Our weakness is exchanged for His strength.
- Our healing is possible.

Let us declare Jesus as "Mighty God" and give Him the glory that He alone deserves!

December 7

Honor and Respect

I am concerned about the extreme to which our society has gone with the cult of the child during the past thirty to forty years in the United States. Ordering our worlds around not only the needs, but the whims of our children has caused a great distortion. There will be left no center of authority around the child where he or she can order his or her life, no clear guidelines or directions, no well-defined values. And so, respect has diminished and the health of our communities has declined.

This is not so much the child's fault as the parent's default. Seeds of disrespect left unchecked will only grow. Teaching our children to honor and respect others requires clear standards, loving restraints, and consistent discipline. Dishonor is a social offense. When you are taught to dishonor parents you are removing a pillar from the foundation of society. Unless people learn to live together in the family, they aren't likely to learn to get along with anybody anywhere.

As we reflect on the Lord's command to "*Honor your father and your mother*" (Exodus 20:12; Deuteronomy 5:16; Ephesians 6:1-4), may we consider the implications of obeying this command. We cannot do this as a one-day thing. We must set this as a principle in our lives, one that carries a great deal of weight! The command comes with a promise "*that your days may be long . . . and that it may be well with you.*"

Can you imagine the difference that walking in this principle would make in the world that we live in? While we cannot make everyone do this, we can do our part to be an example of this principle in our lives and in our families.

DECEMBER 8

CONTEND FOR THE FAITH

In reading Jude's letter this morning, it is apparent that he is sounding an alarm. It is a call to battle, to fight for truth, to contend for the faith. Only believers who are prepared can answer the summons. The danger he is speaking of is real. Christians should not be caught off guard. The enemy has used the same tactics in past generations. However, God is able to keep those whose minds are on Him strong.

Jude wrote:

"Beloved, while I was very diligent to write to you concerning our common salvation, I found it necessary to write to you exhorting you to contend earnestly for the faith which was once for all delivered to the saints. For certain men have crept in unnoticed, who long ago were marked out for this condemnation, ungodly men, who turn the grace of our God into lewdness and deny the only Lord God and our Lord Jesus Christ." Jude 3-4

Jude uses many different metaphors to describe what we are dealing with: "*spots in your love feast...clouds without water...late autumn trees without fruit*." The key is they have no fear. They serve self. They are fruitless and stir up trouble. Therefore, vigilance is needed on our part. Unless one is growing in the faith, exercising discernment and confronting apostasy in all forms, the deposit of faith will not remain true.

But the great thing is that we have a great God that we can trust to lead us. As Jude concludes his letter he writes these words which we can also declare:

"Now to Him who is able to keep you from stumbling, and to present you faultless before the presence of His glory with exceeding joy, to God our Savior, Who alone is wise, be glory and majesty, dominion and power, both now and forever, Amen." Jude 24-25

DECEMBER 9

A LAST LETTER

2 Timothy is the last of Paul's letters recorded in the Bible. It has me thinking of what I would write if this was my last writing? What would be important for me to communicate?

This week I found out that someone who has just recently been coming to our church suddenly died. The last conversation that I had with her was that she was going to be traveling to be with her family for Thanksgiving. I wished her to have a wonderful time with them. I never expected that I would never see her again. Last words are important. But you never know when it will be last words. That is why it is so important that we guard our speech.

Paul, in his last letter was concerned for his young leader, Timothy. He was releasing him to his full capacity as a leader. He has many important things to say to him. *"Stir up the gift of God" ... "Do not be ashamed of the testimony of God" ... "Hold fast the pattern of sound words which you have heard from me" ... "The things you have heard from me among many witnesses, commit these to faithful men who will be able to teach others also" ... "Endure hardship" ... "Keep a clear focus" ... "Be diligent to present yourself approved to God, a workman who does not need to be ashamed, rightly dividing the word of truth" ... "Confront apostasy" ... "Preach the Word! Be ready in season and out of season"*. Most of all Timothy stay the course. Many have strayed for various reasons.

This was not a letter of unimportance. It was filled with clear direction, encouragement and even endearment. There was guidance but also warning. A clear example had been given, and now Timothy would need to rely on God's Spirit and Word to continue to direct his path. He was not left without a pattern. I hope that in my life what I leave gives clear guidance, encouragement and a personal example that can be followed along with patterns that helps another generation continue to steward their call.

What if you had to write a last letter? What if what you said to someone was the last thing they would remember about you? Choose wisely!

DECEMBER 10

MY REDEEMER LIVES!

Job had experienced such great suffering in his life. Those who were supposedly his friends accuse him instead of comforting him. When things in our lives do not go as planned or expected, there is something in us that searches for answers, even reasons. Maybe we begin to think of some fault. We think, or we might even come out and say, "they must have done something to deserve what they are experiencing."

After enduring this dialog from his friends for too long, Job responds with an affirmation of his faith in God. His faith transcends his present experience. He knows to Whom he belongs and to Whom he will go. So much so, that he wants or greatly desires that the words he is about to declare are written in stone.

"Oh, that my words were written! Oh, that they were inscribed in a book! That they were engraved on a rock with an iron pen and lead, forever! For I know that my Redeemer lives. And He shall stand at last on earth: and after my skin is destroyed, this I know, that in my flesh I shall see God, Whom I shall see for myself, and my eyes shall behold, and not another. How my heart yearns within me! Job 19:23-27

Well Job's words were written. They were written for all of us to read. They have been placed in God's Word, the Bible. Generations of people have been comforted with these words. His faith in his Redeemer inspires our faith in our Redeemer.

Life's circumstances might get rough, but we do not need to despair. With great confidence we can declare "my Redeemer lives!" When all is said and done, we can be assured that we will see Jesus face to face!

DECEMBER 11

SEE I HAVE SET BEFORE YOU AN OPEN DOOR...

Today as I reread a section of scripture that was prophetically expounded to our church at our 20th anniversary, I couldn't help focus on a particular verse: "*See I have set before you an open door, and no one can shut it*" (Rev. 3:8). This door was in relation to a particular key, the key of David. The door that is opened is the one that the Lord has set open. That door no man can shut. It is God's plan and strategy for our lives laid in eternity. It is a door of God's choosing for us, not a door we choose for ourselves.

Paul wrote that, "*a great and effective door has opened to me, and there are many adversaries*" (1 Cor. 16:9). Great doors have great adversaries. Adversaries are opponents who desire to shut the door and stop us from entering. However, they cannot shut the door that God has opened. They can try to discourage us from walking through that door, but only by God's grace are we enabled to walk through these doors.

It is not the same with the doors of our own choosing. There is no guarantee of God's grace. What we do in our own strength will have to be continued in our own strength. The flesh profits nothing and only brings death, but the Spirit brings life.

As I look back at the years of ministry, I can see that the doors that have been opened by the Lord were not doors of my choosing. Even now, I see doors that are opened that He is directing us through that I would not have imagined, or chosen. It is all part of His great strategic plan. These doors are also part of a corporate call. For me, personally, and in unity with our own church leadership, it is important that we discern just what that door is. It does not mean there won't be adversaries, but it does mean that God's blessing and grace to proceed will be there.

What about you? Have you considered the open door that God has for you? Even effective doors have challenges. But not walking through those doors means never having possibilities. May we discern wisely, and walk confidently through what the Lord has opened for us!

DECEMBER 12

OPEN DOORS ...(CONTINUED)

Yesterday's devotional thought focused on the fact that God has opened doors for us through His sovereign plan. We must discern His plan and by faith go through those doors. When we create our own doors, it does not guarantee that His grace will be there for us, since they are doors of our own choosing. His doors will allow for effective ministry, although we will need to combat adversaries.

One observation from my own life and ministry might be helpful. Many of the doors that the Lord has opened for me personally, or our ministries corporately, were not planned doors. Surely, we have obeyed the intention of the commission to go and make disciples of all nations; but which ones? What manner? What order? What timing?

While we continue to prepare by teaching and forming disciples, we also have considered the opportunities that are before us. Oftentimes, the opportunity has come as a result of simply caring and serving. Seeing needs that move our hearts and doing what we can with the resources God has given us expands the direction of ministry into the door that has been planned for us to walk in.

While we believed at the formation of our church we would minister from neighborhoods to nations, the reality has unfolded through one story after another. Little did we know we might be doing effective work in Ukraine, Belarus, Kenya, Ghana, Zimbabwe, South Africa and now India; not to mention the start of a Portuguese speaking congregation and working among the Portuguese in our region and beyond. All the time we have been working in the various cultures of the world, we have also been working locally with many different agencies, churches, including leadership development and Christian education.

You see, the door is made known through service. You might have the best laid out plan, but it is the Holy Spirit that directs us one person and one need at a time. Like the vision of Paul with the Macedonian call (see Acts 16:9-10), we, too, will be directed by God as we continue in humble service to Him.

DECEMBER 13

TO WHOM SHALL WE GO?

Not everything in life is easy. Our paths have enough fog to keep us guessing which way to go. Sometimes even the Scriptural admonitions are hard to understand or apply. That is what is happening in the life of the disciples as they listen to a tough teaching of Jesus. They themselves responded to His teaching by saying:

"This is a hard saying; who can understand it?" John 6:60

Jesus had referred to Himself as the Bread of Life, and the fact that we must consume Him to have a part of Him. Though He was speaking of the intimate covenantal relationship we should commit to, the disciples had a hard time separating the physical description with the reality of the message.

Many decided to turn away from following Jesus, because of their lack of understanding, or the cost that following Him might entail. In experiencing this, Jesus asked His closest disciples, "*Do you also want to go away*" (John 6:67). Peter was quick to respond:

"Lord, to whom shall we go? You have the words of eternal life. Also we have come to believe and know that You are the Christ, the Son of the living God" (John 6:68-69).

I can't tell you that you will always have the answers to difficult sayings or times in your life. But what I can assure you is to Whom you can turn in the difficulties of life. Jesus has the words of eternal life. Instead of walking away when times are tough, turn closer to the One who is the answer.

Lord, help me know that You are with me and will give me what is necessary through the different seasons of life. I put my trust in You.

DECEMBER 14

GO INTO ALL THE WORLD!

While we acknowledge we are to make disciples of all nations, we are inclined to remain in our own personal comfortable surroundings. It was no different in the Early Church. Given the Great Commission, it took years for the Apostles to move out of the Jerusalem region and culture. In fact, it often took serious circumstances to make them uncomfortable to cause them to move into the realms that God had purposed, whether through famine or persecution, etc.

In the story of Jesus' encounter with the woman at the well, do not forget that she was a Samaritan. You can see that first the disciples questioned within themselves why Jesus would be talking to this woman, not just that she was a woman but a Samaritan woman, not a Jew. It seems that it took them a long time to get what Jesus was teaching them. Blinded by their own prejudices, their hearts were not open to see the potential and pending harvest.

When Jesus said to them, "*My food is to do the will of Him who sent Me, and to finish His work*" (John 4:34), it was in response to their reasoning that He had eaten some food prior to them bringing Him some. How often we are only concerned with our temporal existence.

Jesus now instructs them to "*lift up your eyes and look at the fields, for they are already white for harvest*" (John 4:35).

In our humanness, we see obstacles, but in the Spirit, we see the potential. There are people all around us who are ripe for harvest. We will not recognize this until we lift up our eyes.

Lord, help us lift up our eyes today. May we see the potential harvest that is right before us, and see people as You see them! Remove our own blindness so that we can obey Your command to go!

DECEMBER 15

SOME DOORS NEED TO BE OPENED FROM THE OUTSIDE

I read an account of Dietrich Bonhoeffer while he was about to face his first Christmas imprisoned. He had already spent nine months in this Nazi prison with not much hope of his being released. He was in a cell next to other prisoners awaiting execution. He wrote about being kept awake often by the clanking chains of the cots as the unsettled, condemned men tossed and turned.

The suffocating suffering of this 37-year-old pastor seemed to take on new meaning this particular Christmas. He wrote to a friend, "*One waits, hopes, does this or that - ultimately negligible things - the door is locked and can only be opened from the outside.*"

For Bonhoeffer, there were two sides of Christmas. There is a hopeless precursor side to Advent. Until God arrives, we have no hope for release from this imprisonment of our own sin. We are stuck and condemned, and the door is locked from the outside. We depend completely on Someone from the outside to free us.

The hope of Christmas is that Someone does come and open the door from the outside. The sins that have kept us imprisoned have been paid for. We are set free. For me the issue is, why then do we still act and behave like the door is still locked? Why has life in the church sometimes become so complacent, unimportant, empty, shallow even lifeless? Haven't we heard the door has been unlocked? He whom the Son sets free is free indeed!

I consider that another door must be unlocked from the outside. It's the door of revival; to make alive what was once already alive; to breath new breath in the bones that have become dry; to release the Spirit of God in a new freshness that the chains that we have somehow become entangled with again are released. Only God can turn the key.

As we await Christmas this year, can we turn our prayer to Jesus and proclaim once again "Come Lord Jesus!" He already has the keys. But you and I need to walk through the door He has opened. In fact, He is the door.

DECEMBER 16

THE OTHER SIDE OF CHRISTMAS

Yesterday, I made reference to what Dietrich Bonhoeffer had written while in a Nazi prison in 1943. He referred to the locked door that could only be opened from the outside. Not that we completely depend on Someone from the outside to free us. This he said was the hope of Christmas, that Christ came and did just that.

Bonhoeffer also referred to what happens on the other side of Christmas. On the other side of the birth of Christ the King, we find suffering remains. We do find freedom and hope, but suffering is not washed away. In a very real way, what he experienced and tried to convey is that in the suffering of the Son of God, we find God.

Consider for a moment that from Jesus' birth in a despised manger, to His death on the cross, the Son of God suffered. Christ was acquainted with pain (Isaiah 53:3). And because He was familiar with pain, we, too, are made familiar with suffering (2 Corinthians 1:5; 1 Peter 4:13).

If we are all honest, the wisdom of God in the suffering of His Son baffles us. Christ Jesus became weak and vulnerable in order to suffer for us in His full payment of our sin (Philippians 3:9). What this means is that the child of God suffers, but not because God has withdrawn from us, but because God has drawn close. We are united to Christ and we share in His sufferings (Philippians 3:10).

I believe this is all a part of what Paul meant when he said he would press on. It's one thing to know the power of Christ's resurrection, and another to know the fellowship of His sufferings. Being perfected requires both. Be encouraged, press on! Know Him! Stretch forward!

DECEMBER 17

CAN WISDOM BE MINED?

This morning in my reading of Job, he asks an important question. After spending much time explaining how silver, gold, iron and copper are mined, and many other precious minerals and stones are brought to light, he asks:

"But where can wisdom be found? And where is the place of understanding." Job 28:12

He adds:

"Man does not know its value, nor is it found in the land of the living." Job 28:13

Not only can't you find wisdom the same way that you mine precious stones, these same precious stones cannot be used to purchase it either. So, it can't be found the same way, but does anyone want to search for it? Does anyone even value wisdom? Again Job asks:

"From where does wisdom come? And where is the place of understanding?" Job 28:20

He comes to understand that wisdom is hidden from the eyes of the living, but not hidden from God. He knows the place of wisdom and established it.

So what are we to do? How might we search it out? If God sees wisdom and declares it and even prepares wisdom, what can a man do? Job's concluding summation is, *"Behold, the fear of the Lord, that is wisdom, and to depart from evil is understanding"* (Job 28:28). What a privilege we have to know God. As His people, we can know Him and value Him above all else. Here is where we learn wisdom. It reminds me of a chorus we used to sing:

"Lord you are more precious than silver...Lord you are more costly than gold...Lord you are more beautiful than diamonds...and nothing I desire compares to you." Do you value Him in the same way? Let Him know it with your words and with your life! Then you, too, will know wisdom and get understanding.

DECEMBER 18

OPEN DOOR TO THE CITY

I have returned again this morning to study the church of Philadelphia in Revelations 3:7-13. This city of Philadelphia was an outpost settlement at the doorway of the land routes to the east. This letter was sent to the church in this city, to honor them and challenge them. They are honored for their works and their loyalty to the Word and Name of Christ. But beyond that, they are promised that they will experience amazing breakthroughs of evangelism within their own city. The challenge to the Christians at Philadelphia is to faithfully point to the Word and Name of Christ.

All I can think of is what the Lord wants to do in our city. In the church of Philadelphia is an important feature of evangelism. It is Jesus Christ who opens and shuts doors. He holds the decisive key in His hand. It is the same Lord who has set Christians in this outpost city before He opens a door which no one is able to shut.

The church is given a fourfold task:

1. Remain loyal disciples of the Lord;
2. Affirm to the people around them of their own loyalty and trust in the Word and Name of Jesus Christ;
3. Live in the realm of Christ's love; and
4. Welcome the people who will surprise them by responding to this witness.

In other words, we are to be people of integrity in word and deed. The reality of our love for each other and those whom Christ opens the door to will verify our reality.

My prayer is that we recognize the doors that the Lord has opened for our churches. Be prepared to walk through them. Have the integrity that He calls us to have. And most of all, demonstrate genuine love which is the fruit of His Spirit. Our city is about to change. How about yours? It's not about how much strength we have. It is all about the strength that our Mighty God has. Whatever He opens, no man can close! But it will require that we walk through these doors!

DECEMBER 19

MY RIGHTEOUS SERVANT SHALL JUSTIFY MANY

I have read Isaiah 53 several times this morning. I have read it slowly, pausing, reflecting on these words that Isaiah prophesied about Jesus so many years before His coming. There would be no fanfare. No great reception. No special physical features that would attract people. He says that Jesus would be "*a man of sorrows and acquainted with grief, and we hid, as it were, our faces from Him: He was despised, and we did not esteem Him*" (Isaiah 53:3).

I wonder as I read these words how so many today still do not believe this report? How many still hide their faces from Him, not realizing all that was experienced on their behalf? That Jesus took upon Himself what we deserve? The Good News is not that He suffered, but WHY He suffered and WHAT that suffering accomplished. Look at the great exchange that Isaiah speaks of:

"But He was wounded for our transgressions, He was bruised for our iniquities; the chastisement for our peace was upon Him, and by His stripes we are healed. All we like sheep have gone astray; We have turned, every one, to his own way; And the Lord has laid on Him the iniquity of us all." Isaiah 53:5-6

Jesus bore all that separates us from the Father. He was the payment for the penalty for what we deserve. He did so with the joy of knowing what we could have. He bore all our iniquities so that we might be declared righteous, being justified by Him. Not only that, but He continues to intercede for transgressors.

What great love has been demonstrated to us; self-sacrificial love. While Jesus deserved to be treated like a king, He identified with our most detestable kind of existence. He stooped down, became the most humble of men, identified fully with all that we struggle with, and after defeating sin and death made the way for us to be over-comers. Surely the arm of the Lord has been revealed. May we not hide our faces in our own generation, but instead turn towards our Redeemer and receive His glorious life.

DECEMBER 20

YOU KNOW ME – SEARCH ME AN KNOW ME!

Psalm 139 begins with the psalmist declaring the perfect knowledge of God:

"O Lord, You have searched me and know me." Psalm 139:1

The psalmist continues to describe God's knowledge – *"You know...You comprehend ...You understand...You are acquainted."*

God has perfect knowledge for He is our Creator, forming us and determines our purpose:

"The days fashioned for me, when as yet there were none of them." Psalm 139:16

I could go on with so much more here, but as I look to the end of this Psalm, I can see something important that sticks out and causes me to ponder. With the rehearsal of the intimate knowledge of God, the psalmist turns and gives God permission to continue to know him:

"Search me, O God, and know my heart; Try me, and know my anxieties; and see if there is any wicked way in me, and lead me in the way everlasting." Psalm 139:23-24

Here is a statement of relationship. While many people run from an all-knowing God, this psalmist runs to Him. He is extending an invitation for the Lord to be close, interactive and even corrective in His life; to be intimate, leading to the transformation and forming destiny that will enable a solid peaceful walk in the presence of God.

Are we willing to pray this prayer? "Search me, O God." It doesn't end with that. God wants you and I to know Him. He is "The Way." So, I finish my prayer, "Lord, with the intimate knowledge you have of me, lead me in the way everlasting." Amen.

DECEMBER 21

HEALING FOR BROKEN HEARTS

This time of year sometimes amplifies the pain that some carry. It might be the loss of someone they have loved, or the anguish of being separated from another because of turmoil, misunderstanding, disagreements or even abuse. Our hurt can be emotional or physical. In either case, we can be comforted if we will allow it. Among many other things, the psalmist speaks words that should give us hope:

"[The Lord] heals the broken hearted and binds up their wounds." Psalm 147:3

There is an important thing to note here. Surely, there is the acknowledgement that wounds are present. But the condition of our hearts must also be open to healing. If our hearts have become hard, where we are carrying resentment, pride or vindictiveness, we will not allow another to help us heal. We choose to go it alone, festering in us, with recovery being slim or none.

I have learned that if the circulation of blood in our body does not work properly, the wound will not heal. The blood must flow if healing is to take place. We must open our heart to the Lord. He alone can bring comfort. He will guide us in the steps we must take. He will bind up the wound. Given enough time, healing will come. He will nurse you back to health.

The good news is that you do not need to stay in your present condition. Open up your heart, healing is available. Each day there are new mercies from the Lord. Jesus bore stripes on His back for you, so that you might be healed. Give Him your condition today. He will love you, care for you, bind up your wounds and restore you.

Lord, today, we look to You to bring healing and comfort to our wounds. Heal our hearts, renew our minds, let forgiveness flow and restore the oil of gladness in our lives. Amen.

BOW DOWN YOUR HEAVENS

It is getting close to Christmas, and for most of us, that speaks to some tradition that we are accustomed to. I know that for my wife and I, that tradition is changing some. We are moving from one season to another, not firmly fixed in one or the other. But there is one thing that remains a constant. That is the devotion and awe inspiring understanding of the wonderful God we serve.

The psalmist declares: *"Lord, what is man, that You take knowledge of Him? Or the son of man, that You are mindful of him? Man is like a breath; His days are like a passing shadow, Bow down Your heavens, O Lord, and come down"* (Psalm 144:3-4). And that is exactly what He has done – come down. Great was His humility. Paul writes about Jesus:

"[He] made Himself of no reputation, taking the form of a bondservant, and coming in the likeness of men, and being found in appearance as a man, He humbled Himself and became obedient to the point of death, even the death of the cross." Philippians 2:7-8.

God, Incarnate, Emanuel, God with us- How wonderful is God's love for us! This revelation is so great that the angels sang "*Glory to God in the highest, and on earth peace, goodwill toward men*" (Luke 2:14). Heaven did bow down. As a result, "*God has also exalted Jesus and given Him the name which is above every name, that at the name of Jesus every knee should bow, of those in heaven, and of those on earth, and of those under the earth, and that every tongue should confess that Jesus Christ is Lord, to the glory of God the Father"* (Philippians 2:9-11).

You see – heaven did bow down, and now so must we! This is the message of Christmas! While things and seasons change, we must never forget the reason for this season. As you give this some thought, quiet yourself, take a breath and think of the wonder of God. Let your voice give God the glory that He alone deserves. He alone is worthy!

DECEMBER 23

I WILL REJOICE IN THE LORD

When Mary heard the greeting of Elizabeth, she responded by declaring:

"My soul magnifies the Lord, and my spirit rejoices in God my Savior." Luke 1:46-47

These words of praise and adoration poured out of Mary as she prophesied as a river flowing from deep within her. She was filled with the Spirit of God and with the Word of God. Such a deep reservoir of God's Word is intertwined with her prophetic song. This tells me that Mary, even in her young age, had a deep understanding of the Scriptures.

We, too, must worship with a deep resource of the Spirit and Word if we are to magnify the Lord in our lives. We are called to hide God's Word in our hearts so that we might not sin against Him. These words also flow through the river of the Spirit to be a blessing in our prayers, praise, and exhortations to others.

All week, I have been saying to myself, "My soul magnifies the Lord, and my spirit rejoices in God my Savior." Each day has its own share of difficulties that can cause us anguish from the depths of our hearts. However, we are called to cry out to God, and then wait for Him to answer with hopefulness. Only God can give us peace in difficult circumstances. Only He can give us the strength to be victorious. Paul, too, tells us about this great reservoir of God's Word that is to be turned to song:

"Let the word of Christ dwell in you richly in all wisdom, teaching and admonishing one another in psalms and hymns and spiritual songs, singing with grace in your hearts to the Lord." Colossians 3:16

Let us declare the praises of our Lord with joy.

DECEMBER 24

HUMBLE SERVANT IS HIGHLY EXALTED!

When I was a 14 year old boy, I made an attempt to build a manger for my mom for Christmas. Some 42 years later we still have that manger to remind us of the humility of Christ's coming. Can you imagine the love that expressed through His humility.

Paul writes that we, too, should have this same mind of humility that was in Christ Jesus:

[He] "made Himself of no reputation, taking the form of a bond servant, and coming in the likeness of men, and being found in appearance as a man, He humbled Himself and became obedient to the point of death, even the death of the cross." Philippians 2:7-8

Such obedience, humility, servanthood to the Father and love for us, was demonstrated through the life of Jesus. He made the way for us to be joined with the Father through Him. Truly love came down. But that is not the end of the story. Paul goes on to say:

"Therefore God also has highly exalted Him and given Him the name which is above every name, that at the name of Jesus every knee should bow, of those in heaven, and of those on earth, and of those under the earth, and that every tongue should confess that Jesus Christ is Lord, to the glory of God the Father." Philippians 2:9-11

To all our family and friends around the world, we have much to rejoice over! The humble Servant is our exalted Lord! My wife, Bernice, and I want to wish you a most blessed Christmas! May His mind be in us as we continue to be His example of love and service to our fellow man - from neighborhoods to nations.

DECEMBER 25

HARK! DO I HEAR ANGELS SINGING?

This Christmas morning is quiet. There are the remains of a family gathering last evening still evident in our house. Having our children grown and with children of their own, our home is pausing, reflecting, renewing strength this morning for another go-at-it of family gathering this afternoon.

I have taken some time to respond to people's greetings and communicate greetings of my own, along with well wishes and blessings this morning. For one day, a special day, people from all over the world look for peace, joy and strength. People love and want to be loved in return. At the same time, it can be a difficult time for people who are separated by miles, difficulties, circumstances, sickness, or even through the death of loved ones.

The coming of Jesus to us was not without its struggles, separation, aloneness, and stresses. Yet, His coming changed everything. Jesus came to identify with us in our weakness, so that we could exchange our weakness for His strength. This is what gives all of us hope. This is what keeps us going. This is the invitation that we can give to others.

When we exchange with Jesus our life for His, we are most joyful. No wonder singing accompanied His coming. Even in the silence of the morning, I think I can hear something special. Wait a minute, don't you hear it also? Hark! The Angels are singing!

"Glory to the newborn King! Peace on earth and mercy mild, God and sinners reconciled! Joyful all ye nations rise. Join the triumph of the skies; With the Angels host proclaim 'Christ is born in Bethlehem'. Hark! The herald angels sing, Glory to the newborn King."

May His joy be your strength today and always. Merry Christmas to all who read these words! May God's peace continue to be your portion.

DECEMBER 26

UP, UP AND AWAY!

We have begun our first leg of travel today. The hum of the flight and an occasional cough are about all the noises that I hear. We left our home early, my brother Russell bringing Bernice and I to the airport. The roads were clear and the check-in no problem. Just before boarding, we saw a friendly face going by our gate. I had to chase him down. David Wyns was traveling back home with his daughter and grandchildren accompanying him. It was so good to see him. I had thought about driving to his home this week while in his neck of the woods, but this was even better. He looked great and full of strength.

We are on our way to visit my son and his family. We will celebrate Christmas southern style, a first birthday for our youngest grandchild, and just enjoy visiting with the other two grandchildren, daughter-in law and the entire extended family as well. My wife has taken her preferred position on the plane, napping. I'm glad she has a window seat so she can just dream away.

I hope you all had a wonderful Christmas. Now we must live with the reality that Christ has come. Otherwise, our family and friends will think of Christmas as just a holiday, instead of a breakthrough in history. Even more so, Christ's coming has been a breakthrough in our lives also. His light has shown in the darkness, and all who come to Him, He by no means casts out.

Ask yourself today, "How might His light shine through me." When He shows you, all you have to do is shine in that direction. May we all have many of these opportunities today.

"And the Word became flesh and dwelt among us, and we beheld His glory, the glory as the only begotten of the Father, full of grace and truth." John 1:14

December 27

Ambassadors for Christ!

Yesterday, when we landed at our final destination, we arrived at the baggage claim ahead of our son and grandchildren. My wife could see them coming, so she positioned herself near the main entrance with her arms wide opened. I caught a picture of when she first embraced the two oldest. The look on her face can tell you all you need to know about the emotion of the moment. The love of being reunited together.

This morning, I am thinking about the Father's great love for us. He sent Jesus on a mission of reconciliation, to bring all who were estranged from Him back to Himself. He spared no expense. He left nothing undone. All that was required for the payment for any penalty was provided for. Jesus completed the mission. He also appoints those who are reconciled to the Father to continue this mission as ambassadors and representatives of His great kingdom.

Paul wrote to the Corinthians:

"Now then, we are ambassadors for Christ, as though God were pleading through us: we implore you on God's behalf, be reconciled to God. For He made Him who knew no sin to be sin for us, that we might become the righteousness of God in Him." 2 Corinthians 5:20-21

We are representatives of God, called to open our arms wide to all whom He calls. His arms are already opened wide. Know that He sees you from the other side of the door. When you walk through you will get the most powerful embrace.

"Behold, I stand at the door and knock. If anyone hears My voice and opens the door, I will come in to Him and dine with Him, and He with Me." Revelation 3:20

DECEMBER 28

GOD'S WAYS LEAD TO LIFE!

Yesterday, we had a wonderful day. First, attending Living Faith Fellowship to worship with the family there. We heard a wonderful message by Angelina's brother David. He exhorted us that while we might have a tendency to get anxious, we can have joy in the presence of the Lord. His wife had just delivered a fifth child the day before. She encouraged him to deliver the Word of the Lord as had been planned.

We went to Angelina's family home following the service to celebrate Eva's first birthday (a week early because we would not be there on January 3rd). We had time to spend with the extended family and were so at home. I began thinking about how Angelina's dad and I had become friends through ministry so many years before. Neither one of us expected then that we would have our families entwined. Surely God orders our steps, and it is good.

"The steps of a good man are ordered by the Lord, and He delights in his way. Though he fall, he shall not be utterly cast down; for the Lord upholds him with His hand." Psalm 37:23-24

"A man's heart plans his way, but the Lord directs his steps." Proverbs 16:19

This morning Bernice and I were able to listen to the sermon that Pastor Adelson preached back home at MBM. I am so proud of the people that the Lord has brought close to us. It is comforting to know that God is with us. We are in His hands. We have nothing to fear. He is our Emmanuel.

Blessings to all of you this morning.

DECEMBER 29

THE BEGINNING AND THE END

This morning I finished another year of reading through the Bible. Jesus reveals Himself as the "*Alpha and Omega, the Beginning and the End, the First and the Last*" (Revelations 22:13). This has me thinking about the seasons of life. We are always looking forward to something new, but to enter the new, we must also come to the end of something. You can't enter spring without leaving winter. You can't start a New year without ending the past year.

Life is filled with those things which are first and last, new and old, beginning and ending. To finish reading through the Bible, I can either check it off as something accomplished or begin to renew the process again. If I just read the Bible to finish it as a goal, there is some benefit, but is this the only reason that I do this?

The reality is that life is not lived in these two extremes but everywhere in between. While I may look forward to something new, I don't want to miss the process and all the important people and events that become so important to the reality of life. In reaching the new, I might have much sorrow saying good bye to those whom I loved whose life might have come to an end. There are joys and sorrows for the journey we are called to.

When Jesus reveals Himself as the Alpha and Omega, the Beginning and the End, the First and the Last, He isn't revealing Himself as the extreme poles of our lives, but the entire reality of our lives. Only through Christ can we have a beginning. Only Christ will see us through to the end. This is comforting to our lives. However, what is even more exciting is that we can live each and every day under the shadow of the Almighty. He is with us. He leads and guides us. He will never forsake us. He is our present help in time of need.

He summons us today through His Spirit and Bride saying, *"Come! And let him who hears say, Come! And let him who thirsts come. Whoever desires, let him take the water of life freely"* (Revelation 22:17). Let today be a new beginning for you. You don't need to wait for the New Year.

DECEMBER 30

WHAT MORE COULD WE NEED OR WANT?

I have been thinking this week how blessed my life has been. God has given me all I need. My wife has walked with me for 36 plus years. We have raised our children and now are seeing our grandchildren being raised. My wife's quiet nature and servant spirit have given our home such peace and joy. It is a place where we can reflect on God's great hand and be refreshed.

We have a loving church family; people who are genuine, loving, faithful, and true friends. Peter also adds something that I believe centers our lives well. In writing to the dispersion, in part of his greeting, he included the following words:

"Grace and peace be multiplied to you in the knowledge of God and of Jesus our Lord, as His divine power has given us all things that pertain to life and godliness, through the knowledge of Him who called us by glory and virtue." 2 Peter 1:2-3

If you carefully look at this scripture, you can see that what God has given us is "*all things that pertain to life*." In other words, all that is important has been given to us. There are many pursuits in life that actually take life away. However, if we walk in what God has given us, we will always experience an abundant life. A life that is well satisfied. Note, this has nothing to do with materialism. Surely, God knows what our needs are. But only when we understand His great blessing to us, will we find the contentment that we otherwise can't find.

As our year is coming to a close, I wonder how many people are placing their hope for the New Year on something that is a fantasy, on what cannot bring real joy or satisfaction? We just can't hope in nothingness! However, when we place our hope in God, we can walk by faith with a great assurance. God has given us His precious promises. I can attest that He is faithful to His word. Because of this my hope is secure. Yours can be also!

DECEMBER 31

WISE OF FOOLISH? TWO WAYS - TWO STARK DIFFERENT REALITIES!

This morning I was having a conversation with two of my grandchildren. I asked them a question, "What is the difference between being wise and foolish?" Kids, like many adults, have a difficulty transitioning from hearing something to actually doing something. For some, it can be selective hearing, for others, it can be outright disobedience. In any case, they are not paying much attention to what someone says because they are decided on doing something regardless. They need to learn what happens when they forgo listening to instruction.

Jesus gives this same instruction to adults. In the concluding comments of what we know as His "Sermon on the Mount", Jesus explains the difference between the foolish and the wise. The foolish hears only. The wise hears and does what Jesus instructed (see Matthew 7:24-27). The results couldn't be more opposed. For the foolish man, his building collapses under the weight and strain of storms. Storms come to all of us at some point of our lives. The wise man, who built with the sayings of Jesus in mind, following His instructions, had a house that prevailed despite storms.

I wonder how much we are like my grandchildren. They are not old enough to yet understand the significance of their obedience. However, that does not mean we should not be teaching them. But as adults, we should know better. Given the fact that we are beginning a new year, should it be appropriate for us to consider first time obedience ourselves? How are we responding to the Father's words? If it has been with indifference, or even disobedience, may we turn and ask for forgiveness. If we don't turn, what we build will suffer loss. If we obey, what we build will endure.

He who has ears, may he understand and do! Let us build with wisdom! Blessings to you as you prepare for the beginning of a New Year!

www.ingramcontent.com/pod-product-compliance
Lightning Source LLC
Chambersburg PA
CBHW070841100426
42813CB00003B/700
* 9 7 8 1 6 1 5 2 9 1 9 7 7 *